DOUBLE HAPPINESS:
TWO LIVES IN CHINA

BY

DAVID ALLAN EVANS
AND
JAN EVANS

THE SOUTH DAKOTA PRESS

1995

Double Happiness
Two Lives in China

by
David Allan Evans
and
Jan Evans

Library of Congress Cataloging-in-Publication Data

Evans, David Allan.
    Double happiness : two lives in China / David Allan Evans and Jan Evans.
    p.   cm.
    ISBN 0-929925-31-9
    1. China--Description and travel. 2. Evans, David Allan--Diaries. 3. Evans, Jan --
Diaries. 4. Evans, David Allan--Correspondence. 5. Evans, Jan--Correspondence. I.
Evans, Jan.
DS712.E88 1995
951.05'9'0922--dc20   95-15884
[B]   CIP

Primary Editor
Patricia M. Peterson

Cover Design
Patricia M. Peterson

To

Dustin, Brandyn, Nicholas, Nathan,
Justine, Joshua and Tempest

FOREWORD

China is a large stone to drop into the lives of middle-class, middle-aged, middle-American people. It calls itself, of course, the middle Kingdom----between heaven and earth, but by American definition it is the house of extremity: too much poverty, dirt, inefficiency, noise, corruption, bureaucratic dissembling. It is too old, too big, too complicated to take into your American psyche in a single year----or decade or century, should you live so long. It sticks in the interior craw and upsets your conventional notions of what the world should be like. That is why it is a good journey for you to undertake, should you be lucky enough to have the chance, and why so many books have come from westerners trying to make sense of their experience----to describe it so that fellow citizens can have some glimmering of its power and how it alters forever your notions of home, normality and your own life.

Here in *Double Happiness,* you are given another try at description, another image, another interior weighing of the China stone. It takes the exterior form of a journal by a husband and wife of a year's teaching in Nanjing----a city of great antiquity and greater contradiction. I think it is not a journal at all but an epistolary novel that happens to be true----in one sense. The characters are Dave, a poet from a college in South Dakota who loves the life of the body----sports, exercise, fitness, physical alertness. He makes literature passionately and worries a lot. Middle age weighs on him in a very male fashion. I know this: it weighs on me too and I am his contemporary. In China he begins to construct an image of his own death----and of his connection to his father and to his son and grandchildren, a tree of men whose bottom branches don't leaf out quite so easily as a new sapling. The other character is Jan, a middle-class wife and mother from South Dakota, an affectionate, even-tempered, good-humored woman who likes cleanliness, order, plain-dealing, and her husband and children, not necessarily in that order. She is curious about the world and other people, is game to plunge into the new worlds of teaching, writing and adventure. She has raised her children, done her duty, and wants to give the world a try to see what it's made of. Her middle age is quintessentially female----a time of opening, of putting away worries and having a new look at experience. These two have been happily married to each other for a long time----almost their whole lives.

This book is at least partly a praise of marriage and what it can amount to if people are lucky----and patient. Poor marriage has suffered so many body blows in this generation that the honest and unsentimental praise it gets here is lovely and unexpected music.

Yet China drops its heavy stone into marriage too, and that is honestly faced and described by the two voices in this novel-journal. Jan begins uncertainly----appalled by filthy houses, dead rats, flies on meat, the difficulties of teaching, ignorance of language and custom, homesickness. She flowers as time passes, and discovers the joy of going nose-to-nose with the strange. Dave begins strong and confident, pleased with his literary work, surprised by the magnificence of the old books he's teaching to quick and eager students. But a little flickering of mortality----a racing heart----catches him off balance, terrifies him, and brings on a sort of dark night of the soul, a black depression.

To be sick in China is to encrust the stone with concrete and lead. So far from home----a rational medicine----but even further from silence, order, harmony, space. China is an unrelenting cement mixer with a wheezing motor----continual noise, crowding, flashes of violence and misery. I was once sick there myself, and Dave Evans does not exaggerate the pure terror he describes here. I felt it too; so would you. Because he describes it with an ironic view of his own self-pity and psychic paralysis, and because we know----since this is a true novel----that he survives intact, we can bear his description. Fiction might want a darker denouement for its literary power, but here we are glad for simple fact.

But these two characters----Dave and Jan (and since they are also real, I may as well confess that they are old friends and neighbors just across the border) ----also give readers the battiness, joy, affection and sweetness that are equally a part of Chinese life. This contradiction is a sort of ground base in China books: the simultaneous loathing for the lies and bureaucratic chiseling of public China, and a true friendship and admiration for the Chinese citizens and students whom one comes to know: their courage, generosity and good humor in the face of the awful. Maybe that's the stone that China drops into the middle of your life----irreconcilable contradiction, a paradox inside a paradox like a set of interior Chinese boxes.

It is both a good stone and a bad stone, and Americans who seem obsessed with single vision these days need to be reminded that the world is larger and more complicated than talk radio will ever imagine.

So you are lucky readers to have this book in your hand. These two voices have things to tell you----not just about China or marriage, or dog meat or sleeping pills----but about your own life and the strange and unexpected ways that it can grow larger and richer when you least expect it.

Bill Holm
March 1995

PROLOGUE

So far, in a little over half a century, I've had only a few experiences traumatic enough to leave deep psychological scars. At the age of four I was swept into a culvert in a flash flood a block from my home in Sioux City, Iowa. A neighbor man happened to see me go under and sent his German Shepherd, an experienced war dog, into the culvert after me. The dog apparently aided my passage through the cornstalks and other debris in the culvert, and when the two of us came out the other end, we were retrieved by the neighbor. The newspaper reported that I could have drowned if it hadn't been for the man and his dog, and that although I hadn't suffered any injuries, I had been "severely shaken" by the experience.

When I was 12 or 13 I was nearly electrocuted trying to capture pigeons on the roof of a soybean mill. I still have an exaggerated fear of electricity.

Then, when I was in my early 20s, my father suddenly dropped dead of a heart attack at the age of 52. His death may have been the main reason I became a writer; in retrospect, spending so much time at making poems since the age of about 24 has been, at least in part, a diversion from the pain of loss.

I would have to wait several decades to experience another major trauma, this time in a foreign country.

My wife Jan and I spent one semester teaching in China in 1988. I had been selected as a visiting professor in an exchange program between South Dakota State University and Yunnan Normal University in Kunming, which is located in the southern-most province of China. We enjoyed our brief stay in China and we wanted to go back. So I applied for a grant through the United States Fulbright program, which sends professors, teachers and researchers all over the world. We went back to China for an entire school year, starting in August of 1992, and this time I was a Fulbright Scholar in American Literature and Jan taught oral English and writing at Nanjing University in Nanjing, a city in eastern China, several train hours inland from Shanghai.

This book consists of journal entries and letters Jan and I wrote during our year in Nanjing. The "two lives" in our subtitle refers to the lives of two persons, wife and husband. But it also means two different lives lived in one year in China: the first, a "double happiness," which is a Chinese phrase signifying an essentially happy and contented marriage; and the second, a relationship distracted by another trauma in my life.

During our semester break when we flew back to the U. S. for a few weeks to see our children, grandchildren and friends, I experienced a brief episode of irregular heartbeat, apparently from an overload of caffeine and alcohol. A heart test revealed a "tiny defect," which may have been real----but nothing significant----or an error made by the sensitive scanning machine. My doctors cautioned me about excessive caffeine and alcohol use, and released me. Just as Jan and I were about to fly back to China for our second semester, I became anxious, assuming I had a serious heart disease, even though I had been told by several physicians that my heart was strong.

When we got back to Nanjing, my anxiety----magnified many times by the fact that I was 52, the same age my father was when he died----intensified into a crisis. The crisis was compounded by the relentless noise and crowds, the fear of having to spend time in a third-world hospital, and the disturbing feelings that one can have from being too far from home for too long a time. The four-year-old boy who had been swept into a culvert and came out the other end alive but severely shaken, was now a man who had been swept into a psychological culvert----in a strange country on the other side of the world.

This book, then, is a chronicle of our year in that splendid and varied country called China: travel, work, friendships, food, entertainment----the day-to-day give-and-take lives of two persons married for over 30 years. The book is also about trying to cope with a personal crisis----Jan's attempt to cope with my distress is a story in itself----trying to maintain equilibrium both separately and together, and to get back to a double happiness again.

Dave Evans
January 1995

x

DOUBLE HAPPINESS
TWO LIVES IN CHINA

"WHEN YOU CLIMB THE MOUNTAIN, SING
THE MOUNTAIN'S SONG."
--ANCIENT CHINESE PROVERB

LATE AUGUST

August 25

Dave

Our first morning in China—Beijing, at the Landmark Hotel. I woke up and looked out the window. The buildings and mountains beyond were shrouded in fog and haze. I couldn't help but wonder how this year would go.

So far, it's been a lazy year.

Self control is everything. I must get control. Slothful summer. I virtually did no writing, only some reading. Lots of drinking and eating. Must get control of my body, my emotions. My stomach is too round, too soft. I'll do something about that. With control comes confidence. With control comes good work. Self-control. And then, with control, I'll do as the Gullah proverb says to do: "roll your apple cart right on."

August 24

Jan

Dear Shelly, David, Kari, and all,

Your parents have arrived once again in China! On our trip over we had doubts about coming back, but we are less apprehensive this time. It will be crowded; our living conditions won't be as nice as what we have in the U.S.; we will have to do without certain foods; we will struggle with the language barrier; and we won't have the luxury of driving a car. We talked about how cold we were in Kunming in 1988, where it was supposed to be warm, but wasn't, and about how difficult it can be to live in China, so far from friends and family, and how lonely we were at times. But then we talked about how much we liked the endless variety of scenery, the ancient relics, the culture so unlike ours, the warmth and graciousness of the Chinese people and their love of Americans.

When we came here the first time to live for five months, it was a major event in our lives. This time, knowing we will be here for eleven months is almost overwhelming. It's difficult to leave all of you for such a long time, but here we are. We are optimistic and apprehensive at the same time.

While we were in the air, looking around at the other passengers, I realized we were in the minority; almost all the people on board were Asian. The pilots and flight attendants announced the messages in Chinese first and then in English. I tried to use my new Chinese language skills, but quickly lost my confidence.

We landed in Shanghai and made it through customs easily. I went into a bathroom and, as I walked through the entrance, the attendant tore a small piece of toilet paper off the roll she was holding (just enough, she thought) and handed it to me. This is China, I thought; others will decide for you what you need. The toilet was a squatter, something I had blocked out of my memory. Now it came back rather suddenly. I'd get used to it again, I kept telling myself.

We boarded the plane again for a two-hour ride to Beijing. Our contact person from Nanjing University, Qian, met us. She was holding up a sign with our names on it. We were whisked right through customs—no questions asked, nothing checked. It helps to have contacts. It was midnight Beijing time (11:00 a.m. your time) when we arrived at our luxurious hotel, the Landmark. This is not how we remembered China, but we accepted it and retired to our room with twin beds (not our choice). We are on the top floor (15 floors up) in a beautiful area. We will enjoy it for five days.

We miss all of you and hope you'll write to us soon. Just wanted to let you know we have arrived.
Love you all,

Mom (from Beijing)

August 25

Jan

On the way home from sight-seeing around Beijing today, we were able to get a seat on the bus—a lucky break. We were exhausted. I'm not used to having so many people so close to me—arms touching my arms, legs touching my legs. I felt claustrophobic and conspicuous. Dave and I both fell asleep, however, with people surrounding us, touching us, bouncing up and down with the bus.

A man reached out and touched Qian after we got off the bus. She swore at him. We asked her what she had said to him. She said it was the equivalent of "damn you."

August 26

Dave

First problem, and we're not even in Nanjing yet: we're scheduled for a two-room apartment on campus, and we thought it was three rooms. This we hear from Qian. Living in a two-room apartment will be intolerable. One bedroom, one living room and a tiny, closet-like kitchen. We have fifteen boxes of books that have supposedly been delivered to our apartment in Nanjing, and more books in suitcases with us. We wouldn't have space enough to be by ourselves. I know that living in China is difficult, but this is unacceptable. I must insist to whoever is in charge of foreigners that we be given another room. Tom, the other Fulbright scholar who will be teaching at Nanjing University along with his wife Deb, has two bedrooms. This should give our argument some credibility.

...I need to get some space to write, and then write. Sometimes, I think my writing is over, yet I know it isn't. I know that once I can sit down for a period of time, I will be back at it. I don't function well when I don't write. My poems, stories and essays in many ways define me, have been defining me for decades. Writing is connected with my well being, my relationships with others, my sense of accomplishment.

August 26

Jan

Our schedule today was filled with meetings, a noon luncheon and an evening reception in an exquisite hotel ballroom. A Chinese Deputy Director of the State Education Commission spoke to our group of Fulbright scholars, spouses and the U.S. Fulbright directors through an interpreter for 1 1/2 hours. He talked about all kinds of reforms in the Chinese educational system. It was all I could do to stay awake. Dave and I suspect the man's information may have sounded better than it actually is. His aim was to make a good impression for the Fulbright people. In China I think presentation is often more important than substance.

...Dave has a cold—new environment, not enough sleep, new germs. He's in a quiet, introspective mood—probably thinking about what's ahead for him, and for us together, this year.

August 27

Dave

Yesterday, meetings all day, Jan and I grew tired at around 3:00 p.m. Still jet-lagging, and I have my first cold. Good start. Tom said that most viruses in China start in eastern China, where we'll be living, and that colds and even flu are inevitable. "Good way to lose weight," he said. And he reminded me of the wonderful Chinese tradition of sitting by a person's bed when he or she is sick, waiting out the death of the sickness. As Montaine says, even illness has its troubles: It gets sick, it lingers and dies.

...Jan visited my bed about 4:30 this morning. We have twin beds here, and the closeness is especially good.

August 27

Jan

Our hotel room looked good on the surface, but we found a cockroach; the doorknob on the front door is loose; the shower knob is loose; the shower curtain is torn; the drapes aren't completely attached with hooks; and various small items are in need of repair. These things bother me some, but I think I'll be able to overlook them after a while. I know it won't take me as long to adjust to China this time as it did when we were here in 1988-89. We were told this morning that we couldn't get <u>kaishui</u> (hot drinking water) because the water heater is broken. Even so, we are grateful to be in such a fine hotel in China. Patience and adaptability are necessary to survive.

...A few U.S. Embassy people gave us information today about Chinese economics and politics, and then former Fulbrighters who had spent the past year in China held a round-table discussion. We attended a luncheon at the International Club hosted by the United States International Service (USIS). The Chinese International Cooperation Department later hosted a dinner reception at the former home of a person who introduced Mao to one of his wives. What a place—like the one I envision when I read about China's wealthy war lords and other important people in China's history. Members of the Beijing Symphony played Mozart for us in the evening.

After dinner Dave and I went across the street from our hotel to the Great Wall Sheraton Hotel. To us, it illustrated just how much China is changing. It is decadent, with an expensive decor—high ceilings, numerous candelabra, shiny brass pillars, plush overstuffed furniture, a huge waterfall, flowering plants and ivies, thick carpet and hotel attendants dressed in crisp, snazzy uniforms. The gifts in the numerous shops are exorbitantly priced.

...Dave's cold is getting worse.

August 28

Dave

Daily banquets are killing me. Still have a cold; who will win, me or the cold? I'm winning, right now. Stomach ache early this morning. Jan warned me yesterday not to eat the uncooked veggies (after I had eaten them). Maybe that's the problem.

...The waitresses in the hotel dining room here—exquisite, so serene, such beautiful indifference. They wait on you, but won't give you much on the menu—

"Sorry."

"Sorry."

Yet all the stuff on the menu is in the buffet line! You buy the buffet, it's yours.

Such incredible, beautiful indifference—only women can look like that—so cool, so aloof, so...such exquisite disinterestedness. Is this how they are in bed? How can a man make them smile? How do they handle joy with those slow, deliberate, cool moves—how to excite them.

6

August 28

Jan

Several people in our group have sinus problems and diarrhea, including Dave. He feels miserable. I hate it when he's sick. He doesn't handle discomfort well.

...An evening buffet reception at the U.S. Embassy was an unusual experience. As we were getting out of our bus, a siren sounded and a delegation of U.S. congressmen arrived. They were in China to look at the Chinese transportation system. They had no connection to our education group, but we were combined with them for a reception. They definitely were the main focus of the hosts at the reception. I believe our group was just being "fitted in" to the evening. The Chinese served lots of American food and plenty to drink. The caviar was horrible, in my opinion, but I'm not a connoisseur. I was never certain who the ambassador was since I was introduced to so many people. It was mass confusion. Maybe we shook his hand at the door? I'm not sure.

August 29

Jan

Today our hosts took all of the Fulbrighters and their spouses to the Great Wall. We had climbed about 900 steps when Qian told us we were almost half-way to the top! I stopped often to rest and was dripping with sweat. I wasn't sure I could make it all the way up. Qian didn't seem to have even worked up a sweat. She tactfully told me, as I was catching my breath, that most temples and scenic spots in China are up high, so Chinese people are used to climbing. I know they also do a lot more walking than we do—and eat less. They are generally thinner and in better shape.

We ate our picnic lunches on some rocks and enjoyed the magnificent view of the mountains surrounding the Great Wall. Some in our group had taken the cable car up; others decided to take it down. A Fulbrighter named Charles had taken the cable up and said it was flimsy, and that they might just as well have tied him to a kite as far as safety was concerned. Walking down was almost as difficult as walking up. My legs were literally trembling and my right knee hurt. Near the bottom of the hill we saw a Chinese woman coming up the steps in high-heeled shoes! We felt like wimps.

August 29

Dave

The Wall
Jan's legs were shaky coming down. I felt decent, but I'm lugging a little too much gut these days. Lovely sights. Walked up 2,000 steps or more. Lots of hawkers, selling everything from fans to warm orange pop China is discovering it can make money on foreigners.

...Jan—how beautiful she looks asleep or awake. Last night, while she slept, I wrote post cards to friends and family and had a few beers. I was thinking of how willingly Jan organizes our lives together. She needs to organize, and I need to be organized. To kiss her bare back in bed is a privilege. And too much of a joy to put into words.

August 30

Dave

5:00 a.m.
Flying out of Beijing to Nanjing—apprehensive about Chinese planes. We both know about the crash in Nanjing a few months ago, on take-off— many killed. I want to get up and get down quick.

August 30

Jan

Dear Sisters,
Hi, Bev and Delores. Just a note to let you know we have just arrived in Nanjing and to tell you a little about what we've been doing. I'll send one letter for you to share and will continue to do so. We hope everything is going well in Sioux City.

We spent several days in Beijing having meetings and sightseeing. It was fun to see the Great Wall again. Beijing is great. We were thankful to have a Chinese person with us when we boarded the plane from Beijing to Nanjing—there were so many details to handle. We had to pay excess baggage fees plus an airport tax, after being directed to one window after another. The meal on the plane was decent, as was the plane ride (not the same China Airlines we experienced before). Dave was apprehensive, though, about the flight. Nanjing is more modern than Kunming, especially the airport. We are impressed with the lushness of the countryside. Jiangsu Province, of which Nanjing is the capital, is known as the richest province in China. We were met at the airport by Mr. Wu from the Foreign Language Department and Mr. Dai from the Waiban (Foreign Affairs Office).

Our apartment is bigger than we expected. It has a living room, a bedroom, a modern bathroom with a hand-held shower and a kitchen area with a two-plate burner. The hall closet has a rack for hanging clothes, but it's too high for me to reach. The bathroom mirror is also high. I can only see the top of my head in it. These apartments were apparently designed for tall foreigners.

Apartment kitchen

The kitchen and bathroom have tile floors, and the kitchen counter and sink have tiles (some are broken). We have been told we will have hot water most of the time. The bed is comfortable. The living room contains a T.V., two book-cases, a dining table, various small tables and a small refrigerator. There were no sitting chairs or a sofa, so we asked for them. We were given two soft chairs without arms—not so comfortable, but better than none. We put them to-gether to make a sofa. There is an air-conditioner in the bedroom, but it doesn't work right now. The kitchen is out of cooking gas; the floors are dirty; there are ants all over. There are curtains on the living room and bedroom windows, but none on the bathroom and kitchen windows, and no shower curtain. We have a small porch off the living room. Construction work is going on all around our building, so it is quite noisy. Qian told us the maids were supposed to have cleaned this apartment, but since their leader has been away they have been lazy.

You would not like this apartment; in fact, we have trouble imagining either of you here. I'm stressed about the ants mostly, but we'll get something to get rid of them. (I hope.)

Besides all this, it is terribly hot and humid. I was dripping wet as I put clothes, toiletries and books away and realized that I didn't bring enough cool clothes.

Qian, our contact person, took us to the campus cafeteria for lunch, and we decided that this would probably not be a favorite lunch spot. It's dirty, noisy and crowded—not a good atmosphere.

A servicemen from the apartment building came to help us with our tape player. He plugged it directly into the 220 socket. It hummed loudly and then quit. Now it won't work at all. I'm sure he blew out the transformer. He didn't know about the 110 voltage of our machine. I was mad at Dave. He shouldn't have assumed the serviceman knew anything about our voltage.

Later this evening we went to eat at a street restaurant. Dave wanted noodles, so Qian found a noodle shop not far from our apartment. Dave ate, but I just drank some soda out of a bottle with a straw. I was starving, but I wasn't ready to eat on the street just yet. Street cafes don't appear to be very sanitary.

My legs are sore from the climb up the Great Wall. I can't clean; I can't cook anything because we are out of gas. I was so hungry that I ate the M&Ms we brought along, while Dave went to bed early.

I'm feeling depressed right now. How can we live here for a year? It hasn't been a great beginning. Forgive my complaining, but I feel better doing it. Things will get better. Stay in touch.

Love to all,

Jan (apprehensive)

August 31

Dave

My first journal entry in Nanjing. As we were moving into our apartment at Nanjing University, Mr. Wu Y. (from the Foreign Language Department) had a young maintenance man reconnect our wall sockets. He screwed them back into the wall with a screwdriver. I thought I'd take the opportunity to "ask him" to show us how to work the stereo/CD player we'd brought from the States. I pointed to the player, then to the cord. He promptly picked up the plug and plugged in it, and hit the switch. It came on, hummed weirdly a few seconds. Then Jan seeing what was going on as she came into the room, motioned for him to pull out the plug.

The guy didn't know a fucking thing about electricity, all he knew, all his job required, was a knowledge of screwdrivers and how to screw in wall outlets—our new expensive stereo may be ruined, mostly because of my haste and stupidity. When we plug the machine in now, using the converter, nothing happens. No red light, nothing.

Adding to the gloom that first day:

The apartment is filthy,

there's no gas left for the two-plate burner,

our boxes, containing cooking utensils and other everyday important items for survival, have not arrived.

Jan's so disgusted she's decided _not_ to eat out in street restaurants, not just tonight but _never_ in China—she thinks they're too dirty.

It's extremely hot, and Jan didn't bring a single light T-shirt (though she did bring about 115 blouses).

We ate out last night, accompanied by Qian; but Jan, being very hungry, had nothing to eat. I saw her lying in bed in the sweaty heat after we got back to the apartment—and there was frustration and a little despair on her face. Her eyes, as I looked, began to get wet—and I was feeling sorry for her, but dammit, she could've had something to eat at the noodle shop. We've had hepatitis shots, after all.

Is this the settling-in syndrome? We did experience similar feelings in Kunming in 1988. We need to get organized. Jan is also uptight about her classes—what to do the first day, how to conduct her classes.

One more woe: the booklet accompanying the converter says you can't use it for computers. Now what? I'm not going to be able to hook up my PC?

... Right now, sitting in this hot, dirty, two-room apartment at 7:00 a.m., without hot water (I need <u>coffee!</u>), I'm not sure about a lot of things.

August 31

Jan

We took our medical records to the Waiban (Foreign Affairs Office) and paid Y150 (Y = yaun; with the current exchange rate, about one American dollar to five or six Chinese yuan) for various kinds of necessary documents. Later on, for lunch, we went to the Jinling Hotel to eat with Deb and Tom (Tom is a Fulbright professor; Deb, his wife, is a teacher). The Jinling is a fancy hotel with Western food. It was expensive but we pigged out anyway. We all agreed that we deserved it and wanted to have a dinner celebration for our arrival in Nanjing. Western food in China isn't the same as what we can get in the U.S., but it's a good imitation—just as the Chinese food in the U.S. isn't the same as Chinese food in China. There are so many different and unusual kinds of vegetables here, and the beef doesn't taste anything like the beef from South Dakota. Here it's tougher and has a strong flavor. The local ingredients and the cooking styles make a lot of difference, too. But when you're in a foreign country you make exceptions and adapt to what you can get. If they call it "Western," we'll try it.

...This afternoon Mr. D. from the Waiban called to tell me I had to have blood drawn tomorrow morning for a liver-function test. I am upset. I already had the test in Brookings, but it apparently wasn't noted on the forms. If I don't get the test, I can't get a work permit. If I don't get a work permit, I can't teach. So I have to go. I do not want a needle stuck in my arm. I fear that it will be a used needle, since I've heard that they re-use them in China.

...We had dinner at Professor Wu K.'s this evening. He has a new, attractive apartment—better than any apartment I've seen in China so far. He has a ceiling fan and other comforts. Wu K., the acting head of the English section, was dressed casually in what looked like pajama bottoms and a tank top shirt—a cool fashion statement. Professor Wu Y., another administrator from the Foreign Language Department, was also there. For dinner we had carp, crayfish, cucumbers, peanut chicken, plain chicken, peas, beans, green vegetable, rice, soup, tea, beer and a strong liquor. I liked the beans, vegetables, chicken and rice but was not crazy about the carp and crayfish. Wu Y. apparently likes strong liquor and kept urging us to finish the bottle he had brought along. We tried but couldn't. It was strong and wicked tasting. Wu K.'s wife speaks no English, so she was very quiet. She busied herself waiting on us, making sure we had plenty to eat and drink. Her husband and Mr. Wu didn't talk to her very much. It was frustrating for me not being able to communicate with her. I tried to say a few things in Chinese, but my Chinese is equivalent to uttering a few words, not exactly communicating. I suspect she understands more English than she admits to. Her husband is an English teacher and she's been exposed to English for many years with him and their daughter, who is currently living in the U.S.

When it was time to leave, the three of them walked us down five flights of cement stairs and out onto the street. It is customary to do this in China.

SEPTEMBER

September 1

Dave

First day of classes:

Jan is apprehensive about at least two things: classes and having to go to the Quarantine Center for a liver test. We worked so hard in Brookings to get everything right on the medical reports, but somebody screwed up. I told Jan I'd go with her, and that she must simply insist on a disposable needle, and make sure they bring it out in the package for us to see before they stick it in her arm. And we'll bring one of our own along, just in case. We know from our experience in Kunming that Chinese hospitals and clinics can be filthy. Needles, like chopsticks in restaurants, tend to be re-used.

September 1

Jan

Mr. D., Dave and I left for what we were told would be a ten-minute walk to the Quarantine Center. (It took 20 minutes.) I paid Y12 to have my blood drawn for the liver-function test. I was afraid and angry because I was required to do this, but it went okay. They used a new disposable needle—at least it appeared to be new.

Because of this blood-letting, I was almost late for my first class—Sophomore Composition. I feel somewhat out of my element teaching, since I'm not trained to be a teacher, but I think I'll like the group and can do a good job with them.

...I'm finding China a little difficult to get used to again. The odors, pollution and crowds are often bothersome. Today we saw various sites while walking: a man on a motorcycle who had just been hit by a bus (he was apparently okay); the shortest possible mini-shirt on a young attractive girl; a young woman sitting right in the middle of a busy sidewalk nursing her baby while thousands of people walked by her, not looking. China is changing. We would not have seen this kind of mini-skirt, for example, in Kunming in 1988. Nanjing seems more liberal.

The traffic here is incredible, and I'm apprehensive about riding a bike. Deb said she saw a person killed on a bike two days ago. She made it sound like an everyday occurrence, something you observe and walk on by. I know riding a bike here requires skill. At this point, I don't know if I have the skill. We see a lot of spitting and tissueless nose blowing on the streets. That is culturally acceptable here, but it doesn't make it any easier for me to see. Nanjing doesn't have the horse-drawn carts we saw in Kunming, and we see more high-fashion clothes in Nanjing. Nanjing is not the rural city that Kunming is; but we still get the stares and crowds when we stop to buy things.

...A new foreigner, from California, arrived today as we were coming home. He looked like we must have looked that first day—confused.

...Our air-conditioner was replaced today with one that works! Our lamp was fixed. Things are looking up, except that we still have hundreds (maybe thousands or millions) of ants. I especially hate ants in my cupboards. Our laundry came back today, and it looks great. The apartment workers will do it for a small fee.

September 2

Jan

The first thing I heard, when I finally found VOA (Voice of America) on our short-wave radio, was that a Chinese student who had been in exile in the U.S. since the Tiananmen incident had just returned to China—and was arrested immediately. Students have been asked by the Chinese government to return home, but then they are promptly taken into custody. I wonder if this will lead to any demonstrations, and I feel somewhat uneasy about it. Apparently there is quite a network of underground activity for reform in China.

...We ran into Fred, the new foreigner, downtown near the Jinling Hotel today. He was getting adjusted to China in his own way, which was with tall shots of gin. The price he paid was high; he could have bought a large bottle of gin for that amount. He'll learn. Fred is a playwright, very outspoken and somewhat irreverent. When asked why he came to China, he said, "I don't know why the hell I'm here."

We saw two fights today. Chinese people don't seem to get physical in their arguments, but they can really abuse one another verbally, and they don't care who is watching. We always stop to watch with fascination and usually sympathize with the person who appears to be losing. With so many people, so few resources and so little space, fights are apt to break out.

...Deb brought some Miracle Whip to us tonight—a special treat. She also brought us a wall calendar. We were delighted. Little things like this mean a lot right now. Deb tells horror stories about the food stands around here and about people getting sick. Jeff, on the other hand, a teacher who will be leaving China in a month, is pretty casual about his eating, and he hasn't been sick. He's lived in China for five years and has no doubt built up immunities. I'm somewhat apprehensive about eating food cooked in outdoor food stands, because of the visible lack of sanitary conditions and the pollution, but then I think: if something is cooked thoroughly, it should be okay. I'll be discriminating in my food choices.

Fred

We ate at the Sprite Outlet, a small street restaurant near our apartment that caters to foreigners. The food was good and the restaurant was relatively clean (just a few cats roaming around eating the scraps on the floor). We're going there again on Friday night with a group of foreigners.

September 2

Dave

Whatever I touch turns to shit. Yesterday they fixed the air conditioner. It took four men. Then, last night, it turned cool and I wanted to turn the machine to low. I moved the switch one notch and—presto!—the machine quit. Then I got hasty and let the shortwave radio fall on the floor. Luckily it still works.

...The other night we were invited out for a fine supper at the apartment of Mr. Wu K., acting head of the English Department. Good, congenial, witty talk by him and Mr. Wu Y., another administrator. Then yesterday morning I saw both of these men when I went to the department for the first time. They acted as though they hadn't seen me before. When a young American colleague asked him if the two of us had met, Mr. Wu Y. said that he had met me at the airport (which was true). There was no smiling, no real recognition. What's going on?

...Depression has set in. I must start working out, somehow. Qian said she was going to bring me a permit to get into the weight room; I didn't see her yesterday except very briefly. I don't know what to make of her. I know she's been assigned to us as a sort of guide for the school year, to help us around, answer questions. She has been good, for sure, but there's something about her, and about Mr. D., the Waiban person also in charge of our welfare—both seem beset, stressed out. I know they are very busy.

...When we went walking around town trying to find our way to a large department store. I couldn't help but think about what sort of mindset the Chinese possess or are possessed by. I think it must have to do with one's relationship to the group, to society as a whole. In the U.S. a citizen is an individual. There's nothing, supposedly, more important to an American than his or her individuality—not the State, not a group, a neighborhood, a town or a city. Individuals, of course, are _influenced_ by groups, and obviously the behavior of individuals has a lot to do with the behavior of groups. But the individual is supreme, the individual has rights the State cannot compromise or tamper with.

Not so in China. Here, the individual is secondary. The State, which means the power to make things happen—the Party, in other words—is supreme. The Party knows what is best for the individual. And that fact explains, as far as I'm concerned, the suspicion and fear and general discontent of the Chinese. I believe that a system in which the State (or any group) asserts itself as more important than the individual violates something basic in human nature. Humans are social animals, obviously. We have to cooperate, we have to reciprocate. We do, of course, all the time.

But there is a fundamental difference in China that has to do with historical matters that reach back to Confucius and beyond. Some writer, referring to Chinese attitudes toward individualism, used the phrase "the ethics of subservience." Good way of saying what goes on here, obviously. We have to cooperate, we have to reciprocate.

Subservience to something bigger than oneself—the Emperor, the State—has always been a matter of morality in China. In the West, subservience is considered <u>unethical</u>. Ever since towns established their own sovereignty, independent of feudal powers, human rights or civil rights, the State has, in effect, been subservient to the individual. In China the Bill of Rights, written ostensibly for the people, is more or less the equivalent of a platform written by one of the two U.S. political parties vying for votes. In China legislative and executive powers have never been separate. Which means that the legislative body is more or less a branch of the executive body.

Back to my point: The Chinese always seem to be sneaking around, suspicious and fearful, afraid they're going to be ratted on by somebody. Individuals here—I mean the ones who really do feel separate and non-subservient—must have the toughest time of all, because they don't kowtow to authority; they don't identify with the group; they don't hang out with the bosses. I can see how independent thinkers and doers would suffer in this society. It's the ass-kissers who get along. To a lesser degree, this is true in the U.S. There are those who are independent, separate persons, those who don't need the group. And there are those who stay close to bosses, who need always to be sanctioned by the group and by the bosses, and who, as a result, are probably more comfortable than individualists.

September 3

Dave

Dear Dustin:

I decided to write my first letter here to you, my dear grandson. I just hooked up my printer and I hope it works. Otherwise, I'll have to use a typewriter, which I don't want to do because it's too much work compared to having a computer—you see, if you make a mistake like this: if you maake a mistakkkkeelikethis all you have to do is punchafewpunchafewbuttons and prestooooooopres Presto!, it's fixxxxxxed.

China is very crowded, which is like saying that water is very wet. But we have a really fancy hotel here with American food if we really get lonesome for home.

Your grandma and I will be taking trips around the area. Nanjing was once the capitol of China, so lots of emperors have lived here, and their tombs, which go back over a thousand years, are still here. Actually, they can't find some of the tombs. The emperors wanted to hide them so they couldn't be found, since their servants buried a lot of beautiful art work and other expensive things along with the emperors. There are also remnants of a city wall that goes back about a thousand years, along with a bell tower where they used to ring the bells announcing ceremonies of the Empire.

Well, I have lots to do. I hope your new school is a good one. You need to study hard so you can do well later. That's all for now. Give my love to all. Love,

Grandpa Evans

September 3

Jan

Dear Sarah & Chuck,

We're surviving, and sometimes even thriving, but we do miss our Brookings friends like you. Nanjing is an exciting city. Today we had our first experience at an open food market. There were so many kinds of food that were unidentifiable and unappealing to us. Meat was arranged on worn-down, weathered, wood blocks. Flies were swarming all around. The narrow aisle between the food stalls was difficult to get through because of so many people (some with bikes), trucks and cars working their way through. The ground was strewn with trampled bits of food. A young man who spoke English and said he was the manager of the market, came up and offered to help us find what we needed. We bought several kinds of vegetables and some fruit. He seemed curious about us not buying meat. (I slipped on a piece of some kind of meat, and almost fell down, as he was questioning us about it.) The people selling food in the market are from the countryside, and don't speak Mandarin Chinese. They didn't understand my limited Chinese very well and I didn't understand what they were saying at all. We were stared at and talked about openly. I sense that it will be difficult and challenging to shop at the food market. We didn't have to buy food when we lived in Kunming because the university there provided us with a cook.

Preparing food is a chore, but you know how I like challenges. We have limited facilities and cooking utensils. We do like the simpler life we have here, with fewer "things" around, but we miss some of our American conveniences. I have a cold and feel congested. Dave has already had his first cold. I had my afternoon nap (I never took naps in the U.S., but here in China it feels right since almost everyone does) and took some of the medicine we brought along with us. We brought medicine for any and every possible kind of illness. I'm covered with mosquito bites. Dave doesn't have any. They never bite him. Why me?

We are anxious to get our 15 boxes that we shipped from the U.S. There are so many items in these boxes we really need, such as food.

I had to throw out our new large bag of rice today because it was filled with ants and black bugs. And I was actually looking forward to rice tonight! When I told our friend Qian about it later, she said, "It's not necessary for you to throw it out, the bugs will come to the top when you cook it." That is an insight I don't like to think about.

Then I burned the bottom out of our borrowed teakettle. I was boiling water for drinking, and by the time I smelled it burning, it was too late to save the teakettle. I was embarrassed putting it in our garbage for the maids to take. They are curious about us anyway and must think we're strange. I'm sure we were the topic of their conversation today.

For dinner tonight we had plain noodles. Our lunch consisted of scrambled eggs with tomatoes. Maybe we'll lose some weight? Write soon to tell us everything we're missing out on in Brookings. We love to get mail from home. Bye for now.

Love,

Jan (looking for a new teakettle)

September 3

Dave

Settling in.

Got the air-conditioner fixed but it keeps blowing a fuse.

...Deb says she knows of a couple of Americans who had "heart problems" in late fall or winter. Thinks it's the MSG. My blood pressure went up the last time I was in China—maybe from the MSG? So, we must eat intelligently. And eat Chinese food only sporadically.

...Fred, a playwright and professor who's been in China only a couple of days, looking around, said with a straight face: "There's a lot of people here, have you noticed?"

I said, "No, I hadn't noticed," and laughed.

...I talked with Jeff, who has helped translate some Chinese poetry into English. It's interesting how Chinese poetry over the centuries has tended to be sanctioned by the State and by the people (the literate ones). American poetry has become more and more aesthetic, narrowed, useless as statement, even though it makes statements, argues for this or that. It seems, when I think about it, that American poetry, because it's written by individuals, appeals mostly to individuals. Whereas Chinese poetry, written in a collectivistic society, is more for the group, more useful to society, at least potentially. The Chinese poet has to take his task differently from the way his American counterpart takes his. The American poet says, "I celebrate myself, and sing myself." The Chinese poet is subservient to the State, the group, the people. The American poet is subservient to nobody. Hence, the failure of American poetry to have much effect on life in America. Auden: "For poetry makes nothing happen..."

Of course, that's not true. A poet in the West can have a terrific effect on individuals. So he or she can be useful, too, in an accumulative, less conspicuous way.

September 4

Jan

In desperation, I cut off a pair of pants to make shorts, since it is so uncomfortably hot and humid. I feel like the guy in that scene from the movie Airplane who had sweat literally running off his face and body.

We went out to eat at the Sprite Outlet with a group of foreigners. One person in the group ordered for all of us—13 dishes, with beer and Sprite. (What other kind of soda would you expect to order in the "Sprite" Outlet?) Sprite is proudly displayed in large plastic bottles and in small glass ones. After dinner we went to Pam's and Marianna's apartments to look at various items that had been left by other foreigners. We picked up some plates, knives, a pitcher and a few books. It was almost like a rummage sale. Our group tonight consisted of two Japanese couples, two German women, a Canadian, a man from England and the rest Americans. We have almost a year to spend with these people.

September 4

Dave

Yesterday afternoon, for the first time in months, while reading stories for my class, I felt that work was possible again. I sat there, while Jan slept, and read in peace, and nothing else entered my mind but the stuff I was reading. This is what I need right now. A calmness of mind and body—and then a steady and patient and consistent progress with my writing.

...Last night I had a dream about the great golfer Sam Snead coming to our hometown, Sioux City, Iowa, and people sitting on benches in the club house after playing a round, asking him questions. I asked him a few questions, praised his accomplishments over half a century. I asked him what he thought of Jack Nicklaus, but he put me off, saying that he might say something that would be misinterpreted. Then he showed off his money by taking out bunches of bills and throwing them to the audience. I got two or three 20-dollar bills and a one-dollar bill.

When I woke up I realized that, to me, Sam Snead may be a symbol of work, of staying in there, of doing your work without worrying about distractions and intrusions. And then I realized that, if I have accomplished anything in my life as a writer, it's because I've done the work necessary to produce a good poem or story. It can't be done by just hoping it will happen. One has to plug away, day after day, on a poem or a story. Revising, reshaping, redoing, throwing this away and keeping that; but it happens only through goddamn stubborn hard work. Fuck the world, the working writer says: I'm making a story. Nothing can stop me.

Be calm, Dave. Be patient. And work. And be confident that the time you spend writing and revising will be productive. If one has talent, something has to come from the effort.

...China is not nearly the physical challenge this time that it was the last time, living in Kunming, in the sticks. Here we have pretty much the conveniences we have at home. We have a flush toilet, refrigerator—even an air-conditioner. Winter will be more of a challenge, of course.

September 5

Dear Children (Shelly, David, Kari, et al.),

We haven't heard from you yet, but know it takes 10 to 15 days for mail to reach us from the U.S., and it's still only September. We think about all of you often and wonder how you're doing. (Again, share this letter among yourselves.)

We're fine and actually feel more free and less involved in China (which is ironic in a communist country). Our daily routine involves searching for and buying mundane items like toilet paper, bananas and beer. We spend time preparing our simple meals, reading, writing, preparing for classes, correcting papers, listening to VOA and taking afternoon naps. We enjoy being together.

Today we attended a reception in the Foreign Language Department, and each of us received two boxes of mooncakes, along with some bananas, cookies and candy. We all introduced ourselves and told what we would be teaching. The reception was over when they handed out the tins of mooncakes. I don't much like them, but your dad does. They are little round cakes filled with bean paste or meat.

Our apartment was made for unusual-sized people. I have to bend way over to do the dishes in the kitchen sink. The hand-held shower in the bathroom is mounted so low that the water hits the middle-to-bottom of my back. But when I look into the bathroom mirror, all I can see is the top of my head. The clothes rack in the closet is so high I can't reach it. Even your dad has trouble reaching it. One clothesline on the porch is too high for me to reach; the one hanging in from the porch is so low I have a fear of falling over the ledge while bending over to get the clothes. None of the doors and windows fit properly. There are big gaps, so bugs and cold air can get through in the winter. Sometimes we wonder if these apartments are designed for foreigners on purpose, to help drive us crazy while we're in China? I suspect it's just poor workmanship in general—lack of motivation by government workers who have no choice in what they are doing.

We bought a teakettle and a pail. Our colleague Jeff told us it is a good idea to have a pail around in case the water is turned off, as it sometimes is. He's been here almost five years, so he speaks from experience. Deb says that, if there is any threat to the government, we should have containers for water and also a week's supply of food. That sounds ominous.

Tonight we were both so itchy that I got out our magnifying glass to look for bugs on us. I couldn't find any.

When we were at the market this morning, I only wanted five eggs (wu jidan), but I got nine. Apparently they are sold by the weight, or the seller didn't understand me, which is quite possible. Your dad seemed to enjoy watching the chickens being killed and cleaned. I preferred not to watch. I accused him of being weird or sick.

We miss you all and look forward to hearing from you soon.
We Love you,

Mom (afraid of falling)

September 5

Dave

Beginning today, a new idea for my journal: DETAIL OF THE DAY (If there is one).

First DETAIL OF THE DAY:
Walking down the street, suddenly Jan and I were following a young woman wearing an extremely short miniskirt. For a few minutes, at least, I was in focus.

September 6

Dave

The Chinese are ambitious. I talked with Wu Y., who said that the Yangtze dam will create a huge lake in the Three Gorges area, which is already being evacuated. Whole villages are being moved out. He says there was once a fear that if China were at war, the enemy could zero in on the dam, which would release so much water it would drown cities downstream, such as Nanjing and Shanghai. Fortunately, China seems to be under no threat at this time. There's already a "small" dam that has backed up the water in the Gorges about 500 feet.

...Yesterday I worked for hours on a poem, and made something I felt was half-way decent. But I was able to focus on some images and get some work done. I must keep at it. If you're a fisherman, you make sure you keep moving, keep your hook baited and in the water. It's an active process, not simply a matter of sitting on a bank sipping beer. The writer's hook is baited with words.

... Met some people last night who belong to a Christian organization. The Chinese government forbids proselytizing for religion. I find it impossible to believe that at least some of these people don't proselytize, even if they don't do it overtly. Over the years I've known some Christian extremists. I don't blame China for not allowing them to spread the Gospel. China has been burned before, in big ways, by Christian zealots. The Taiping Rebellion in the 19th century, for instance. A man claiming to be Jesus' brother got an insurrection going that might have leveled the Empire if it hadn't been for a strong defense backed up with British troops.

There's something almost weirdly persistent about these extremists. They're here ostensibly to teach English, but their real mission is to convert. Hence, they are hypocrites; they are living in China with false credentials. If they want to teach they should teach. If they want to convert, they should go elsewhere. Their religious convictions should be, as in the U.S., a private matter. True believers scare the hell out of me. Anybody who gets in their way will be trampled. The sociobiologist Edward Wilson says that the best actors are the ones who believe they are not acting. They <u>are</u> the characters they play, and they have an attitude that doesn't include humor.

September 7

Jan

Dear Patti & Jerry,

Hello from China! Having our lap-top computer makes it easier for us to write letters. We hope you'll write too, since we know you have a computer.

We're happy to be here again, even though everything isn't ideal. There are times that we wonder about spending almost a whole year here, especially when things don't go quite right or when we miss you and other family and friends. But mostly, we're satisfied and look forward to new and different experiences.

We, along with the other foreigners, live in a place called "The Foreign Experts Building." One of our neighbors, Reggie, a professor in his late 60s from Canada, told us about his recent China hospital experience when a group of us were on our way to dinner the other night.

First, you should know that being sick in China is a fear shared by most of us foreigners, as I'm sure it is by most foreigners in the U.S. but China, of course, is a third-world country.

Reggie told us he thought he was having a "mild heart attack" and was taken to the hospital at 3:00 a.m. in a van. The vivid description of his experience in the hospital was grim and frightening to the rest of us. The last thing we want to do in China is to have to go to a hospital. He sent a message to his contact person on campus and found out that there is no ambulance service at that time of morning. So a van was found to take him. When they arrived at the hospital, they had to knock on many doors to get in, the building was all locked up. Reggie apparently had been having diarrhea for about eight days, which may have brought on his problems. I'm not sure that it was actually a heart attack, since that seems to be what the Chinese doctors typically assume foreigners have when they get sick. Reggie said he had to sit on a portable toilet placed in a row with other sick people. The toilet was made from a piece of board with a hole cut in the center, held up by two wobbly legs. It was placed over a trench. At one point, he heard loud gushing sounds as all of the waste from the long line of squatters went by him. He said the smell of the room plus the smell of the bed, was intolerable. The doctors stood over him smoking, sometimes blowing smoke in his face, while they were examining him. Sick people surrounded him, some naked. A naked old man wandered up to him and stared at him with, in Reggie's words, "his dick near my nose..." In Chinese hospitals you have to provide your own washrags, towels, soap and <u>food</u>. There are no nurses to wait on you. Basically, that means you have to have someone else take care of you.

When Reggie had to be moved to another area of the hospital for a test, they put him on a cart which he described as having "square wheels" and clunked him along outside, across the road. Before entering the elevator, he had to pay some money. He said you must pay whether you are near death or not. The EKG monitor they used was, he said, for a veterinarian's use. He was sweating so much because of the heat and humidity, and because of the anxiety he had from being in such a place, that the suction cups wouldn't stick on his chest. They shaved his chest hair, but they still had to hold the monitors on. Reggie previously had heart bypass surgery. He's probably not a good candidate for China. Reggie convinced the hospital personnel to let him come back to his apartment where he promised to rest. They gave him some medicine to help him with his diarrhea and let him go. I think that a person needs three basic qualifications to come to China: good health, a strong stomach and a sense of humor. Reggie doesn't have particularly good health or a strong stomach. But he does have a sense of humor. Do we have these qualifications? We hope so. As I read this over, it sounds like a nightmare. (It actually was for Reggie.) But we were laughing hysterically as we listened to him describing all of this in such vivid detail.

...We hope to hear from you soon. Tell all the boys hello for us. Write and let us know what's going on with you.

Love,

Jan (trying to stay healthy)

September 7

Dave

On Sunday we were walking down a street overflowing with people. I saw a large man about my size, but slightly shorter, pedaling newspapers loudly. When he saw me through the mess of people, he came toward me, raising his voice, and thrust out his hand. I took it, and then he said something to me I couldn't understand. He kept repeating the words. Did he want me to buy a paper? I couldn't tell, and he acted as though he thought I understood him. It was a bit startling. I didn't feel threatened, although his voice was loud and he was in my face. Finally, I smiled him off and dodged away. It's easy to become anonymous in those crowds, especially on Sunday when everybody is out on the streets.

...There's something in our furniture, or in the bed, that's making us itch. Chiggers? Fleas? We're both scratching constantly—me, mostly my head and beard and pubic hair. What the hell is it? Can we get rid of it? How? When? The bugs bug Jan.

...There were six or so workers outside our window this morning, filling in the big hole where they laid pipe last week. They have no stomachs. The ends of their belts hang out like flat, black tongues in the heavy heat. Do they ever take a break? They work from early morning to darkness every day, including Sunday. Is this typical of Chinese workers? I can see why so many were conscripted into building dams and railroads in the U.S. back in the early days of the century. Grand Coolie Dam, and soon. They know how to work. They don't seem to complain.

September 8

Jan

I found out that I'll have two conversation classes with 40 students each, and meet each class twice a week. This irritates me, since I think 40 students are too many for a conversation class. I think they are giving me this many students because I refused to teach more hours than the ten hours we originally agreed on. They just doubled up the students in the two classes. Serves me right for refusing to teach another class.

September 8

Dave

Sweltering heat. Sometimes you think it's letting up, and then it's just as hot as ever.

...I finished a poem today.

NANJING MORNING WALK

Following a miniskirt
along Guangzhou street
just to see where it'll
take me
following a black
miniskirt, skinny
legs, white blouse
black high heels
dark rings of nylons
just under the skinny
ass, a little
hand now and
then reaching
back, pulling the
skirt down—
if it comes up
any higher I'll
see everything

or trip over it
or both—
following a miniskirt
along Guangzhou Street.

September 9

Jan

I took my class plans and some books when I went to the graduate office to talk about my conversation classes with Mr. Z. I wanted to express to him how unhappy I was about having 40 students in my conversation classes. He was supposed to be there, but, Ms. Xia, his assistant, told me "he had to go somewhere." I waited for him to return and tried to talk to Ms. Xia. Her English is almost non-existent and my Chinese is not good, so it was an extremely awkward situation. We struggled along, not feeling very productive, when a student walked by, heard us and stopped to help interpret. Finally, Mr. Z. came. His English is not good either; better than Ms. Xia's, but not good. The three of them talked at length in animated tones while sipping tea from Tang jars (the swollen tea leaves floating like seaweed). I was able to get only bits and pieces of the conversation. I told Mr. Z. that I thought 40 students were too many for a conversation class. But he seemed more interested in quantity than quality. He said there was no other teacher who could take these students, that they would have to double up, or I would have to teach more classes. I thought this meeting would be uncomplicated, but it turned out to be the opposite. I went home feeling angry and disappointed. It's so difficult to communicate a point when no one seems to be under-standing, or even interested, in what you're trying to say. And these students are non-English majors.

September 9

Dave

DETAIL OF THE DAY:
At the government market, which is enclosed and stinky, two women run the chicken operation. The chickens are bunched up in crates—tense

and crowded. When a customer points to a chicken, a man reaches into the crate and grabs it by the neck, then hands it to one of the women, who binds its feet and weighs it by tying it upside down to a scale pan. Then the customer feels the chicken all over, poking the breast to decide if it's what she wants. If she wants it alive, she pays, ties the chicken to her bike and leaves. If she wants it de-feathered and ready for cooking, one of the women takes the chicken back to a long, rusty trough.

There are two methods of execution, one used by each woman. One involves scissors. In this case the chicken is held up, and its throat is pinched and clipped several times with the scissors until there's a big enough slit for the blood to stream into the trough. The second method involves using a small knife, which is simply thrust into the neck like a letter opener until the blood spurts, then runs out. In both cases there is no protest by the chicken—no protest, that is, until the scissors or knife has been firmly embedded. Then, there's a terrific squawk, a thrashing of wings, a kicking. The chicken, after it has bled for about 20 seconds, while being held in mid-air, is dropped into a bloody, rectangular basket, where it runs and leaps and flutters, trying to fly free. Then, gradually, finally, it runs down like a child's wind-up toy, stopping in any position—upside down, sideways, on its neck. The customer, meanwhile, is not watching, doesn't seem to be interested enough to give the procedure a first glance. It's a grim process.

September 10

Jan

Today we foreigners officially met the university president, the vice president and other important university people. We met in a huge, well decorated, air-conditioned room in the library. We sat around on soft over-stuffed chairs with white doilies on them, and each of us introduced ourselves and told the group what we are teaching. The director of our apartment complex spoke through an interpreter and then answered some questions. Two German teachers seemed overly aggressive with their questions and comments. We haven't lived here as long as they have and don't know what they've been through. They were concerned about all the construction going on around our building—especially the noise, which begins before 6:00 a.m. at least six days a week—and with the lack of cooking facilities in some of the apartments. I wouldn't have attacked these apartment managers the way they did, with the various heads of the departments around. The criticism may have caused someone to "lose face." I was uncomfortable. After the meeting Fred said, "It's always good to have some Germans around. They make us Americans look good."

...We stopped at the Waiban so I could get paid, the tenth of the month being payday. I was paid more than they said I would get. I'm not even going to try to figure out their system. Dave got his passport, work card, registration card and name tag; but I didn't get mine since I had to have that darned blood test. I almost feel like a criminal. Who knows, maybe I didn't pass the liver-function test and they'll deport me.

September 10

Dave

DETAIL OF THE DAY:
Last evening, near sunset, I saw, downtown, a man with burning eyes. There's a poem there; the way the sun hit his eyes and lit them up, like mercury, was spooky. I had just yesterday re-read, for my American Literature class, "The Tell-Tale Heart" by Poe, about a young man's obsession with an old man's "evil eye."

September 11

Jan

Open market shopping never fails to be an education. Qian came by at 7:00 a.m., and she and Dave and I walked for 20 minutes with our egg basket, plastic bags and backpacks to get to the market. Qian identified various items for us: fish balls, plant roots, lotus, bamboo, quail eggs, duck gizzards (sliced and prepared in a sauce that is a specialty here), duck eggs (with a damp, brownish dough on the outside and rolled in some kind of seed) and other strange foods (to my eyes). While that food was intriguing, we bought food that I could identify: tomatoes, potatoes, eggs, bean sprouts, tofu and

32

rice. Qian argued loudly with the vendors over prices, just as everyone else seemed to do. I stood there watching and thinking how much fun it would be to yell and complain about a price, at which time the vendor would either reduce the price or yell at me. If I only knew the language well enough...

In the market, if a fish is lying on the ground in front of a pan of water, it means it is already dead and is cheaper. Today there were live ducks and geese, along with the chickens, to be sold and killed on the spot. Qian says 6:00 a.m. is an even better time to go shopping. Then it's not as crowded and the food is fresher.

Just as we were leaving the market, a huge bus came rumbling by us at a very high speed, its horn blaring. People scattered. Qian said she dares not challenge the buses. Dave and I agreed—or the cars, or the motorcycles, or the bicycles. Apparently, Qian will take chances with cars and bikes— we won't.

...When we returned from having dinner tonight, we found that Qian had left some gifts for us at the desk: apples, two large bottles of beer, a large bottle of soy sauce and a greeting card. It's the Moon Festival celebration. The card (which was actually a Christmas card) had a thoughtful message on it, and she also copied down a poem she'd written.

September 11

Dave

DETAIL OF THE DAY:

Some bastard stole my hat, my good green seed hat! I was jogging (hurrying) on the track, and my habit is to run with only my headband on; so I stuck my hat between two bars of a fence separating the track from the concrete spectator seats. Every time I came around I checked on it, and then, when I finished and came back, it was gone. An older man pointed down the street toward someone. I walked toward a group of men, but when I came abreast of them, I saw that none of them had the hat. I'm pissed. I would've given the damn hat to the guy if he'd asked for it.

September 12

Dave

Last night about six of us foreigners went to the Pizza Place and about an hour and a half later I noticed five or six large, empty Steinbrau bottles close to my plate. Too much beer. Susanna, the big woman from Germany, said that most Westerners, when asked to <u>ganbei</u> (drink it all down) at a banquet, are expected to back off.

"I don't back off," she said.

I believe her. She has to weigh well over 200 pounds and stand 6'2". No wimp!

September 13

Dave

Yesterday I wanted to buy the cheapest cigarettes (for pipe tobacco) but the woman in the little shop on the street made it clear in Chinese (although I didn't understand her) that the cigarettes were not worth it. So, no sweat, I went for the Y220 pack instead of the cheap Y80 variety. That pleased her.

As far as pipe smoking goes, I can smoke anything. At one point I considered using tea leaves, since I can't find pipe tobacco in Nanjing. Now, what I do is buy cigarettes, peel them open one by one and dump the tobacco into a "Baggie." It's a slow, deliberate process that I actually sort of enjoy. There are lots of little details I'm getting into here that I wouldn't indulge in back in the States because life is so much easier there: hanging out shirts, taking the little alarm clock from the bedroom every morning and putting it on the living room shelf by the window, moving the upright fan to different places according to where we are (if in the bedroom, toward the bedroom; if in the living room, that way). I appreciate tasks such as taking my chair out the door and onto the "porch," which Brian the Brit calls the veranda—it barely fits, but I'm afraid to leave it outside during the day when I'm gone, scared that the maids will take it away because they think it'll get rained on. Everything is a little chore. Which means that my life—our lives—here are more physical, more caught up in details. To get on, we simply have to do more things, stay more active. There's not much time for just sitting or lying around with a remote control in my hand, clicking the world by my eyes, forward and backward.

...Still dreaming sometimes of my dead sister Bonnie. In the dream she's still alive, but brain damaged. She's alive and yet her life is not important enough, it seems, to matter much. I go back to Sioux City, where we both grew up and, even though I know she is there where she always was, in her house on the hill, I don't go to see her. I feel guilty. Does the dream mean that I <u>did</u> feel guilty when she was alive about not going to see her much? But I did go to see her, frequently. She was a bright star in my life. She died at 39, a young woman. I have long since passed that age. At 52 now, my dad's age when he died, I have a perspective on Bonnie that would have been roughly equivalent to my father's. It's a sad dream; I've had it maybe a half dozen times over the last five years. A dream of a living death.

...Yesterday we were read the riot act by a local security officer. He said it's good to make friends in China with the Chinese, but cautioned that it shouldn't be taken too far. Two proscriptions: no sex with Chinese women (the fine is 5,000 yuan) and no proselytizing for religion. As for the former, the officer said an American of high status was caught in a hotel room recently with a young lady. He told the police he only wanted to take her back to the U.S. and make a movie star out of her. He didn't want the police to let his wife and children know this. And then the officer told us: "If you are caught, besides the fine, you will be detained and the woman will be punished."

What's interesting is that the officer didn't say anything about ideology. He <u>did</u> say that we should observe China, and then make up our minds about it "later," whatever that meant. (Did it mean that any conclusion we came to, we shouldn't start lecturing about?) But the proscriptions had to do with emotion, not intellect. Ideology is one thing, but emotion is what carries the day, what leads people astray. Sex and religion. China has never had a separation of State and church, never had a separation of State and <u>anything</u>, since the State has always been in charge of ideology and morality.

Just follow the emperors. If they believe in a higher cause, then you can believe in a higher cause.

After the meeting, Tom, a brilliant fellow who knows a great deal about Chinese history and politics, made a good point: whether the people of a country are religious or not depends on the kinds of questions they ask. Western people have always asked about the relationship between the individual and God; the Chinese always ask moral questions having to do with relationships between people. Hence, no God is assumed. What is assumed is the importance of how one relates to his/her fellow humans. That's what counts in China. Relationships. Hence, the importance of guanxi (connections). Who do you know? Not what do you know? We say that's important in the U.S., too, and it is, obviously. But in China it's 100 times more important. It has to do with fundamental questions, such as: What is my relationship with others? Who am I responsible to? and so on. Consequently, the importance of the work unit: danwei. For whom do you work? Who are your fellow workers? Who is your boss? The pecking order in China's work place is extremely formal and complicated. This is a secular idea. If a person is screwed over, he has to do something "on earth" and in terms of relationships, to get even or get peace. In the U.S. you can go to church on Sunday and get in cahoots with your god. The Chinese person has to work out his problems in his danwei. That fact would make personal relationships extremely important. Friendship to the Chinese person has to be much more important than it is among us.

The great theme of Tang and Sung poetry is friendship—especially missing a friend.

September 14

Jan

Dear Pat & Chuck,

If you're looking for a vacation spot, friends, why not come to China? We'd love to have you here and show you around. China is a place to be for excitement. Just living day-to-day is an adventure, and I know you two like adventure. Think about it.

This is exactly the kind of adventure I'm talking about. This morning I sat down in our most comfortable chair to eat my oatmeal with bananas and raisins from home, and I discovered ants in the oatmeal! I hadn't put the cereal in a zip-lock bag, a big mistake. The ants ruined my appetite. I know I shouldn't be so picky, but....

Today we walked to town to find some tennis shoes for Dave, size 11, or 45 (si shi wu) in Chinese. We looked all over. Most of the clerks laughed at us and said "meiyou" (don't have). We had some trouble in Kunming buying shoes for Dave, but didn't think we would have trouble in Nanjing. Wouldn't you think a few men would have feet as big as Dave's in a city of nearly five million? I bought a new "fanny pack," as a crowd grew around us and watched me make the strap bigger, try it on and decide whether I liked it.

We saw a man and a woman fighting over a bag. They were getting physical, which we haven't seen here before in all the fights we've witnessed. The woman was squeezing the man's neck, and his face was turning red. We watched until people started to watch us watching them.

Later, as we were walking down another street, we heard the familiar tune "Happy Birthday." It was a street cleaner truck rumbling along with its loud speaker on. They often alternated this song with "Jingle Bells" or "Here Comes the Bride." It cracks us up. American music is also played over and over on the campus loud speakers. "Moon River" seems to be a favorite on the campus loud speakers. I like it, but not ten times a day.

A majority of the women here wear nylon hose like those worn in the U.S. before panty hose. Do you remember them? The women roll them down just above or below the knee. Some of these hose aren't very sheer, and they often fit loosely. My mother and grandmother used to wear this type of hosiery rolled down in a similar fashion. It looks unattractive to us, but it seems to be all the rage here.

Letters from home today made us feel good. In the U.S. we're accustomed to using the telephone for communication—not letters. So writing letters is almost like a new means of communication for all of us.

So, it's your turn! Write and let us know how you are. Take care.
Love,

Jan (avoiding ants)

September 14

Dave

DETAIL OF THE DAY:

The poet Li Bai lived in Nanjing for a time.

...Saw a really good <u>qigong</u> (Chinese martial art) workout the other day—a guy dressed in a white suit doing all sorts of things at the track. Very good, obviously advanced.

...Worked on a poem today:

THE GLEAM

Walking at dusk along
busy Guangzhou Street
I caught in the crowd
a pair of eyes—
liquefied, like mercury,
by the dying sun.
I took a few more steps,
looked again, and
they were just an
old man's eyes.
A few more steps, and
they were back to mercury.

I turned the corner
and left them there—
on that dark street
in my brain where
gleaming things live.

September 15

Jan

Dear Herb & Sydna,

How are things in Brookings? I'm sure you're as involved and busy as ever. I think you two would like Nanjing. I know you were in Shanghai, but did you visit Nanjing? Nanjing University has about 2,000 more students than SDSU. We are often told that is the #3 university of China, with #1 and #2 being in Beijing. We're enjoying it here and have met many new foreigners, as well as Chinese people.

I sometimes feel like we're in a time-warp here, reliving the '50s. Hoola hoops are popular. Disco music is popular. Telephones are becoming more common. One of my students wrote in his journal about his friend calling to tell him that he has a "new phone call" (telephone) at his home. He said he congratulated his friend and was happy to have the convenience of talking to him so easily. He also said that "the quality of the 'machine' is just so-so." He said he was awakened at 11:00 the other night only to receive "a useless call." It was someone dialing the wrong number. He says this is a chief problem, and also asks, "What if I don't want to talk to someone who calls me? This could be a serious problem." He says, "Using fingers to 'walk' instead of legs is a great development." I wonder if he has heard of the ad, "Let your fingers do the walking." I don't think so.

We have maid service in our apartment three times a week. Tuesdays are "clean sheet" days. We are given one roll of scratchy toilet paper (about 1/4 the size of what you buy in the U.S.) and exactly four clean towels. The service people work in a completely objective manner and speak no English. On Thursdays and Saturdays they mop the floors with a dirty-looking rag mop and swab out the bathroom sink and tub. They have their jobs to do, and go about doing them in sequence. They also bring us hot water twice a day.

Our students are delightful and upbeat, even though they have a lot of stress in their lives. Since they live eight to a dorm room, they have various problems. It's difficult for them to study, and they complain of roommates' habits. The lights go off in all dorms at a certain time each night, so even if they want to read or study late, they can't.

Recently we ate dinner at a neighborhood restaurant with Angela and Pam, two of our American colleagues. Angela was doctoring her first bad cold with tofu soup—a tofu-based soup with "tree ears" (rubber-like mushrooms). It's probably the equivalent of eating chicken soup for a cold in the U.S.

I'm so thirsty all the time here, probably from walking and sweating so much. The beer tastes extra good, maybe too good. Knowing I can't go to the faucet and get a drink of water no doubt makes me more thirsty. I don't like the taste of the water chilled. Maybe the Chinese are right in thinking cold water isn't healthy. They don't drink it cold, as you know.

Today was the first day for one of my conversation classes. Mr. Zhang, head of the Graduate School, came for the first hour, probably to check up on me. Most of the students are Ph.D. candidates in various science fields such as Nuclear Physics, Applied Mathematics, Pure Mathematics, Algebra, Biology, etc.—bright students. I told them each to prepare questions for me for the next class. That might have been too brave a request, since I don't have an endless amount of knowledge on the tip of my tongue.

Several students came over to our apartment during my office hours this afternoon to pick up their journals and to visit. (We foreigners don't have offices at the university, so we have office hours in our apartments.) One older student is a teacher who wants to learn English "very fast." I gave him some reading materials and told him to practice writing every day. He wants to get a job in journalism in some other city. He's taking a chance leaving his teaching here at the university to do something different. If he doesn't get the job he applies for, he won't have the security of having his assigned job. I hope he's successful and that I can help him.

When students visit us foreigners in our apartments, they are required to leave their ID cards at the service desk. They, and we, are being monitored. I don't remember that from Kunming. Maybe you do.

The university is doing construction in front and in back of our building, connecting it to the restaurant in front of us and to the hotel behind us. This means more money for the university because it will be convenient for the hotel customers to walk through and eat at the new restaurant. With this construction going on, it's becoming more and more difficult to exit and enter our building. Brian, an older teacher from Britain, banged his head fairly hard on a steel bar the other night when he was coming home. There were no lights and it was very dark. He must have complained because now there is a very bright light out there at night. I think they are building a wall in front to "wall" all of us foreign teachers in. One morning we'll go down to leave and find that we can't get out. China loves walls. This city is surrounded by a wall that goes back almost 1000 years. The university is walled in, as are all other universities and businesses, as you know. Most people in China live within walls, and here we are.

Have a good semester. Write and let us know what's going on. Sydna, are you working on your journal? I'd like to read it when we get home. Love,

Jan (walled in)

September 16

Dave

My hips are beginning to ache like they did in Kunming. That arthritic ache. It's a good ache, though, because I know the legs are getting into fairly good shape.

...The air is very subtly, very slowly, cooling off. But certainly it's warmer here than in Brookings, South Dakota in September. That means, I believe, that October and even into November will be good, crisp sweater weather. December? We might half freeze. We'll need to buy a space heater, for sure.

...Yesterday Jan worked for over an hour on the computer revising, spell-checking, etc. Then, suddenly, the electricity went off. She panicked and turned off the machine, which meant that, because she hadn't yet saved all of her revisions and corrections, she lost them. I tell her: save, save, save. And that the battery is a safety auxiliary. It will take over when the lights go out. SAVE, Jan, SAVE, I tell her.

She was upset, and I can understand. It's such a marvelous machine, but it can screw things up, too. The Yin and Yang of writing. Not all good, not all bad—a mix, like everything else in China, in life.

...Jan is starting to think more about writing, her own writing, too. She pours over her students' papers; she's really interested in what they have to say and how they say it. She reads a single batch of papers two or three times before she grades them. Wait until she's had about the 20th batch coming at her, I tell her. She heard that if a student gets a "C" in a class, he or she might jump off a bridge. Well, Nanjing is the place to be when that happens, with that huge bridge—the longest, if not the tallest, in China—over the Yangtze.

September 16

Dave

Walking is the best thing homo sapiens can do for the body. That and sex.

...Yesterday I saw from a distance a young black man coming up the street; when he saw us close enough, he noticed my hat, which says "IOWA."

"Hey, you from Iowa?"

He came over, I said, "yeah," and we started to talk. He was a good looking young man of about 25, not very black but obviously African American, with a T-shirt on that advertised a boxing club. He said he'd gone to the University of Iowa, and I told him I had too. He was out of the Marines and was taking Chinese classes at Nanjing U., was apparently nearly fluent in Chinese, having studied it formally before he came to China. He said he was going home soon, but would come back later to finish his year. Apparently, he had some time off, so he was going back to the

Our apartment building in Nanjing

States for awhile. When I asked him why he was going back and then returning after a short time, he said: "It's tough living in China if you're black." I nodded, understood, since I'd heard this before. Many Chinese tend to hate blacks.

"I could write a book," he said.

He was an intelligent, sensitive young man, I could tell. He was using not a main street but a lane, sort of an alley. I got a glimpse of his situation. I was thinking to myself: he's in his 20s and normally looking for girls, and these Chinese girls are so incredibly attractive-though-innocent—in their high heels and miniskirts, so many of them. He has to be extremely frustrated, since back in the States he wouldn't have such a problem.

"I miss Iowa City," he said, and I understood. It's a liberal town, a university town where anybody goes with anybody, no matter the skin color, and where, just last year, a Chinese student, having come in second for a post-graduate fellowship, opened up with a pistol on a room full of people, professors or administrators. It is a goofy world.

...Jan is so accommodating. Several of her students stopped over for Wednesday office hours. She talks slowly so they can understand. They obviously like her. She works with them one-on-one, patiently, and likes to read and correct their papers. She's very indulgent, and they like that.

I see her working at her journal at night, like tonight—she's becoming a writer I'm thinking.

"Did you like that book on writing?" I ask her. I'd recommended a book called Writing Down the Bones.

"I'm becoming a writer," she says, smiling, because she knows that's sort of what I had in mind when I asked the question.

"Good," I say. "That means you'll start neglecting me."

She laughs. And then saves what she's written—it's time for dinner.

"What're we having, Jan?" I ask.

"I don't know," she says, "but it'll be good."

September 17

Jan

We heard today that Reggie is still sick and had to go back to the hospital. He was having heart palpitations and still has diarrhea. He plans to fly home as soon as possible. Fred said Reggie left some "rubbers" (condoms) for him, and that he had some photo-developing material to leave to anyone who wants it. Reggie was a bombardier in the Canadian Air Force and, for that reason, he says, the Chinese are suspicious of him. He said someone was in his apartment checking over his things when he was in the hospital. When whomever it was found his photo-developing solution in a bottle in his refrigerator, they had a drink of it. "Served them right for snooping," he said. He is a very outspoken person, not necessarily a virtue in China.

September 17

Dave

The construction noise around here is relentless. It starts at around 6:00 a.m. and goes until dark: hammering, sawing, loud voices, drilling. If only we could have a little let up, once in awhile.

...My American literature students are very smart, that's for sure. They know American poetry well. They haven't had much opportunity to read it, but what they've read, they've absorbed completely. I like their smartness and eagerness. They'll be fun to work with, and a challenge.

September 18

Jan

TGIF...Fridays are good for us, but for most Chinese, Fridays are just another day. They work six days a week, and some also work on Sundays—especially the construction workers. They work from sun-up to sun-down and beyond, and not by the hour. We were told they worked during the night last semester. The foreigners complained about the noise and it was stopped. We don't need an alarm clock here to wake us up. We hear the first loud pounding of a hammer at 6:00 a.m., and it doesn't let up until dark. We're not bothered by the noise quite as much as some of the other foreigners.

...About 20 to 25 of us foreigners went out to dinner for Jeff's farewell party. He's going back to the U.S. after having been in China for almost five years. The restaurant we ate in wasn't very clean, with stained tablecloths, chipped glasses and used chopsticks. But the food was decent. An American medical doctor from the Hopkins Center (a joint Chinese/American education venture) joined us. We feel a little more secure knowing he is around, in case we need a doctor—one we can communicate with. Reggie had a hard time communicating with his doctors through his interpreter. For some reason he didn't get checked by Steve, the American doctor. He probably didn't know Steve was here. Reggie said he had gone into potassium shock. He thought he was within a half-hour of dying. Parts of his body were numb and his face was starting to contort. At this point his contact person wanted to put him on his bike and ride Reggie to the hospital. Reggie is overweight and besides that, was in no condition for a bike ride. He was taken to a hospital in a car. He had a difficult time making the Chinese understand him when he tried to tell them to feed him some bananas. He was finally given some bananas and four quarts of an I.V. solution. He came out of the shock within 15 to 20 minutes. He will, nevertheless, leave tomorrow to go home. He was told there were no plane tickets available, but when he offered them an extra 100 U.S. dollars, a seat was found for him. We spent some time talking to him this afternoon telling him goodbye. We'll miss having him around.

September 18

Dave

DETAIL OF THE DAY:

This morning I was awake but drowsy and suddenly heard two abrupt hard hits from a hammer on a pipe. I checked my clock and it was exactly 6:00. Then I heard very little pounding for the next few minutes, which leads me to believe that the two hits were a deliberate, mean-spirited wake-up call. The men know the foreigners are in this building, and they know we're tired of their pounding. It goes on and on.

...How fun Jan is. Last night we had some old '50s songs playing and she grabbed me in the middle of the room, and we danced a little. We'd had such a great time in bed after lunch. Then we rested, got up and took a two-hour walk. I felt animated, rejuvenated. Jan's a joy to hang out with. Lots of others are here without companions. I wouldn't be able to stand it long without Jan. Solitariness has one good thing going for it: you can pace yourself and get work done. But I'd still choose being with Jan any day over that. I still get work done because she wants me to get it done, and she has her own work to do. The extra room will make a difference. I'll be hiding out.

September 19

Dave

Met a doctor at the Hopkins Center—Steve. Congenial fellow. He'll be available if we need help. He says there's a decent foreigners' ward in the Renmin (Peoples') hospital, where they even have a machine for blasting kidney stones into oblivion. And Shanghai has a very modern, Western hospital. That's only about four to five hours away. Good to know. He told us to make sure we do two things while we're in China: boil our water and cook our vegetables. And, he added, number three: peel the skins of fruits, including grapes.

...I got my weight-room "tickets," which are good for 24 workouts. I'll use them this time. Jan remarked last night in bed, looking at my arms and shoulders: "You don't have any mass." I'll show her some mass. Hard, hard mass. Soon. Just watch me.

...My running is improving; my legs, which have been a little sore lately, are holding up. Chugged two miles in around 20 minutes. Not like a decade ago when I did ten miles twice, one time averaging around 8 1/2 minutes a mile. To think that I was once, 30 years ago, a sprinter who could cover 100 yards in around 10 seconds, could be at full speed in about 10 yards. Once, light footed, light hearted.

September 19

Jan

Dear Delores & Bev,

When you talk about cold weather in your letters, I feel envious. We're suffering terribly from the heat and humidity of Nanjing—one of the "four ovens of China." Besides being overheated, we also think we have fleas and/or worms. We spent a miserable night last night itching and scratching.

Today we went with a group to tour the sites of Nanjing. We started off visiting one of the gates to the city and part of the 1000-year-old city wall, and then went to the Taiping Memorial. The Taiping Revolution happened in the 19th century, when some religious fanatics wanted to take over China. They were put down by the Empire, with the help of the British. The huge and numerous pictures on the wall described the sequence of the rebellion in and around Nanjing.

We had a decent buffet lunch in a Chinese hotel. As we pulled up to our next stop, the Sun Yat-Sen Memorial, we smelled something burning. The van had lost its brakes. Seeing the way people drive here, it's not surprising for brakes to burn out. Drivers speed along and are continuously having to stop suddenly for bikers and walkers. It scares us to watch while we ride. It often appears as if we're about to hit someone or be hit.

We climbed the 395 steps up to the top of the Sun Yat-Sen Memorial. Sun Yat-Sen is called the Father of Modern China. He helped overthrow the empire and start the Republic in the early years of the 20th century. The climb was easy for us, compared to the Great Wall climb. The view was wonderful; we could see the city of Nanjing, with the famous Purple Mountain in the distance. It is actually purple.

We got tickets for the movie Ju Dou, which was nominated for an Oscar for best foreign film. It was actually banned in China until just recently because of its so-called sensitive theme, but it is now openly shown. We felt it was neither anti- nor pro-China, just a moving, powerful film. The theater was large and all of the seats were reserved seats. No popcorn or cold drinks were available, only crackers and dried foods. Dave especially missed the popcorn, since he's used to eating one "monster bucket" per movie. A movie without popcorn is hard to deal with.

I didn't like Dave much today (at least not this morning). He was crabby when I asked him to put some of his things away. Maybe the stress of living in two rooms has gotten to us. We can't get away from each other. It's the "little" things he does that get on my nerves—like being crabby, not putting things away, or leaving the lid off the water thermos. I probably bug him, too, at times; in fact, I'm sure I do.

Deb, a colleague, told us that the maids, when they are done cleaning, go through all of our stuff and play our radios and tape players and mess with our cameras, that they are actually working for campus security. Maybe that's why we've already used up new batteries in our tape player and short wave radio, and why our camera lens doesn't close any more. I don't know what to think. She said she and Tom came home unexpectedly one time and caught the same maids—in security uniforms—going through their stuff. But who knows? I do know that the bank statement we received the other day obviously had been opened.

Deb also told us that the trip to Yellow Mountain we're supposed to take in two weeks is dangerous. People die every day on that mountain by falling, she said. Now I'm apprehensive about going. You know how afraid I am of heights and sharp drop-offs, especially when there are no protective rails. Deb an d Tom are not going. Our friend, Qian, seems so excited about going, and if we don't go, she won't be able to go either.

We found that going for a walk on a Sunday is too difficult. The crowds then, since many people have the day off, are elbow-to-elbow, bike wheel-to-bike wheel. We'll probably save our walks for other days of the week.

We recently went to a small "dive" for dinner with Jeff, an English teacher, and a Chinese friend. The restaurant owners were happy to see us come in and greeted us warmly. The food and service were good. Someone at another table was hacking and spitting, which was a bit distracting. As the waitress opened the beer bottles for us, she let the caps pop right off onto the floor. While we were eating, we heard a huge explosion outside that caused me to duck for cover. Apparently, it was a celebration with firecrackers for some big event, a wedding or the opening of a new shop. It went on for about five minutes, until the outside air became smoky, and then the restaurant filled with smoke. Just a typical night out in China.

The other day at the market a clerk tried to charge us too much money for two green peppers. An older Chinese woman, who happened to be there buying green peppers herself, shamed the clerk into charging us less. We're often at their mercy, since we don't know prices. It sounds trivial, but it's the principle of the thing. In the U.S. you know what you have to pay and usually *don't* argue about it.

Well, this is going on and on. Write and let us know what's happening in Sioux City. We miss you all.

Love,

Jan (avoiding fireworks)

September 20

Dave

Dear Friends,

With this letter I will kill two birds with one lap-top, making it both a letter and a day's journal entry. So, you get to look in as I do my self-reporting and at the same time you get news from your friends in China!

Okay, here goes: Evans you dumb bastard, you hypocrite, you dolt. You panicked. You broke the first rule of the East: don't panic, but take the Middle Way, the way of the Tao, which you should've learned in two years of Shotokan karate if not in China. You broke the calmness rule; you let your emotions run your life long enough to...to wipe out a brilliant, four-page letter to friends called LETTER TO FRIENDS, a letter in which you brilliantly and humorously and energetically and even calmly (but not without significant emotion) described your life in China in the past month, describing your weight loss of at least six pounds because of all the walking, all because you turned the goddamn computer off when the battery light went on and the buzzer buzzed, indicating you were low on battery power.

You did the same thing Jan did the other day when she was at the computer when the power went off, and, instead of <u>SAVING</u> what you'd written <u>before</u> you turned off the machine (I was smug, I'll admit it; I reminded Jan, calmly, to always save what she's written—she was not, let's say, in a mood of celebration at the time), the implication being: <u>I</u>

always save what I write—and then I do the same goddamn thing. I panic. And lose this brilliant letter to friends, called, as I said before, simply, plainly, calmly: LETTER TO FRIENDS. In which I described my life in China to date, a brilliant summary, dealing with how much I (with Jan, of course, who reminds me, not without a calm and penetrating irony, to always save what I write before I turn the machine off—she's one up on me in a two-room apartment now) enjoying walking down the street and seeing all the wonderful, incredibly varied sights of Nanjing, streets lined with Sycamore trees whose branches hang over the bike paths, creating a tunnel effect; streets where, second-to-second anything can happen—a man selling papers can suddenly spot you in the crowd, come running up, grab your elbow and get in your face—a big man, bigger than you are (and you are big in China), large-boned and tall and wide shouldered, different looking and different feeling, and that man can fix you with a look and start yelling at you for some reason, and you simply remove (as I did) your elbow from his hand, calmly, and smile at him, and back away and disappear into the crowd, which is easy to disappear into, like a rain forest.

Or about meeting the unlucky young African American (the PC rhetoric has a way of lingering, doesn't it?) from Iowa City who sees your Iowa hat from a distance and shouts out: "You from Iowa?" and you say, if you are from Iowa and by God I am and proud of it, you almost instinctively say, recalling the movie, "No, I'm from Heaven," and the guy comes over and tells you, within 20 seconds, that he's headed back to the States because the Chinese can't stand blacks, that he could write a book about his experiences here in the last two weeks, since classes started (he's studying Chinese language and culture at Nanjing University); or about the terrific movie that our friend and contact person, Qian, took us to last night: Ju Dou, which I was going to recommend to all my friends, which I was going to describe for you if you haven't seen it, and recommend it as a must-see, two-thumbs-up movie in which a beautiful young woman falls in love with a man twice her age—partly to escape her impotent, abusive and rich husband, the lover being a dye worker who dyes and sells cloth, a richly symbolic movie whose symbols I was going to explain in great unboring detail unlike I sometimes am guilty of in classrooms with literature; about going to see the Sun Yat-Sen Memorial yesterday, walking up all those stairs (about 400), looking out over Nanjing, seeing the Purple Mountain to the south, the city to the west of the mountain, of having a perspective, the way Li Bai might have had hundreds of years ago, long before Sun Yat-Sen took the Empire down and set up the brief and violent republic, making way for Mao and the triumphant peasants, the Long March and all, having Li Bai's perspective sort of because Li Bai actually lived for a time in this city; about, also, our living quarters here...

(This journal entry-letter is going on, I can see, and Jan says it can't be more than two pages, then we can print it on both sides of a page and save money in the sending of it, which, by the way, is a whole letter in itself—I mean, all the work you have to do in China to send a letter—they make written communication difficult for one big reason and that is that words on paper have tremendous power, much more power than words out of the mouth because—well, it's a whole letter. But you have to go to the post office, buy your stamp, then go to the paste box and get your fingers all gooey and sticky because the stamps and the envelope don't have any paste on them, the kind that you could just run your tongue over, you know, like we have in the U.S.—very ironic, this, since I was told that the students demonstrating in China's major cities in 1989 stole the glue boxes and pasted their huge, extravagant slogans all over the walls of cities, campuses and so on.)

But I was onto another subject, I'm forgetting exactly which, but I was, in the first four pages which I, stupid stupid me, lost somewhere in the guts of my Zenith lap-top, talking about our living quarters, which are fine, we have a real Western bathroom with shower in tub, mostly hot water though sometimes only hot water, two huge rooms, one lamp (dim light), a desk, two over-stuffed chairs, usually with a stuffed and wordy and panicky writer occupying one of them, a porch, a bedroom with a bed with something, apparently, in it that wants to bite the hell out of my ankles every night but I solved the problem with Skin So Soft last night, finally, I think. And I was writing about the fact that we'll be moving downstairs to a three-room apartment next month, what absolute LUX-URY, I'll be able to hide in one room sometimes...about. (This is by far the longest of my journal entries so far, the others run anywhere from...but that's not the point, that's not what I'm doing here, I'm telling you about China also, killing two birds) about walking down the streets and just looking around, watching things happen so magically as people

make a living, a woman now and then coming up to you with a child for appeasement purposes and asking you for money, a man selling rain-flower-rocks spread out on his cloth, and, need to get this printed, front and back, more later, later, back to the apartment (don't expect order here, this is a journal, too) all the goddamn noise around us on both sides, the feeling of being entombed like Fortunado by Montressor because they're building a corridor into a hotel on the south of us and a corridor into a restaurant on the north side: pounding, sawing, vibrating, yelling, sometimes singing—you know, those serious, casual voices of young workmen—a constant, relentless noise which makes it difficult to think or write or read or sleep—and all you can do is take a long, two-hour walk every day to get yourself tired enough to plop on the slim, armless chair, sans remote control, sans potato chips, sans stereo even, since our transformer was blown out by a so-called electrician who, when I "asked" him if he could hook it up, urging him by gesture to show us how to work the converter, plugged the thing into the 220 outlet: the machine hummed weirdly, and died, all three of us witnessing the death—a quiet, unmistakenly electronic, cold, painless death of a machine (which we're trying to get fixed by having a Chinese transformer stuck into it). About how much China has changed since we were here last, how you can get canned tuna, canned ham, even a sort of "Spam," thousands of kinds of cookies in packages, mayonnaise, cooking oil, several varieties of toilet paper, almost everything available in the West because China has discovered the free market.
As Ever,

Dave

September 21

Jan

My Ph.D. students asked me various kinds of questions today: about Bush, American politics, American lives and customs, the town I'm from, what they need to do in order to go to America to study, about "black humor," my hobbies and how old I am. I tried to answer most of the questions, but told them half jokingly (half not) that it's not polite to ask a woman her age. I enjoy talking with them.

...Tom told us that at 1:00 a.m. he was awakened by a loud fluttering noise. It was a bat with a huge wing span that had squeezed in through the crack in the bedroom window. With an accurate toss of one of his shoes, he killed it. It is bat season and we see a lot of them flying around outside our apartment building at night. The windows in these apartments don't fit properly, so bats and other little creatures can get through easily.

September 22

Jan

I took some cartoons from the U.S. to my conversation class to show them some American humor. Chinese people generally look for political undertones in cartoons, even when there aren't any there. I think that a lot of the cartoons in Chinese publications <u>are</u> political in nature, but I also know that in China you can't criticize the government. So, I suppose they are very subtle cartoons.

...Dong, one of my writing students, walked along with me after class. I asked him where his flat was in Nanjing. He misunderstood the question and went into detail about the town where he was born and how beautiful it is. I tried again to ask where he lived in Nanjing, but got the same kind of answer. He still didn't understand what I meant, but he felt he had to answer me anyway.

Xu, another writing student, interviewed me for a paper and wrote, after I told her I didn't like to cook: "In spite of this dislike, I think she must <u>still</u> be a good wife." I asked Dave about this after I told him I was fixing green lima beans and applesauce for dinner. He said I was a "good wife" but then began to reconsider. I told him that he couldn't find a better wife than he has, not even here in China.

...Qian is great at bargaining in the stores. When I'm looking at something with interest, she says, excitedly, "Do you want to buy it? I can get it cheaper." If I want it, she goes about bargaining and always comes up with a lower price. I don't know what she's saying, but she starts out by pointing out some minor flaw in the item, and goes from there.

Sometimes she and the clerk appear to be yelling and saying terrible things to each other, with spirit. It's fun to watch, even if I don't know what they're saying. I do sometimes feel a little uncomfortable, especially if the yelling seems more heated than usual. I'm not used to shopping like that. That's not to say that I haven't felt like yelling at times.

September 22

Dave

Here's an idea:

If a Chinese ant suddenly evolved with the ability to live inside refrigerators, Chinese civilization would finally, after 4,000 years, quickly collapse.

...Mr. Zhang wants me to fill out his survey about American writers. He called and said—after he'd put it in my box yesterday—that it was urgent that he get the survey back tonight. He, of course, took us out to dinner. Reciprocity in China is much more obvious than it is among Americans.

...There's so much show among the Chinese. The men put on a tie and suddenly they have substance. I like that innocence. Put on a good outward face and that means something important, that means there is substance. A holdover from the imperial days, no doubt. Put on a good show and keep the rabble astonished. Extravagance. Ceremony. Flourish. It all can easily stand for real substance. The medium is the message.

September 23

Dave

Mr. Zhang says he's happy—he's doing what he likes to do. He edits a journal, talks with American and Chinese poets, is putting together several books. He's happy but for one thing: his apartment. It's too small. He appreciated being in the U.S. about a decade ago, where people have room to entertain guests. Home is important. Home, the place, is important. Locale. The physical house or apartment. Maybe home is about 80 percent of happiness, whatever happiness means.

...Mr. Zhang wants me to go to Wuhan to give a talk about American poetry. He's especially interested in Midwest literature. He questioned the quote from Lao Tzu I used as an epigraph to a poem I wrote: "The strong are without ambition." But I looked over the translation I have of Lao Tzu's <u>The Way of Life</u> again and found that it really is not a bad quote, though "striving" might be a better word than "ambition." The strong don't need to strive because they <u>are</u> strong. You don't need to show your strength if you are strong. It's the weak ones who have to flex their muscles.

September 24

Jan

The bites I have on me are itching intensely and I'm developing scars from scratching holes in them. I don't know what's biting us—spiders, mosquitoes, fleas, bedbugs? Besides, we both had stomach problems today.

September 24

Dave

I enjoy watching Jan go over her students' essays. She first goes through them—she's so curious, brings me the ones she likes or the ones that have interesting sentences or images. Then she reads them again, and this time makes marks on them, and then she goes over them again and gives them a grade. She wants to be more articulate about things like imagery and figures of speech. I tell her she knows all these things, she just doesn't have the vocabulary down yet. She'll get it by listening to me and looking over my shoulder as I grade papers.

...Tomorrow, to Shanghai. I told Jan: I don't want to get waylaid in Shanghai, or Shanghaied in Shanghai, though I wouldn't mind getting laid in Shanghai.

September 25

Jan

Dave suffered with severe stomach pains during the night, but we

(Tom, Deb, Dave and I) still left at 8:00 a.m. to go to Shanghai. I told Dave if he was going to be sick, Shanghai was a good place to be. There are good doctors there, we were told.

...The countryside on the way to Shanghai is some of the richest land in China. The farms are lush and well cared for, and the homes are large.

When we got to Shanghai, Dave felt better, so we had pizza for lunch at the Peace Hotel, the same hotel where President Nixon stayed when he visited China in the early '70s. It's an old, elegant hotel with good Western food.

September 27

Jan

Dear Winnie & Phil,

Just wanted to let you know we are doing fine in China and to thank you for sending the tape of Philip and the various clippings from newspapers. We enjoyed them. You know from having lived abroad, how important these kinds of things are.

We just returned from a trip to Shanghai, where Dave and I went with a couple of friends, Tom and Deb. It is the most crowded place I have ever seen, or even imagined. I first thought Kunming, was the most crowded city, with two million people; then Nanjing, with almost five million; but Shanghai with almost 14 million people makes these two cities seem like small towns. It's the largest city in China. At times, you literally can't move because of the density of people. A ride in a cab is life-threatening, not only for those in the cab, but for the people and vehicles on the street the cab is speeding down. This goes on all day every day. When people get home at night, they must feel like, "Well, I've been 'lucky' for another day; I wasn't killed or run down." I'm afraid there are many unlucky ones; we heard lots of sirens.

We found a KFC restaurant in Shanghai and ate there a couple of times. It was wonderful, and I don't usually like KFC food. When you can't get it, it tastes better than it should.

The hotel we stayed in was comfortable and cheap—$30.00 per

night, but we each found a cockroach in our rooms. The beds were okay and we had warm water in the shower. It's funny how grateful we are for a warm shower. The location was especially good for walking to the shops. We were also close to a river and it happened to be opening day on the newly remodeled Bund (river front) the day we arrived. We watched the huge freighters, junks and barges making their way up the river. We bought wonderful down comforters which we watched being made. We had a choice of three types of down filling (all the way from 70% to 95% down). After making our choice, a huge blower forced the down into the comforter. We went grocery shopping in a Western food shop and found it satisfying being able to buy cheese, butter, American soups, brown sugar, American or European cereal, prunes, raisins, U.S. chocolate and pancake mix. But we paid a high price. American food is very expensive in China. A regular-size jar of Skippy peanut butter, for example, cost $8.00 U.S. Even so, we felt like we deserved it. Deb, was exuberant and kept saying how happy she was.

One afternoon, we caught a cab to take a letter and a package a Chinese friend in the U.S. had asked us to deliver to her mother. The cab driver took us there, after stopping several times to ask directions, one time in the middle of a busy street. He parked, we all got out and he locked the doors to his cab. He led us to an old, shabby-looking building. He spoke no English, nor did anyone in the area. We went up several flights of stairs and knocked on several doors. Only one older couple was at home. To say they were surprised to see us would be an extreme understatement. They frantically tried to find the people we were looking for, but they had no luck. We decided to leave the package and letter with these people. We created quite a sensation in the neighborhood by going there, and they are probably still talking about it. It gave us an insight into where our Chinese friends grew up—much more modest than we expected. The living conditions were comparable to less than lower standard in the U.S., and from what I could tell, each "apartment" consisted of only one room. There was a Western-style toilet in one corner of an upper floor, without a door on it, probably shared by everyone in the building. We felt bad that we didn't get to meet these people, relay messages from and to our friends and take snapshots of them to give our friends back in the U.S. If it wasn't so difficult to get around in Shanghai, we would try again. But we are limited in time when we visit other cities.

When we left for the train station to come back to Nanjing, we had trouble getting all of our heavy, cumbersome bags full of groceries and other items we'd bought in Shanghai into a cab, and then had trouble dragging it into the train. I suddenly had the feeling we looked like "rich Americans," a label I don't like.

When we got back to Nanjing and were waiting for a cab at the train station, there appeared, out of nowhere, about 15 tattered, dingy-looking people, some begging and others just watching us like vultures. We were afraid of what they might do and were anxious to get into a cab. One cab driver wanted us to go with him, but he didn't have a meter in his cab and seemed to be aligned with these people. We spent several uncomfortable moments before we got into cabs, with the people eyeing our bags. We have been warned many times about thieves. Deb and I rode in one cab and Dave and Tom in another since the cabs were small and we couldn't get all of our baggage in one. Tom argued with the cab driver when they got to the apartment because he changed the meter as soon as he stopped. He was trying to charge too much. The cab driver then came over to me as I was standing waiting, and wanted me to pay for Dave and Tom's fare. After some rather heated discussion, Tom asked for the cab driver's supervisor's name and phone number, and the driver quickly left in anger.

When we got inside our apartment and turned the light on in our kitchen, I screamed. There was a gecko (lizard) stuck to the cupboard above the sink. Dave gallantly came to my rescue and smashed it with a shoe. It curled up and fell into the sink. We then realized we should have let it live in our apartment, since it would have eaten insects. Killing it was just an automatic reaction.

Our trip was fun and we came home with a good supply of Western food. We like the vegetables, rice and fruit here but miss the variety of foods available in the U.S. Dave misses racquetball, Phil, but is trying to stay in shape by jogging and walking. There aren't many available tennis courts, so we haven't used our racquets yet.

Hope you're doing well. Tell Philip Jr. hi from us.
Love,

Jan (Shanghai traveler)

September 27

Dave

Shanghai!

Just got back from Shanghai, my so-far favorite China city. Crowded is not the word you could use with any accuracy, especially for Nanjing Road, the main street, on a Saturday or Sunday. At one point I felt like just giving up in that crowd, it was so suffocating. (If you did give up and go limp, you'd probably be held up by the moving crowd, and nobody would notice anyway!) Shanghai does not have room for all its people.

Cab drivers are something, too. My God, what a way to make a living. To ride in a cab in Shanghai is to put yourself in danger from the moment you get in and close the door to the moment you step out at the end of the trip. And then, not quite, because another cab, or a car or bus or truck or bike may come along and flatten you. But to sit there inside the cab and look through the windshield as you're moving along at an outrageous speed, to see the bikes and walkers clear a path for you, and the kids walking with their parents, the bikes hovering around the center of the street, and other cars—it's like playing one of those video games in a kid's game room, where you're on a racing motorcycle or in a car, and you see the road unfolding before your eyes, and you know that, having paid your quarter or two, that you will not make it to the end of this journey before a major crash, into a tree, another vehicle, a bridge or whatever. There you are, turning the wheel to avoid all those obstacles threatening to break you up every second, coming at you, coming at you, or are you coming at them?—it's an optical illusion, of course. It's only a screen, and the steering wheel is working but it's not a real one. But that's what it looks like. With one difference. In Shanghai, it is real, and you pay a hell of a lot more than a quarter or two. Hard to describe. A

Tom , Deb, Jan and Dave in Shanghai

person with a weak heart would be advised not to attempt it.

But Shanghai is wonderful. It's a place to live for awhile, not just to visit. Shanghai has everything—hotels, food, rivers, the ocean, ships, junks, a beautiful walkway along the water, huge excursion boats, tankers, coal boats, you name it. But the water is absolutely and totally polluted. You can't drink it even after you boil it, because it has metal particles in it. I wouldn't think an expert swimmer would last in the water around Shanghai more than a few minutes. I can't imagine water any dirtier. Back to taxis. One day Jan and I were in one and stalled in heavy traffic—which in Shanghai is as common as breathing; the bikes move a lot faster because the bikers can weave better, can fit into smaller holes in the traffic. We sat there, and outside my window on the right was an old woman with only one tooth, waiting to cross the street. When she saw us she began making threatening gestures, criticizing us, pointing at us, her voice very insistent and angry, her mouth spittled over with haranguing. About every ten seconds we could make out the word "meiguo" (America). If I'd thought about it, I would've taken her picture. But we sat there, half surprised, half stunned, while a shower of epithets came over us in the middle of heavy traffic in the middle of Shanghai.

Earlier that day I'd gotten another stare from an old man on the sidewalk as the taxi was halted. And then the stare was transferred to the taxi driver, as if to say: "And you are giving those two foreign devils a ride?" The older generation, born before Liberation, evidently still has some things to say about capitalists.

Ah, Shanghai. It's another country more than another city.

September 28

Jan

When we took our new toaster that we had bought in Shanghai out of the box, we discovered that it had no plug on it. I was angry. I thought we had been ripped off and considered sending it back (as I would have at home), but later I learned that it's often the way appliances are sold here. Besides having no plug, it had an awful smell—as though it had sat in some dank, moldy basement since the Qing Dynasty. We took it to an electric shop and, with sign language, had a clerk put a plug on for us. At first he thought we just wanted to buy the plug, but we wanted them to put it on for us too. (Most people probably put their own plugs on. We are not capable.)

September 28

Dave

Recently I was having some xeroxing done at the campus library. The man in charge made a mistake, didn't have the paper in properly, so five or six pages had to be voided. He took the copies and put them on a shelf. I hated that, if only for the reason that it was a private letter. But if I'd said anything to him (he spoke English)—that I wanted to keep them or destroy them myself—he may have suspected the content. I said nothing.

September 29

Jan

I had a "visitor" in my conversation class today. Mr. Z. from the graduate office met me before class and pointed out a woman in the classroom and told me not to call on her since she was just visiting for a few classes. I'm sure she was checking up on me. I wanted to catch this visitor/spy after class and tell her just how much I enjoyed having her with us, but I didn't.

...Dinner tonight, by invitation only, was a dress-up affair. It was sponsored by the provincial government and is considered to be "the event of the year." I'm not fond of stand-up buffet banquets. The food was typical, and excessive amounts had been prepared. Fred was having a good time. He had consumed many beers and became somewhat bois-terous. He was clapping with the music and yelling at a female singer on stage in an organdy dress. He said he wanted to go up there and "suck her toes." He also said, over and over, how much he loves women in organdy dresses. It's probably a good thing most people couldn't under-stand what he was saying. We keep reminding him of the No. 1 Rule here —no sex with Chinese women.

...We bought a new "glow-in-the-dark" clock today for about $3.50. (It doesn't glow in the dark.) At home I would have immediately taken it back. Here we probably wouldn't be able to find the shop again. We'll keep it.

September 29

Dave

Lots of professors here suffered, even physically, during the Cul-tural Revolution. Some are crippled for life, psychologically if not physi-cally. And Red Guards who persecuted some people are now working side-by-side with them.

September 30

Jan

I read in my student LiLi's journal today that her friend's father just died. Her friend said this about his father: "The big tree has fallen."

He said that he would have to take on the responsibility of his household now, since he was the man of the house. She also wrote, in another entry, that the university had an abundance of ads around the campus these days. One ad said in big red letters: "Let's go shooting"; and in parentheses: "Those who have heart disease can't go." Direct and to the point.

OCTOBER

October 1

Dave

A holiday (National Day), and still, they're banging away on both sides of our apartment.

...Why can't students check books out of the campus library? My student Wang says that the library administrators want to make money, so they force students to use the copy machine, which brings in money. Is it true? Universities are doing what they can anymore to make money. Putting up hotels, fancy restaurants, shops, etc.

...Stay on your feet, Dave. That's the trick. Buy a bike? Maybe, though I know a bike will make it easier for me and, just as the Chinese when they come to the U.S. always get a car if they can afford it, I'll no doubt end up with a bike here. But I will keep walking; I know I need to.

October 3 & 4

Dave

Nantong trip on Thursday, Friday and Saturday, back on Sunday.

In Nantong:

(I write these words in my little notebook on Saturday at the Wengfeng hotel):

The mini-bus ride to Nantong was so terrifying that, should I get back to Nanjing in one piece tomorrow, I will never again go any distance in a mini-bus in China. It's either a train, or a plane or a boat—period. The people on bikes, cycles, three-wheel cars, and smaller vans—all parting as our bus approached, some bikes—even people on foot—especially in the villages, nonchalantly, vaguely veering to the left into the center of the road—our driver constantly beeping his horn—and missing them routinely by a few inches—it's only a matter of time—somebody's going to get hit, clipped, run over, flattened—

63

And the semis coming at us, the trucks, all this is a danger. (I told Deb that my body knows when it's in danger.) I told Tom and Fred I thought the driver was going too fast, but they didn't seem to be bothered by it.

I wanted to fly back home (no flights), take the train (no trains), take the boat (too long a trip up-river to Nanjing), so I'll have to submit to it.

I'll hate it—but maybe, since we're leaving at 6:30 a.m. on Sunday, it'll be less crowded on the "highway," and it won't be as bad as it was on National Day. We'll see—I fear it more than I can describe.

But there was more to the Nantong trip than the drive. We all went clam-digging on Saturday morning. Had to travel about an hour, not on main roads like the ones we used coming to Nantong—and then, when the tide was out, go by hand-tractor across the Yangtze flats. It reminded me of the kid's story, The Five Chinese Brothers, in which one brother can actually swallow up the sea. It was like walking around on the bed of the sea when the water has been sucked up by your kid brother, standing there with his cheeks bulging, his face turning red as he holds his breath. There were stranded junks,

Clam dancer

little pools, crabs sneaking about and darting back quickly into their holes. And clams. If you stood there and moved both feet, first one and then the other, creating a little pool, suddenly the clams, being tricked into "thinking" that the tide was coming in, would pop up and you could reach down and grab them. We saw one old man who tried to show us how you do it. He was very effective, obviously, since his bag of clams was huge. Evidently he'd been doing the dance for years, maybe decades.

We went to an interesting fabrics museum, which displayed in pictures and exhibits a sort of running history of weaving and fabric-making in China over the centuries. We watched one man as he worked on a loom. He reminded me of "The Hunger Artist," a story by Franz Kafka about a man whose art of fasting has become obsolete. There was joy in this Chinese man's work. He obviously loved to show it off. I enjoy watching somebody who is good at something, it doesn't really matter what. I admire a person who gets good by practice and diligence and determination.

...The ride back to Nanjing? We made it, is about all I can say. The driver was pulled over just after he was reported (for something: speeding or reckless driving) by a patrolman. He refused to pay a fine of Y50, and evidently was hoping that his foreign "guests" would chip in. I refused to pay. The bastard's fast driving had turned me off completely. Fred wanted to just pay it so we could get home instead of sitting around in the van waiting to decide what to do next. But I was thinking—why feed the man's fire? Just as I was about to say something, Jan pinched me, so I just sat there, fuming inside. Finally, for some reason the driver was let go without having to pay anything and we took off again. That driver is the reason I will never travel any distance in China in anything smaller than a huge bus.

Period.

October 5

Jan

Dear Don & Phyl,

I'm happy to hear you're going to retire in Arizona. You deserve it. It doesn't seem likely my big brother should be retiring yet. You're not that old, are you? I hope we can come there to visit you sometime, preferably in the winter. After spending time in Nanjing, we should be able to handle the hot weather. It's hotter here than anywhere I've ever been.

We've been mostly enjoying China this second go-round. We didn't have the usual cultural shock to deal with, as we did when we came here the first time in 1988. We were more prepared for what to expect. But some things you can never be prepared for, like a recent trip we took to a city called Nantong.

The University Foreign Affairs Office arranged a bus trip for foreigners who teach at Nanjing University to go to Nantong to go clam digging in the Yangtze River near Shanghai. The eleven of us who chose to go piled into a small van and left one bright sunny morning at 8:00 a.m. We could barely get all the luggage in and the seats were very small and uncomfortable. It was especially uncomfortable for a couple of the tall men who ended up in the back of the van. The back is also the bumpiest, since these university vans are always without shocks. The ride was life-threatening all the way, with no letup, even through the towns along the way. People literally had to dodge the van to keep from being run down. We came within inches many times of crashing into another vehicle or bike rider. The driver seemed to hate being behind anyone. He passed cars and trucks at the most inopportune times. I guess he could be considered skillful since we didn't have any accidents when it seemed certain that we would. Dave was often near panic since he was sitting on the driver's side next to the window. He had a better view of how many close calls we were having. I tried not to look and mostly stayed occupied talking or trying to read.

Near Nantong we pulled up in back of a long line of traffic to catch a ride on the ferry to cross the Yangtze. Our guide said nothing to us as he went up to the front of the line and apparently paid extra money, because we were allowed to go ahead of all the traffic and get right on the ferry. It was an interesting half-hour ride across the Yangtze. We got out of the van and went up on the top deck of the ferry and took pictures of the huge ships, some even from Russia, and enjoyed the view. A Chinese man who worked on the ferry gestured to us to come into his room on the top deck. There was an acrobatic show playing on his T.V. set at the time, which he and his family seemed to be enjoying. There were two couches and a chair, without cushions, in the room. The man kept trying to get his young son to talk to us, but his son was too shy and hid behind a woman, who I assumed was his mother. The man and his family seemed pleased that we were there. When others knew we were there, they came to have a look at us. We felt like circus freaks.

The countryside is filled with large, fairly new-looking cement homes, sitting right alongside homes with sod and thatched roofs. The roofs on the cement homes have designs on them that resemble the curves on canoes or fish tails. This design is prevalent only in the areas near the river. We were told that the roof designs on homes are "house gods," and that they protect the families from danger or bad luck.

After stopping in a small-town hotel for lunch, we arrived in Nantong in mid-afternoon, tired and emotionally drained from the trip. Our hotel room was the worst we ever stayed in. It smelled of mold and smoke and was filthy. Because there were no screens on the windows, swarms of mosquitoes came in when we opened the windows for air. It was unbearably hot (no air-conditioning). Dave and I didn't say much about it to each other; we just thought, as we got in our twin beds and pulled the mosquito nets around us, that we would cope with it.

The next morning when we got up and had showers, our tub filled with water and would not empty. The sink wouldn't drain. The toilet wouldn't flush. Dave had a miserable night and was claustrophobic from sleeping inside the mosquito net; the smoky-moldy smell of the room got to both of us. The carpet was filthy. One corner of the room looked like it had been used for spitting or something else. We didn't dare step on the floor with our bare feet. The towels smelled bad and the thermoses and cracked cups were dirty like everything else in the room. So after a breakfast of cold meat, vegetable dishes, rice gruel, hot milk, greasy fried eggs, tea and assorted bread items, Dave told the guide we would like to change our room to the newer part of the hotel. We had met an American couple who told us their room in that part

Houses with curved roofs

of the hotel was decent. Everyone else in our group, except the four Chinese people, complained about their rooms also but didn't ask to change. We got a great room and thought the extra money we had to pay was worth it. We had discovered our limits as far as comfort goes.

That day we all walked to the top of "Wolf Mountain" to visit the Buddhist monastery there. It was completely packed with people, because of the National Day holiday. There were twelve Buddhist monks painted on large tiles on each side of a huge golden Buddha statue. The artist who painted these has been in exile in Paris since the Tiananmen incident. We watched as people offered incense, money or food for prayers to be said by the monks. The monks chanted in monotone voices, each of them with shaven heads, dressed in loose-fitting, plain, blue cotton robes. Most of them were older men, but a few were young. I was fascinated with these men and wanted to know more about them. They seemed mysterious and exotic to me.

The climb was arduous, and as we were going down, we saw several older people being toted up in carriages (called "sedans") by two young men, each supporting one end. I told Dave that's the way I'm going next time.

We had a dinner of mostly seafood in the old part of the hotel. We prefer not to eat much seafood here. In fact, officials from the Fulbright office in Beijing told us not to eat seafood, especially shellfish. There's too much danger of hepatitis. After dinner we went to the gift shop, bought some imported English chocolate chip cookies and went to enjoy our "new room." We felt a little guilty leaving the rest of our group to their shabby rooms; but we got over it.

One day we piled in the van and went to the Yangtze mud flats to dig for clams (the main purpose of our trip) while the tide was out. Our driver had severe diarrhea, so Deb gave him some of her anti-diarrhea pills. Xiao was nauseated and had to have the driver stop so she could throw up. Fang also felt ill and insisted on having the window wide open, which created a wind storm in the car for the rest of us. I think the abundance of rich food may have gotten to all of them.

When we got to the Yangtze, we had to ride in little tractor-like vehicles to get out to the flats. (I've wanted to ride in one of these vehicles since I saw them in Kunming.) We had to "dance" to get the clams to come to the surface.

On the way back to our hotel, we pulled up to a set of old buildings in the middle of nowhere. We joked about this being the place where we would have lunch. It actually was the place! It looked to me like an old farm with several out buildings. There were many separate rooms filled with people eating. The table in one room was set up nicely for us, since they were expecting our group. Fred, our colleague from California, said when he looked over the food, "everyone has to die sometime," and bit into a snail full of sand. He ate everything. We were served pig intestine, eel, tendrils (of something), fish soup, fish skin soup, mussels, crab, snail, raw crab "nose" meat, duck tea eggs, pork slices, rice, river fish of some kind, something black, and the ever-popular weak orange drink. I ate a little pork, tried an egg, which was mushy and very salty, and drank a beer. It was a difficult lunch for me. The chopsticks were dirty. The dishes were dirty and chipped. People kept staring through the open window at us. After dinner we took a few pictures and then went to look at the kitchen, which we were glad we had not seen before lunch. It was not the kind of kitchen you would like to see in a restaurant where you've just had a meal. Nothing appeared to be clean and there was a lot of trash strewn around. The little kids running around, as well as others, were dirty and unkempt.

There was an argument over the bill, which took some time to settle. Our guide said that in any other restaurant this meal would have been a lot more expensive. We got a "deal" on it.

The next day, our ride back to Nanjing was as treacherous as the ride to Nantong had been. Dave and I decided this would be our last mini-bus trip. We'll go on a train, boat or plane from now on. And then Xiao got sick again and threw up in the van. Besides this, we had all of the smelly clams from the day before under our seats in the van. We were happy to get home alive. Our apartment looked and smelled great.

Don't worry about us. We're doing okay. Write and let us know what your plans are.
Love,

Jan (from the Yangtze mud flats)

October 5

Dave

There was a painting at the Wengfeng Hotel in Nantong, a panoramic scene with a huge lake and mountains in the background, along with several bamboo trees hanging over the edge of the lake. A small boat with a fisherman in it, and calm, dark water. A peaceful scene. Typical classical Chinese—nature was depicted as huge; man as small and yet fitting into the scene comfortably. I was admiring this picture when a moth flew toward the painting, circled it, as if looking for a place to alight, and then did alight—not on the lake or on the boat, but in the branches of the bamboo tree. That made sense. It's as if the moth, surveying the artificial landscape-in-miniature, knew exactly where it could land: where moths land all the time anyway—on a branch, on leaves.

October 5

Jan

Moving day! We moved downstairs to a three-room apartment. A couple of Dave's students helped move books while I was in class. Four female workers came to move the heavy glass-door bookcase. We tried to help them, but they wouldn't let us. They are incredibly strong for being so petite.

October 7

Jan

The ants we had in our upstairs apartment were tiny red ants. The ants in this downstairs apartment are larger black ants (which makes for some variety). Living on the first floor has some drawbacks, but we do have better water pressure and more space. We're happy to be here.

October 7

Dave

So, we've moved in. We now have an extra room. Here I am, sitting at my computer, with plenty of space to write, even with the staccato banging noise of the boiler room through the wall and the banging and sawing outside to the north, as the restaurant goes up. Deadline is supposed to be October 10 or 15th. They have so much to do, I wonder if the man in charge didn't really mean November. He just gave a number because some foreign experts pressed him. It was easy for him to do. Just name a number and smile.

...I miss racquetball. The physical game, and the camaraderie of it. I don't get much vigorous exercise here. I am lifting a little, to keep my arms from shriveling up. And next week I'm going to get a bike. For long trips, I tell myself. A bike in China is the equivalent of a car back home. But we'll be able to take longer trips if we want to, and we can ride all winter. There's much more to Nanjing than we have seen. The natural history museum, for instance, and the bridge—we need to see them.

October 8

Jan

In my conversation class today, I talked about American family life. My students are interested in anything I can tell them about the American family. The two hours went by quickly as they asked all kinds of questions. We also talked about the Miss Nanjing contest that took place here this past weekend—a first of its kind in Nanjing. This is thought to be a bold step (at least in Nanjing). In the past this kind of activity was considered bourgeois. The students, especially the male students, generally like the idea. The few females I have in class, however, aren't sure. One said beauty must come from "inside." One male student said, "It is dangerous to have a beautiful wife." The contest was similar to American beauty contests, with talent, swimsuit and evening gown competition. The winner, a graduate student in a medical school, was awarded a comparatively large amount of money.

...Two students came over, one for help with a letter, and the other just to talk. Neither has very good English skills, so it's a challenge to communicate with them. One asked, when he saw our kitchen area, if that was where I "burned" the fish. I think he meant "cook." I actually do burn food here (I haven't tried cooking "the fish" yet). It's an adjustment cooking with bottle gas on a two-plate burner. The heat is difficult to regulate. We call our big bottle gas tank the "Nanjing bomb."

...Today, on the street, we saw something horrifying. A woman was sitting with a young child (I assume it was her child), who had been burned almost to death. His face was unspeakably scarred. He had no hair and his eyes were taut and barely open. The woman was crying and wanted money. We gave money, but it was very disturbing to look at the child. He looked like a monster in a science fiction movie. We were shaken by the sight.

We also saw, on our daily walk, a man standing beside a tree vomiting. When he was finished he got on his bike, with a heavy load on it, and went on his way. A little farther down the road, we saw a father holding his child next to a tree so he could poop. His little butt, testicles, and penis were exposed for all to see. We often see grown men relieving themselves next to trees or beside buildings. They're a little more discreet, but not much.

October 8

Dave

Yesterday I was in a bad mood. The foul odor of the bathroom and the extra room (mold on the wall), the oncoming cold, the relentless noise of the workers on the south and north of the building—and then all the auditors in my classes. I'm supposed to have only 10 students but I have about six or seven auditors in the literature class and three or four in the writing class. The truth is, I don't want to grade all those papers, and I was told in the first place that I'd have sort of a seminar, a small class in which I could learn all the names, have them do reports, and so on. My ugly mood came out just before I left for class—Jan knows me too too well after 35 or so years.

"How come you're in such an ugly mood?" she asked. (Jan's questions can have such penetrating clarity.)

I mentioned the auditor situation, that I'm tired of dealing with it—I really don't know who's taking the class for credit, or whose papers I need to grade.

"They all want to learn," Jan said. And again, she saw to the bottom of it. They all do want to learn, and I need to treat them all with respect and care.

I went to class and had a good one, I felt. Then I asked the auditors to see me after class, so I could talk to them. The whole class huddled around me. It's hard to isolate students in China. They all want to know what's going on. That's the collectivistic way, I suppose. Nobody has the right to get ahead, to have an edge over the group. So everyone is involved. Anyway, I figured it out. I'll read the auditors' papers and make comments, without giving grades. And I won't have them do reports or take tests. Period. No sweat. Walking back to the apartment, I felt much better.

October 9

Dave

That moth back in Nantong is still fluttering around in my memory:

THE MOTH

In a hotel in Nantong,
near the sea,
I stopped at a painting:
a huge, quiet lake,
a mountain beyond it,
some bamboo trees nearby,
and a boat with a fisherman
standing up, leaning
on a long stick.
Then a moth
fluttered down the hall
and alighted on
the bamboo trees.
I thought of Chaung Tzu,
who once dreamed he was
a butterfly, and then,

waking up, wasn't sure if
he was Chaung Tzu or
the butterfly dreaming
it was Chaung Tzu.
Which moth was real?—
the one fluttering
down the hall,
or the one resting,
quietly,
on bamboo trees
in the painting.

October 10

Jan

Fang and two men—one from the university, and one from a publishing house—came over today to ask if we would write a few "one-minute articles" for a publication about American customs. We agreed that we would each do two; then, as we talked further, we found out that they actually want 70 articles from us. They said they would get back to us and left. Four sounded reasonable, but 66 more? We don't know if we'll do that many or not. Should we feel a little like we're being taken advantage of? We do.

October 10

Dave

Little things get to me. Like...Fred saying to me and to Mike, the other poet/teacher here: "Name one poet right now in America who is great."

Then he goes on to mention all the "great" poets of the post-war period: William Carlos Williams, Robert Frost, T.S. Eliot and a couple of others. I didn't have much of a response except to say that there are a lot of good poets writing right now. I mentioned James Dickey as one who I thought could be considered major. I mentioned good poets like Ted Kooser and Dave Etter. I always think of my answers later, and never, or almost never, at the time they're asked for. I guess I'm a writer more than a speaker. But I could have said something like: "The people who will judge whether poets in America right now are great haven't been born yet..." Whoever thought Melville would be great, or Dickinson, or Whitman or Poe? It takes a long time for posterity to judge these things—decades, sometimes centuries. Leave it to posterity. That was Dylan Thomas' response when he was asked about whether he would be considered a great poet some day. And now, a few decades after his death—sure enough—Dylan Thomas, that little quirky drunk from Swansea, Wales has two immortal lines in Westminster Abbey, along with Shakespeare, et al.

Or, I should have said to Fred that it's more interesting and productive to talk about great poems than great poets. Then I could've mentioned Stanley Kunitz' "End of Summer," "The Well-Fleet Whale," James Dickey's "The Heaven of Animals," and a few others by him, and William Stafford's "The Farm on the Great Plains," and Karl Shapiro's "The Fly," and many other poems by recent American poets. In fact, I could've argued that a great poet is one who has written at least one great poem. But the poet at least should have the chance to write all of his/her poems before one begins to judge.

...What bothers me? Jan taking my jacket off the hall tree. What the hell is a hall tree for if not to hang jackets on?

...So I grab, along with the jacket, my rain jacket, off the hall tree. I'll show her. Now what is <u>she</u> gonna put on the hall tree?

October 11

Jan

Nanjing is known for its beautiful rocks, called "rain flower pebbles," and you can buy them everywhere. They are displayed in dishes of water to show off their beauty. People give these rocks names and attach characteristics to them, depending on what they resemble. We bought some postcards with lines of poetry accompanying pictures of rain flower pebbles. The pebbles are popular tourist gifts and many people have them displayed in their homes.

...The gates to our university, and every other work unit (<u>danwei</u>) in China, have guards sitting near them from early morning to late at night. The guards are usually older, retired men. Everyone who enters must have a purpose, and if a person looks suspicious, he or she will be stopped and checked. Vehicles must stop and the drivers must state their reasons for entering. Cab drivers are required to pay Y2 to enter the campus. People on bikes must stop and walk (not ride) their bikes through the gate.

October 11
Dave

DETAIL OF THE DAY:
   Jan and I stumbled, literally, in Sunday traffic, on a fast-food place called "Gently," went in, had an order of chicken (2 legs; they were out of thighs), fries and a Coke. I asked the young, pleasant waitress where the W.C. was and she pointed upstairs. When I got there the door on the women's showed a drawing of a pair of high-heeled shoes and the men's showed a drawing of a pipe. Pretty snazzy, I thought.

October 12

Jan

   Today we saw a man sitting on a busy sidewalk, with his shoes and socks off, reading a newspaper, while he was having his feet worked on by a woman. He was having his callouses shaved off. His feet were bleeding.
   We also saw "lotus on-a-stick" for sale. Lotus root is actually tasty. It's a versatile vegetable and often served stuffed with rice. To me, that is quintessential Chinese—lotus and rice. The season is here for candied crab apples on a stick. They are bright red, similar to our candied apples, except there are five or six very small apples on each stick.
   We stopped to weigh ourselves on a scale on the street today. To make a living, some older men and women sit all day every day waiting for people to weigh themselves on their scales. It costs one jiao (less than a penny) and we always draw a crowd. People gasp and laugh when Dave steps on the scale. My weight has dropped about 13 pounds since we got here. Dave's hasn't gone down much at all, and he's upset about it. Maybe too much pijiu (beer).

October 12

Dave

DETAIL OF THE MONTH:

Jan brought 19 pairs of shoes to China. (I counted them.) Oh my decadent woman.

...Why is it that, when it comes to couples, you almost always like one and not both? On the way back from the lantern display last night, Jan said: "Sometimes I wish there weren't so many foreigners around." I know what she meant.

...The lantern display we saw yesterday was excellent. What impressed me was the unique combination of machinery/technology on the one hand, and story on the other hand. There were many elaborate displays involving moving animals and figures telling stories of past centuries. The blending of story and machinery is not something you see in America. In China it seems to be a comfortable blending. The Chinese believe in technology; yet they love stories of their past. They're trying all sorts of technological ventures these days, learning as much as they can from the West and from Japan.

But my point is that I don't see in China a separation of story and the machine, which is an American theme in art and literature and has been at least since Thoreau. I was charmed by the display, paid for by individual companies, each showing off its name on the displays. In some cases the individual inventor/artist was there. They seemed proud of their work, and well they should have been.

...You can't ever be sure you are communicating in China, when you don't have the language. What you say often means the very opposite to the person you are speaking to. For instance, when we went to the Pizza Place the other night, we made it very clear—we thought—that we didn't want onions (bu yangcong) and that we wanted two small pizzas instead of one large one. What came back was one large pizza full of onions.

October 13

Jan

Twenty-six years ago today I was in a Colorado hospital giving birth to our younger daughter. I thought about her a lot today and realized how much I miss our family.

...I gave each of my writing students a cartoon I had brought from the U.S., and asked them to write interpretations for me. Their interpretations of American humor were often completely off the mark, but always fun to read. In one cartoon there was a statement about a "collect call." That is a concept they know nothing about. None of these students have telephones.

October 14

Dave

Question:

If the Chinese are, compared to Westerners, short and slight, why are Chinese ants so huge?

October 14

Jan

Today we caught a bus with two of Dave's graduate students, Zhou and Wang, to go to a used bicycle lot to buy bikes. There were many hawkers with bikes to sell and they all wanted us to look at their bikes. They would come up to us, pull on our sleeves, say "hello," and show us their bikes. As expected, a huge crowd gathered around us. Dave's students did the bargaining after we told them what we wanted to pay. Everyone watched intensely as we tried the bikes out. They offered us advice, in Chinese. After making our choices and getting ready to leave, some of the men—whose bikes we didn't buy—were yelling at us. We asked Zhou if they were angry and he said, "Perhaps." (Nice under-statement, we thought.) Then he explained that the men accused Zhou and Wang of helping foreigners, instead of being loyal to Chinese.

October 15

Jan

The fall weather is great here. Days are comfortably warm and nights are cool. The leaves are beginning to fall. Winter quilts have been hung out to air and then distributed to each apartment. We're collecting bricks to put on our heaters for the cold months. We were told that they will help radiate the heat, which is turned on only twice a day for short periods.

...Today I couldn't get the key out of my bike lock, so I left it in the lock. Two hours later I went out and discovered that someone had taken my key, but not my bike. The culprit may have planned to come back later and take it, but I fooled them. I had a new lock put on. I also got a new basket and had my seat adjusted. Dave got a bell and a lock, since his bike wasn't equipped with these necessary items. People pay attention to bike bells and car horns. They mean "move or you'll be hit." The bike repairman and his wife have a booming business in a run-down shack just outside the university gate. They are always busy, and they're quite skilled. They speak no English, but we were able to communicate to them what we wanted done.

They were apparently babysitting for their granddaughter, as most older Chinese people do. The girl, about five or six years old, was inside their flat watching a color T.V., and then came out with a clock in her hand, evidently to show her grandmother what time it was. She then left for school with her red book bag and red-ribboned pigtails bouncing as she skipped across the perilous street all by herself.

October 15

Dave

Joy of joys in China—we bought bikes! Mine is a wonderful green bike, heavy, sturdy, a Long March model—terrific. We rode the bikes home from the bike market and had an easy time. Now we can roam the Nanjing streets, though I'm afraid of the bikes getting stolen, which is common. They can pick the locks. Right now I've got my bike inside the apartment because I don't have a lock. I may just keep it inside, at night.

DETAIL OF THE DAY:

I found the right word to communicate with the bike woman across the street. She was about to close up when I wanted her to put a lock on my bike. She couldn't make me understand; finally I said "mingtian" (tomorrow). She smiled; it worked!

October 16

Jan

A group of 12 male graduate students watched the movie <u>Nine to Five</u> in our apartment this afternoon. It could be considered an attempt on my part at consciousness-raising. We discussed male chauvinism, feminism, bosses, etc. They have some definite ideas on feminism and a woman's place in society. One student said he heard that feminists in the U.S. were homosexuals, that they hated men, family and themselves. They feel strongly that a wife should "take care of" her husband. And yet, when I asked those who are married if they helped with the housework, they all said they did. They also said that if someone is a boss, he (almost always <u>he</u> in China) can do whatever he wants to do to his employees. To them, a leader is not to be questioned. It was an animated and revealing discussion about their ideas of marriage and work relationships.

Chinese movies generally have a political message, one which upholds the virtues of the government and the country. It's difficult for them to enjoy a film just as entertainment or fantasy. They're always looking for the political message.

October 16

Dave

Yesterday Jan and I had our bikes fixed. The woman (who apparently owns the shop with her husband) was trying to extricate one bike basket from the others, and couldn't do it. I offered to help, and took hold to help her, and pulled hard, but nothing happened. She tried it another way, I again offered to help, but this time she waved me off, pointing to her husband. So, the dignity of work is apparently universal. I couldn't interfere with her work because it was <u>her</u> work, not mine. I wouldn't ask her to teach my classes or write my poems and stories either. I do appreciate that. Work is sacred, I don't care what kind of work it is and I don't care what country or culture you're in. Let me do my work. My work defines me. I fix bike tires. I teach poetry. I dig ditches. I build walls. It's all the same.

I'll keep my bike inside. Though I may buy, if I can find one, a cord-type bike lock to supplement the other one I bought. But in the meantime, the beautiful green bike stays in the hall, shiningly, where I can watch over it like a People's Liberation Army guard.

Speaking of which, I heard on Voice of America that the Chinese military wants to engage in more joint ventures, such as Mercedes cars. They can get cheap labor and pay less in taxes. It sounds like the military is losing support, so they need to go into business. They already have much to do with the transportation system: apparently they're in charge of planes and trains.

DETAIL OF THE DAY:
In China <u>leftovers</u> is not a negative concept.

October 17

Jan

Dave went to the campus doctor because he has some sores in his mouth. He was given several vitamins and some powder to put on the sores. He must be lacking something in his diet. The doctor's appointment and the medication were all "no charge."

...We walked to the market for eggs, vegetables and fruit. On our way, we usually stop to watch a monkey that is kept tied to a tree. People feed him everything, and we've seen kids tease him. He looks miserable. He eats some of what is given to him, but automatically rejects other things, such as some candies. We've seen him quite angry, usually at young children. We hate seeing the monkey living like this. We haven't seen many other pets around. Sometimes we see cats, such as in the Sprite. We heard a dog barking one day, but didn't see it.

October 17

Dave

Saw my first fight yesterday, near the Jinling Hotel. Two young women, one a salesgirl, one a customer, were arguing angrily, and the customer said something that caused the other to slap her, then grab her hair. The customer had the salesgirl by the neck, the salesgirl had the customer by the hair, and they were having at it, with enthusiasm. An older woman, maybe the owner of the clothes shop, broke it up, and sent the salesgirl inside, which didn't prevent her from going on with her words through the gaps in the clothes, as the customer went on with her words too. High emotion on both sides.

October 18

Dave

Met with three Nanjing poets last night. I had three of my students there as interpreters. The poets spoke of recent trends in Chinese poetry, and of the poet Bai Dao from Beijing, who is considered very important, but who, as I understand it, has sold out to the political status quo. The poets spoke of a new wave, though they are varied—some narrative, some lyrical, some confessional, some "language poets."

When they asked me about American poetry right now, I mentioned poets like Dickey, Nemerov, Etter and Dacey. One of them asked me about the under-40 poets, and I couldn't come up with any names. Maybe that shows that I'm an "older poet." I hadn't thought of myself as an older poet (though I had, recently, been thinking of myself as an older racquet-ball player). Fifty-two is getting on in years, I suppose. A poet, Frost said, strikes his note long before 40. He's right. The energy it takes, the sort of mind, is a youthful one. Poets at 50 often turn into fiction writers. Or, if they don't know how to make short stories or novels, they go on doing what they know how to do.

But after 50 the poems can be soggy and lack real energy. Stanley Kunitz wrote a good whale poem recently, in his 80s, and William Wordsworth had a reawakening late in life, and W.B. Yeats wrote well all the way to his death—but these are exceptions. Making poems is for the young, mostly. I think it's probably related to the tool-making talent. As a young person you need to be dexterous and ingenious and flexible and unconscious and emotional. You need to make good hunting tools. You have to possess a fierceness that allows you to scream a poem into being, to hit a racquetball or a baseball with great force and timing. You have to be strong and loose. After that youthful storm is over, the poems just don't come as readily. You perhaps turn to fiction or essays. Your life is prosier, less fierce, though not necessarily less happy. Most of your good tools have already been fashioned, and now the younger guys are out there whooping it up and chasing the animals.

Now you look forward to constructing stories, which have their own fascination, and which demand more deliberate, patient thought. They are similar to poems in the making, in that imagination and discovery are still crucial. Now you're not just an image-maker, but more of a teacher. "Pay attention," you say to your community, "I have something to tell you that you need to know. A story."

October 18

Jan

We rode our bikes to the city gate in the south part of town and went to the "bird and flower" market. As we were walking by the various vendors, we saw a tiny bird that had its leg caught in its cage. The owner was working to try to get the bird's leg free but wasn't having much luck.

A group of foreign tourists got out of a brand new tourist bus and made their way through the market, with expensive video cameras, gaudy clothes and tourist hats, hardly looking at anything. One woman had her face covered with a mask so she wouldn't breathe any germs in. We found out that they were from Long Beach, California. The term "ugly American" came to mind.

...The construction workers outside our apartment are still busy working. As we were walking past them to go into our apartment, one of them let a huge metal pipe drop to the ground from the top of the building, creating a deafening sound which made me scream. I think he probably did it on purpose to startle me because he seemed quite amused by my reaction.

October 19

Jan

I spent the entire day, except for a bicycle ride a few blocks to the post office to mail two cards, in the apartment doing class work and being lazy. For dinner I fixed tuna and noodles, which Dave was excited about. I bought the last can of tuna in the hotel gift shop and had a can of cream of mushroom soup that we bought in Shanghai.

...Z. stopped by to visit as we were having popcorn and watching a video. He stayed for quite a while and talked about all of the activities he's involved in. He said he is "too busy." He also said he would ask us over to his "shabby" two-room apartment, where four people live, when he gets back from a conference in Wuhan. He's the kind of guy who seems to be interested in everything and who has a positive, upbeat outlook on life. He says he is absent-minded and doesn't care about money. He has rich relatives, who are farmers, and who think of him as the "poor shabby university professor from the city." People who farm or are in business in China are the ones who are rich. Teachers make very little money.

October 19

Dave

DETAIL OF THE DAY:

The smile on the face of the worker out back who dropped an iron construction pole on the ground just as we were about to enter our apartment yesterday, frightening Jan. I saw the pole coming, so it didn't scare me. But the look on the worker's face—was it a smile of satisfaction or embarrassment? I couldn't tell for sure, but I thought it might have been deliberate. I didn't have a good look for him, but held back a little. Sometimes indifference says more than anything.

October 21

Jan

I thought about my mother today. This would have been her 80th birthday. I wonder how she would have felt about me being in China, so far away from home. She would have worried a lot. Her death (in 1987) is still as vivid to me today as it was then.

...A couple of my graduate students, dermatology majors, stopped over and wanted some reading material. I gave them some magazines I had brought from the U.S., and then we talked at length about the U.S. elections, about U.S./China relations. The Chinese generally favor Bush, since he was an Ambassador to China in 1979. The threat of Clinton's pulling their "most favored nation" status if he is elected is frightening to them. One student pointed out that human rights are not perfect in the U.S., referring to the beating of a black man by cops in L.A. recently. A discussion then took place about the problem with black students in China, which created a major disturbance back in 1988. Recently there have been more problems with black students in Nanjing. Chinese men are very much opposed to blacks dating Chinese women.

October 21

Dave

DETAIL OF THE DAY:

It was a couple of days ago that a construction worker dropped a pole that scared Jan. This morning, I was standing outside with a cup of coffee, when the same worker came by to start his work day. He walked close to me and I said in a friendly tone: "ni hao." And he said, in a friendly tone, "ni hao." It's best to be on friendly terms with people. I could have established enmity between us with a bad look, but I decided not to.

...I don't think we'll be hiring a cook. We'd just as soon go on our own. Maybe eat with Mike and Lida once a week, I don't know. It's amazing how much you keep to yourself, even in a foreign environment. You'd think you'd want to hang around foreigners like yourself. But Jan and I hang around each other. We have our work to do, and we have friends. But we pretty much keep to ourselves, together, alone together. I like being with her. We can be together and yet we can be apart to do our work. She doesn't hang on me and I don't hang on her. We're friends, companions, lovers, married. Husband and wife; wife and husband. I always need her, always will. She is both my wife and my wildest fantasy. What I'd do without her I don't know.

October 22

Dave

My student Lin came over and we talked. He wants to translate an autobiographical book I wrote about six years ago. I asked him about whether China can accommodate the market system, free enterprise, and still be China, and he said that the government has a way of taxing the businesses heavily; and people who are jealous of those who make a lot of money can criticize them, which they do, often. And threaten them as well. He said that China right now is in a look-and-see phase. A feeling-out period. I asked him about the new, younger men just appointed to the Committee in Beijing. He said that the old men are still in charge.

His father and mother, both peasants, were able to do a lot better after the communes broke up around 1984. But his father, he says, worked too hard in the fields as a boy, and ruined his health. Lin feels bad that, even though his family of nine (four brothers and two sisters) was proud of him going away to the university in Nanjing, he cannot, on his wages of Y180 per month teaching two classes (taking 16 class hours as well), help out his parents. And his own little girl of four could be going to school but he and his wife can't afford to send her. His wife is a meat cutter who works on a Normal University campus, and works in the evening selling clothes. Two jobs, and sometimes even three, he says, working some hours in a factory. And still they have a very rough time of it. He is a Party member.

If he and his wife had another child—and she wants to—they might both lose their jobs. They would also be fined Y3,000.00 Not worth it. He studies Qigong and says that it's necessary to do something like that, being usually away from his wife, but that Qigong has a slightly negative effect on his sex life. This is experienced by many Qigong practitioners, he says. Every morning (for the last five years) he does the exercises on his own. He showed me. He's fairly graceful, and large for a Chinese person.

Chinese students, he says, are confused these days. On the one hand they want to go into a profession that their schooling prepared them for; on the other hand, the market system is too enticing, pulls them away. They are poor and vulnerable, obviously. I can see confusion in Lin. He needs to make money, and he'll be a teacher, but teachers are poorly paid. In the meantime, prices are going up all over China.

October 23

Dave

DETAIL OF THE DAY:

A man riding a bike dressed up in a suit and tie and black plastic slippers.

...The rat we saw the other day—I swear it must be a pet. It was as big as a muskrat, and lives virtually under the grocery store it must raid each night. It came out of a big hole as we approached the store, and then, seeing us, went back. There is no way these people can't know that the rat is there. Why haven't they killed it, poisoned it? Maybe they're fattening it up to eat it on some special occasion?

...The good news is that the restaurant next door is finished. The bad news is that they'll be having loud banquets at night.

...The huge German woman, Suzanna, last year got tired of the construction noise, and so one morning (she's a late sleeper) she got up and went outside her door and grabbed a tool away from a worker and took it inside. Nothing happened for five days. Finally she got a few faint knocks on her door and, answering it, saw four men (they came up to her chest, she said), and one of them meekly asked for his tool back (she speaks Chinese). She gave it back, but she's heard no more noise close to her apartment. She is one of the very few women I've ever met that I didn't feel I could whip in a fist fight. I think she'd overwhelm me with her size and booming voice. We do like her.

October 23

Jan

I bought a pair of slip-on shoes today for Y6.5, a little over $1.00 (U.S.) Dave has accused me of bringing too many pairs of shoes to China; he says he counted 19 pairs, but I doubt it.

...A sign on the bulletin board in the apartment reception office says: "You'd better take a bath before 9:00 p.m." In the translation from Chinese to English, the message has become an order. Someone (probably a foreigner) wrote below, "And this means you!" I guess this means we'll be taking a chance, if we wait until after 9:00 p.m., that there may not be any hot water. Actually there often isn't hot water <u>before</u> 9:00 p.m.

October 24

Jan

Robin, a young American teacher, returned from a visit to the U.S. recently and brought 40 videos back with her. She told us we were welcome to borrow any of them, so we asked if we could borrow a couple. When we went to her apartment, she had four old videos set out for us and didn't offer to let us see any of the others. She also said she would like to keep the VCR in her part of the building, since four or five of the foreign teachers there liked to watch videos. The VCR actually belongs to the English section and she and two of the women are not in the English section. We were somewhat offended by her, but will try to maintain good relationships with everyone around here.

October 25

Dave

Well, Jan cut and shaved my beard and mustache off. I looked into the mirror and didn't like what I saw. "A new face, an old life," as the poet James Dickey put it. The line on the right side of my face, extending down from my nostril, is longer than the line on the left side of my face. So, I need to correct this by growing a mustache again. A beard, I think, is partly a way of hiding from the world. Reminds me of the story, "The Minister's Black Veil" by Hawthorne, about a minister who hid from his own community because of some dark sin in his past.

...The university restaurant is open now, but they're segregating foreigners like us, putting us in a back room by ourselves. Now I'll know how certain Americans have felt even in their own country—to be put aside as second-class citizens. Of course, I'm not in America. I'm not a citizen here. And yet, I don't have AIDS either.

October 26

Dave

DEPRESSING DETAIL OF THE DAY:

Bush seems to be gaining on Clinton. It may be that Perot is surging, so Clinton is losing to him, not Bush.

...The weather is changing. A hint of ass-freezing weather at the end of the year. But the sun is out this morning and it looks warm. After all, we're on the same latitude as Atlanta, Georgia. It can't be <u>that</u> cold.

October 27

Jan

Arthur, a 1989 Fulbright professor who is visiting Nanjing, came to our apartment to see us and to talk to a student who wanted information about getting to the U.S. Later, during dinner, he talked about the events that took place in Nanjing during the 1989 Tiananmen uprising. There was a lot of demonstrating going on in Nanjing and people were devastated after the killings. Everyone was depressed and felt hopeless. He and a group of people in the U.S. had a gathering on the first anniversary of Tiananmen in his hometown in Pennsylvania. VOA announcers and other newsmen were there to record the event. He said it was an emotional day for all who were there. He found out that many of his students in China heard about this event on VOA.

October 28

Dave

I woke up in the night. It was unusually warm for the end of October. I heard the ticking of our loud Chinese alarm clock. It was saying, when I listened closely:

"In-teg-ri-ty, in-teg-ri-ty"

Then, a little later, waking up again, I listened closely, and the clock said:

"Coun-try cut-throat, coun-try cut-throat"

I could make it say either "in-teg-ri-ty" or "coun-try cut-throat," but couldn't hear the sayings alternating, one with the other. It was either the one or the other, continuously. Both of us were awake, very awake at 3:00 a.m.

If I were a castaway on a desert island, Jan would be in my daydreams and fantasies, making them wilder and wilder.

October 28

Jan

I started individual conferences with my writing students to go over their essays. Their views and ideas are refreshing. One young man wrote: "I love all of my roommates just the same as they love me. We feel so lucky to have such a room (in the dormitory) and a chance to live together, not only because of the comfort in our room but also because of the friendship among us." He wrote of his room as "a wonderful place with a wooden floor that they swept and mopped every morning"; he said that with all of his roommates sitting at their desks under the light it was "quite a beautiful scene." He's speaking of a small, modest room which houses <u>eight</u> students.

Another student spoke of growing up in a small village where she would awaken to hear women using sticks to beat their clothes on the stone steps while washing them in the river:

"The willows around the river were like beautiful girls standing beside it to see themselves in the water." I think that we Americans, in general, don't appreciate as much of what is around us in our daily lives as Chinese *people do.*

October 29

Dave

I woke up at 5:00 a.m. with the hardest hard-on of the last ten years, at least five. Lord, Lord. Interesting word: hard-on. It must mean, "a hard thing on my body." Hard. On me. Hence, hard-on. It's a noun, a concrete noun at that. But it comes, so to say, from: <u>hard</u>=adjective and <u>on</u>=preposition, or is it <u>propo</u>sition. A propositional phrase, sort of. Hard-on. Hard cock. Stiff dick. Not quite like "the flag of my disposition," as Whitman said.

October 29

Jan

China can provide various types of dramas. On my way home from class today, I saw some of these situations. A female student was struck by a bicycle and hit her head on the pavement (it sounded like a bowling ball being dropped); a male student had to skillfully maneuver so he wouldn't be hit by a bike—it appeared as if he had done this many times before; there was a huge line of students waiting outside the library and winding way around to the back of it, with several policemen there—I didn't know what they were waiting for; several elementary students were involved in an animated fight—verbally and physically (the girls were out-shouting the boys); a man dressed in a suit, vest and tie (and plastic slip-on shoes) rode by on his bike with a basketful of fresh vegetables sticking out; another man rode by on a three-wheeled bike hauling a load of cooked rice on large uncovered trays, and there was a lot of coal dust and other dirt visible in the air; a young elementary student was urinating near the sidewalk and said "hello" to me as I passed him; and I had to dodge a rope being swung around by another young boy, he was oblivious to anyone being near him. If one would have occasion to be bored in China, all he or she need do is to go out onto the streets.

...Richard, a Fulbright professor from Chengdu, is here to present a lecture on American film. He wrote a book about his experiences in China a few years ago called <u>Saturday Night in Baoding</u>. When we met him in Beijing we found out he lives in Mankato, Minnesota, not far from us. He's not having a good experience in Chengdu and says our living conditions and the general atmosphere of the teaching program is better in Nanjing. He says he has not seen the sun since he's been in Chengdu. The sun is so important here. It creates a sense of well-being in our often drab environment.

October 30

Dave

Off to Suzhou. "Above are the Heavens, below are Suzhou and Hangzhou," the saying goes.

NOVEMBER

November 2

Jan

Dear All: (Bev, Delores, et al.),

It was good to get your letters (you know who I'm talking about). We're always happy when we see mail on the apartment office counter, where it's left for us. I'm writing one letter again for you all to share, since we're conserving our printer ink and paper. We did finally get the printer to work but are crossing our fingers.

Yes, we got the package you sent, Delores. Thanks! The apartment desk clerk notified us and we walked 1 1/2 hours to get to the post office to pick it up (and, of course, 1 1/2 hours home in return). It was a beautiful fall day for a walk. We showed our identification papers, paid the small fee and opened the package right in the post office (with people gathered around to see what we got) and immediately ate the candy. It didn't matter that it was smashed. I licked it right off the wrapping and had white frosting all over my face. Dave is happy with the pipe tobacco, and I'm happy not to have to smell the awful stuff he's been using. I came home and used the hair color that evening. The rubber gloves will save my hands, since they're chapped and cracking from the hard water. It took about one week longer to get the package than the letter. Not too bad.

We are settled in our new apartment and have made it as comfortable as possible. We bought a wall clock yesterday, and I picked up things to brighten the place up, like a red silk tablecloth for the table. Living on first floor, instead of on second where we were previously, has its disadvantages. The drains in the kitchen and bathroom smell bad, but we just burn incense when we have to. We also covered the bathroom drain hole with a piece of wood and a brick to hold it down. That helps. We spent a lot of time and muscle on the walls of our study trying to get the black mold off, but we weren't completely successful. Too bad you weren't here to help, Delores; I know how you like to clean mold. Good thing we aren't allergic to it. We like having the extra room, and this apartment is near the boiler room, which will make it warmer in the winter, if a little noisier. We're lucky.

It has not been cold yet, but it is "sweatshirt and sweater weather." The leaves are falling.

How are Thanksgiving plans going? I get hungry, as well as a little lonesome for home and family, when I read of your plans for getting together and having foods like pumpkin pie, lefse, dressing, home-made jelly and tomato juice. Our foreign group will probably get together and fix something. I have a small canned ham that I bought in Shanghai that I've been saving for a special occasion. There will probably <u>not</u> be pumpkin pie for our Thanksgiving.

I generally control my eating, but Dave doesn't always do so well. He's had a stomach problem lately and has developed another cold. I tell him he's a sickly person. We went out to eat recently with two Chinese professors and that meal could have contributed to Dave's stomach problem. He had a fever and chills and has spent more time in the bathroom than usual. I'm sure he's dropped a few pounds in there. I think our "American" stomachs are not adjusted to this kind of food. We try to eat at home as much as we can, but as I've said before, my cooking is nothing that you'd write home about. Dave is excited when we have tuna and noodles, so that's a clue.

My oral classes are presenting debates, and I'm enjoying what they have to say. Dave was a guest lecturer recently in my writing class. His senior students are gone for the whole month of November, so he has a break. He's too lucky. We're generally staying busy with classes and grading papers. I know I have developed a whole new respect for teachers.

Get this: a visiting Chinese professor asked me to give a talk at his university, as well as Dave. He said he thought my voice was "melodic." I agreed to give a talk, but have <u>no</u> idea what I'll talk about. I'm not bothered about being in front of the classroom anymore and actually even enjoy it. There are days, though, that I wonder what I'm doing there. Some classes aren't as good as others. Some things work and some don't. The students are delightful and full of energy, with a great interest in learning English. Anything I have to say seems to hold their attention. A real ego booster.

David Jr. has sent us several FAXs and has called once. Shelly called once in the middle of the night and woke me out of a stupor. She asked,

"Were you sleeping?" We were glad to hear from her. She hasn't written yet, but I know how busy she is with four boys, working full-time, and, of course, she gets <u>no</u> help from her husband.

We hope to get home in mid-January. As soon as we know, we'll let you know. I think it will be good for us to get some R & R, and we'll enjoy seeing everyone.

Better close for now, give the computer a rest and get at some of my class work. Keep writing. We're doing fine and the time is going fairly fast. We miss some of our creature comforts there, and FOOD; but China is endlessly absorbing. Each day brings something new and different. It is in the process of major change.

Love you all,

Jan (future guest lecturer)

...Wait a minute, wait a minute. I read Jan's letter and noticed her foul, ugly, scatological reference to me. I have two things to say: first, it was only <u>one</u> pound I lost, and, what else can a guy do who lives on camel hump, duck webs and water buffalo nose?

Thanks tremendously for sending the pipe tobacco. I've looked all over for two months and finally found some, but it's awful stuff. What you sent me is gloriously good. And the candy, too. You know, we got lost more or less looking for the post office because of Jan's faulty directions—she had made a "PO" on the map, and the "PO" wasn't anywhere near where her marks were. Actually, we could have started out in any direction from our apartment and come as close with her "directions." But we managed to get help.

You should see the markets here, smell them, watch them kill chickens, fish and especially eel. Quite an experience. We eat a balance of Chinese food and our own which, over years I suppose, the stomach adjusts to. We make out, both literally and figuratively.

Yours,

Dave

November 2

Jan

Dear Mitzi & George,

It was good to hear from you. As you know, we are anxiously awaiting the chocolate you said you were sending us. I'll report to you as soon as it arrives. I dream about chocolate candy arriving in the mail. In my dream I get a notice from the desk clerk, and I walk for 1 1/2 hours to the post office. All the way there I'm thinking, "This must be the chocolate from Mitzi." And when I get to the post office, there it is, a whole box of chocolate candy! There is actually some imported chocolate here, but it is old from sitting on the shelves too long and is not fit to eat. We've bought some a few times, only to be sadly disappointed. It tastes like chocolate-flavored wax. We do miss American FOOD, especially treats. Chinese food is okay, but gets to be a drag after a while. Not so much variety, at least not in what we've found. Kunming food was better, we've decided. But maybe we've been away from there so long that we've actually forgotten. We've both lost weight. We walk a lot, and we bought bikes for longer trips around the city.

Recently a group of us foreign teachers from Nanjing University went to Suzhou, a well-known China city, about five hours from Nanjing on a train. Our first night there we were served many kinds of delicacies such as: fish stomach, pig intestine, whole crabs, jelly fish, duck feet webs, eel, "tree ear" mushrooms, sweet black rice with pine nuts, rice, beer and Sprite. So, we were well fed. For breakfast each morning, we had a bowl of hot noodles topped with a spicy sauce with pork pieces and green vegetables. It was actually quite good. It would have been more of a lunch item for us. No cereal, sweet rolls, sausage, eggs, hashbrowns, bacon, pancakes, waffles, or even any bread or toast. And no coffee—only tea.

Suzhou is a small city of two million or so, known for its many gardens and waterways. It's called "the Venice of the East," but that's a misnomer. The water is quite polluted, and the housing is not what I imagine it would be like in Venice. But we enjoyed it. We visited a shoe factory and were allowed to buy shoes at about half price. (I love buying shoes.) We stayed in a hotel owned by the shoe factory in a town near Suzhou.

Our room wasn't great. It had twin beds (which we don't like), two chairs, a desk, two night stands, a dresser, a T.V. that didn't work, a bathroom with a toilet that leaked continuously, and a sink that dripped incessantly. The plastic toilet seat didn't fit properly. The lighting consisted of a couple of bare bulbs hanging on cords from the ceiling. There was, however, a big bowl of fruit for us, two water thermoses, four wet wash rags on a plate and two hand-sized towels. A gas hot water heater hung on the wall above the bathtub, but it didn't work. The first night and the next morning, we had <u>no</u> running water at all! But we did have the two water thermoses, which allowed us to wash up a bit. The bed smelled musty. We decided to commiserate with each other and sleep in one bed instead of the two twin beds.

After dinner one night, Dave and a friend walked out into the countryside of Suzhou. They heard people still working in the fields in the darkness and had to dodge bikes that were passing them in the dark.

On Halloween morning, still in Suzhou (there is no Halloween in China), I wore my pumpkin earrings but that was the only reference to Halloween. I realized that I missed Halloween decorations and celebrations, something I didn't think I would miss. We woke up and discovered that we <u>still</u> had no water. We used the water in the thermoses again for washing. In China we've learned to deal with inconveniences. (There was no "room service" here.)

We went to see a popular tourist site, an elaborately carved set of buildings surrounded by gardens full of shrubbery and flowers and rock formations, which was built about ten years ago and is patterned after the classic novel <u>The Dream of the Red Mansion</u>. It looked ancient, even though it wasn't, and actors were presenting scenes from the novel. A company was also filming a T.V. show or a movie. We stopped to take pictures of the actors with their beautiful costumes and elaborate hair-dos, even took one of Dave in between two beautiful actresses.

We discovered that the gas water heater in our friend Angela's room worked, with some special maneuvering, so we all carried the red plastic basins from our rooms to her room to get some warm water to wash with. We were able to find some humor in this and laugh instead of becoming angry. We had all become weary of not having water to wash up with and were close to the point of complaining. But we didn't want to do that since we were guests. Discovering warm water, I think, made us realize how relatively little things can make us happy here in China.

We were taken to a mountain shrine and a Buddhist temple and then were allowed to shop for a while. I bought silk, and Dave found some great wood cuts. Suzhou is full of various kinds of gift and food shops. We stopped and had some dumplings filled with meat and vegetables. The Chinese we were with knew how to spot a good place. The price was very cheap—Y1.00 for five dumplings (about 20 cents). Dave also had some noodles, his favorite food in China. You'd love the noodles too, Mitzi.

On our way home to Nanjing, we noticed that rice was being harvested all over the countryside, so we asked if we could stop to watch. A peasant man and a woman (with a wet towel wrapped around her head) were very friendly and allowed us to take pictures. The knives they were using were similar to those used in America over a hundred years ago. They were short and curved, almost like a sickle. Most of the farm work in China is done by hand, which means you rarely see large equipment in the countryside. Two men in our group had been sent to the countryside during the Cultural Revolution and had worked in rice fields. Wu took the knife and cut several stalks of rice. It was obvious from his skill at cutting that he had done this before. I wondered if they were thinking about their time spent in the countryside being "re-educated" by the Mao government. I've heard many other Chinese people talk about their experiences in the countryside and know they suffered greatly. Many, however, do not want to talk about it; they want to forget about their suffering.

When we arrived in Nanjing after several days in Suzhou, we had to take a bus home from the train station. We were let off the bus about three blocks from our apartment, and struggled along with our extra baggage, exhausted after a fully-orchestrated weekend. We felt fortunate to get home to our apartment, where we had the luxury of water—hot water.

Are you still working on going to Australia? That would be great. We'd love to have you visit us in China. Write soon. Bye for now.
Love,

Jan (awaiting the chocolate)

November 2

Dave

DETAIL OF THE DAY:
In Suzhou, along the canal streets, many of the flats we peered into had tiny alters.

We toured the Suzhou shoe factory. The young girls, 16 and 17, bent over making shoes, were attractive and seemed happy. Many of them come from far-away provinces such as Szechwan. They work about three years and then go back home and melt into village life. The superintendent, who gave us a talk through an interpreter, said he is a Party secretary as well as head of a company. He's a large, impressive looking man. Very self- confident. He said he'd come up from modesty: started out working in the countryside during the Cultural Revolution, then came back to Suzhou and worked as a carpenter, then got the idea of building a shoe factory from his habit of giving shoes to his girlfriend.

The head of the workers' union is also the head of production. In American industry, of course, union heads are completely removed from management. When I asked about this, I was told that if there's a problem with the workers it has to do, always, with production, (read: manage-ment) and so the problem gets solved. I assume he meant that the Solver of Problems is always the boss and not the worker.

Benefits? If hospital and doctor costs are higher than five per cent of the worker's wages, the company picks up the bill. If lower, the worker handles it. Seems like a decent arrangement.

November 3

Jan

Dear David, Shelly, Kari, and all,
Can you believe this?—we shaved off your dad's beard and mus-tache. It's the first time I've seen his entire face for at least ten years. It's like having a stranger in the house; I don't know him. I'm quite amused by his new white deck shoes (yes, white deck shoes); and now the

nakedness of his face is extremely funny to me. He said he looked at himself in the mirror after he shaved and didn't like what he saw—too many wrinkles. So now he plans to grow his mustache back. We went to a lecture this afternoon, and some of his students were shocked to see his "new look."

I recently bought what I thought was baking powder at the market, but it turned out to be something else. I asked (in good Chinese): "Zhe shi shenme?" which means "what is this?" The woman understood the question and answered me, but I didn't understand her answer. For all I know, it could have been rat poison. Items are often in strange order in markets and shops here, and are in clear plastic bags with Chinese characters only.

I've invented a new kind of pancake (that's why I was looking for baking powder). The grandkids would like them, probably as much as they like the buttermilk pancakes I always make for them. I use a bottle of yogurt (the yogurt is good here), an egg and a cup of flour—nothing else— and they're good. At least your dad thinks so. But you know how easy he is to please when it comes to food. Living here forces one to be creative and conservative. I find myself saving all kinds of things, like ties on boxes, bits of paper, etc., just because supplies of "things" are not always available.

We've been hearing some scratching in our closet, and your dad enjoyed calling it to my attention again today. He said he saw something, when in fact he hadn't; he just heard it. He took all of the shoes out of the closet and tried to find a mouse (or a rat) but couldn't see anything. He then went to the apartment desk for a trap or poison, but they didn't have any. They assured us they would get some. Now every time I open the closet door or any drawer in the bedroom, I'm afraid that something will jump out at me.

Bush won the mock election in one of my classes today (boo), by a large margin, after which I predicted that Clinton would win. Only one student out of both classes voted for Perot. They have a great interest in our political system, more than many American students, I'm afraid.

Zhang and Wang, both professors and writers here, talked to us today about how little money teachers make, and that a waiter in a restaurant makes about three times as much. They both have extra jobs and both have published their writings. Mr. Wang, who is about to retire, makes Y280 per month (around $50.00 U.S.). They said they don't make much money from their publications, but that it makes them happy and gives them some fame. Wang said, "If you don't want to be robbed in China, wear your university faculty identification pin." I'll remember that.

We hope things are going well for all of you. We do miss you and think about you often. Stay in touch.

Love you,

Mom (wearing my faculty pin)

November 3

Dave

There's a mouse in our bedroom closet, and Jan is not happy. The desk person said she may find us a trap today. I think the mouse is eating shoes; I hear him gnawing away on one of Jan's 19 pairs.

November 4

Dave

Election day.

The day was perfect but for one thing: I got sick last night. Here was the day I had:

First, I had promised myself I'd write and pretty much finish my story, "Wheels," which I did, and learned a lot from writing it.

Second, we made love that was as glorious as ever.

Third, I jogged, did two miles without my legs hurting. I may get up to 2 1/2 one of these days, and then, by spring, say, get back up to a slow, steady three miles.

Fourth, VOA said Clinton was in. We will see today, any time now.

November 4

Jan

CLINTON THE WINNER!

We had our ears focused on VOA all morning and are happy with the news. One of my students, Dong, came over to congratulate me on Clinton's victory. Students seem curious about the election and our individual right to vote. We missed seeing the election coverage on T.V. and had to settle for VOA. <u>The China Daily</u> newspaper will not have much coverage. Our impression was that most people in China were hoping that Bush would win. They are afraid of what Clinton might do internationally, especially to China.

...Got a FAX from David telling us about Clinton's victory. We watched the English News on T.V. at 10:30 p.m. to see what coverage they would give it. There was actually very little. It was almost an afterthought at the end of the broadcast. Was this an expression of China's feelings about Clinton?

November 5

Dave

Clinton, the winner! We're happy. Now maybe we've got somebody in power who knows a few people who make under a hundred grand a year.

...Sick last night. Something hit me in the afternoon and then toward dinner time I was chilled and in bed. We had dinner at our place, with the cook hired by Mike and Lida. The food was so so. I'm beginning to think Western bellies aren't made for Eastern food.

...We're anxious to go back to the States and breathe fresh air. South Dakota air is <u>literally</u> fresher. In South Dakota the cold is clean. Snow is wonderfully fresh and white. No coal dust to breathe.

November 5

Jan

We went to a bank for some money, and the process took over an hour. From what we know about bank transactions in China, we were prepared to spend some time there. The bank was packed with people standing shoulder to shoulder, many trying to crowd in ahead and push their way to the front of us. I held fast to my spot, but it still took a long time. While we were standing there, a man came up to ask if we wanted to change money (give them U.S. dollars or F.E.C., foreign exchange currency, for a higher rate of RMB, people's money). I was surprised that they did this inside the bank, since changing money is illegal. Many people change money, but generally in more secluded places. I don't know what happens if one is caught changing money, and I don't want to personally find out.

November 6

Dave

DETAIL OF THE DAY:

Walking up the alley (lane) to classes yesterday morning right by the showers and smelling the young girls' newly washed hair as they emerged from the door and started back to their crowded dorms. There are few things more wonderful to me than the smell of freshly washed women's hair. And Chinese hair is so incredibly, unchangeably black. There is no blackness like it I have ever witnessed. If I were in charge of building a temple I would dedicate it to the hair of Chinese women. I'd have little images of women's faces and heads all over for the worshipers to walk among, and real, black hair hanging down, hair the worshipers could touch, feel, fondle. I have a name for such a shrine: Black Hair Temple.

...Robin wants to monopolize the VCR. Jan is cool; she can let it go. I am different. I have an instinct to strike out against her. Jan says, if I do I'll alienate all the other women up on third floor. Maybe so, but I will probably one of these days let her know my feelings on the matter. I truly don't want to be in charge of the machine, but it belongs to the English Department (not Robin's department) and I don't want anybody to "own" it if I can't "own" it. This is no doubt partly selfish of me. I've got a problem with this person. I sense some enmity building here.

...Sun. Sun is 90 per cent of my happiness today. If I can have sun, I can write. I can survive. I do feel better. My stomach has made its protest, emptied out, as if to say, "Okay, let's get rid of all this poison and start over again. You've got one more chance, Evans. Don't blow it." Jan makes wonderful pancakes; I love to watch her cook.

I love to watch her in the shower too. I'm a voyeur; I peek around the curtain when she isn't paying attention, and look. I use her all up with my eyesight. I ask her, when she sees me gawking: "Would you rather have married a poor horny man or a rich man with ice in his veins?"

"I'd rather marry you," she says.

And just what does that mean? I know some of what it means, but not exactly. I gave her a choice that was too easy, maybe. I'll keep my blood; others can have the ice and the money. Not that the two things are always inseparable.

I've already lost about 12 pounds, I tell Jan.

"Then why didn't you get on the scale yesterday?" (the one on the street that she weighed herself on—she, who hadn't lost any more pounds for a couple of weeks).

"Because I had too many clothes on," I say.

"You can always subtract for that."

"Okay," I say, "Next time I'll do it."

November 7

Jan

Jack, a Fulbright professor teaching in Shanghai, and his wife Evelyn came over to our apartment at 10:00 a.m. and we took a bus to Purple Mountain and visited several spots near there: the Sun Yat-Sen Memorial, Ming Tombs and a pagoda. It was a sunny fall day, with the leaves in full color. This made us feel cheerful and content. We were away from the traffic and noise as well as the huge crowds of people.

We had walked part way there and then paid Y2 to take a mini-bus out to the mountain. When we wanted to come back on the mini-bus, the bus driver said it would be Y5 each. So we got out of the bus and went to another one. The bus driver in the first one smelled strongly of alcohol anyway. The second bus driver also said Y5 each. On the outside of his bus, in big letters, the price was advertised at Y2. We argued (the best we could in English and mixed Chinese) but got on the bus anyway. We had to get back to town and felt the bus drivers were all going to try to charge us as much as they could. It was too far to walk.

Then the bus driver motioned for the four of us to sit in the back of the bus. The driver collected our money first and then collected Y2 each from the Chinese people. He tried to hide what he was collecting from them, but we knew. As we were getting out of the bus, Evelyn shook her finger at the driver and scolded him. It wasn't the amount of money, just the principle of it.

As we were walking the rest of the way home, Evelyn bought me a little wooden dowel to use as a rolling pin. Now I can make pies, or use it for a weapon; neither use is likely. It's a nice little souvenir.

November 7

Dave

The days remain warm and sunny. The saying is, though, that in Nanjing, each day is a full year: spring in the morning, summer in the afternoon, fall in the evening, and winter at night. There is quite a change over the day. In the sun it's quite nice, as in Kunming. The sun is what counts, always.

Children's wear Chinese style!

November 8

Jan

Going to the market in the rain today was especially unpleasant. The squashed vegetables covered with mud, the smelly fish, blood-soaked tofu, crowds of people, noise and confusion made me queasy.

On the way home, we passed a succession of shiny new cars parked behind a limousine, waiting for a bride and groom. The bride was dressed in a beautiful white wedding gown. The contrast of the beautiful bride, the limousine and the run-down, tar-paper shack they were in front of was striking. Sundays are popular wedding days, no doubt because it's the only day people don't have to work. Beautiful white wedding gowns and elaborate, expensive wedding celebrations are fairly new in China. The Chinese seem to have adopted some of our Western customs for weddings, but instead of buying the beautiful gowns, many brides rent them.

November 8

Dave

We're missing our family and friends and, in all the ways you miss it, home. Traveling does affect a person's notions of home. It makes you more aware of the importance of your own people, their habits and ways, the safety of being in your own house, and so on. China is a wonderful place, but it's no place to live for long, as far as I'm concerned. The language barrier is difficult. I want to hear what people are saying when they discuss or argue and bargain. That is a dimension we just don't have here and never will. The food keeps you off balance, too. You have to constantly be vigilant about it—my stomach has not been feeling great for the past week and a half. And, as Jan says, putting up with your colleagues is a chore and sometimes an ordeal. I like Brian's attitude: just let it go, and go on your own steam and avoid the crowd when you feel like it. I like him and his self-reliance.

...Feeling slightly queasy today, and the gloomy, overcast sky doesn't help. First lousy, cold day we've had since we've been here. We probably need it to help clear the dust.

November 9

Dave

The other day coming home with Jack from sightseeing we were walking down the unlighted side of Zhongshan, and suddenly I was grabbed by the arm by a little old woman with fierce eyes. I pulled back. I couldn't believe her strength. For a second I thought I was going to have to fight my way free. She would not let go of me. She wanted money, of course. I finally pulled free and caught up with Jack, who said: "She must like you, Dave."

She might've been the same woman who grabbed Jan one night and wouldn't let go; I had to come between them to break her hold. Jan was shaken by the incident. From now on we'll avoid that side of the street when the sun is down.

...My stomach is still not right. But today: S U N!!!! With sun, all things are possible. Yesterday was gloomy, overcast, cold. Today I don't care how cold it is (actually, 45 degrees). It is wonderful because it's sunny. I know there's something good happening in my body and brain when the sun comes out in the morning. The sun means promise, beginnings; Aurora is the morning star, Thoreau's favorite time of day, too. Now, let's see what we can accomplish between the sunrise and the sunset.

First, to my story.

November 10

Jan

Dear Deb, Roger, and family

Thanks for the card, pictures and Jennifer's nice letter. Your mother said she and your dad spent some time with you recently while Roger was gone.

We're doing well and are keeping busy. We've gone on three trips since we've been here. Friends from Shanghai visited us this past weekend. Also had a friend from the States here a few weeks ago. We're expecting a friend from Iowa in December or May, and David and Karen are coming in June.

We've learned to relax and be patient, which is important in China.

Deb, imagine yourself a Chinese mother. It would be something like this: First, you could have only <u>one</u> child. The law says only one. If you had more than one, you would be punished heavily with a large fine (you have very little money), loss of your job and/or loss of your apartment. You would belong to a work unit which has complete responsibility for you. It would decide when you could marry and when you could have your child. You would live in a two- (maybe one-, or maybe three-) room apartment with cement walls, cement floors, a two-burner gas cooking stove (if you're lucky), no oven; probably a squat-type toilet, with no bathtub or shower. You would wash in a big tub with heated water or go to a public shower. You would have to boil your water every day because you can't drink any water from the faucets. All the water is polluted. You may or may not have a refrigerator. You'd probably have a small T.V. set. You would have to go to the market almost every day if you didn't have a refrigerator. If you did, you would still go several times a week, because you want fresh vegetables. You would not have a car, but most likely a bike with a bamboo car seat on it for your child to ride on. You would get up early to go to work at the job you have been assigned to do, and leave your child at home with your mother-in-law and father-in-law, who may be living with you, along with your grandmother. You would have very little privacy.

Your child would wear pants with a slit in the back with his/her butt always exposed, for convenience when he or she has to go to the bathroom. You would squat her down anywhere you happened to be and let her go. You would work six days a week and not have any paid vacation. Your salary would be determined by your work unit. You would most likely have hot noodles or rice gruel for breakfast, or you might pick up an omelet or meat-filled dumpling on the way to work at an outdoor food stand. No cereal, toast, pancakes, waffles or donuts.

You would drink a lot of tea, since drinking cold water is not considered healthy. You would eat rice and fresh vegetables every day. Dessert, if any, would usually be a piece of fruit. For a treat, you would pick up a sweet potato cooked outside on the street in a coal-filled barrel. You would peel it and eat it on the spot. You would have no heat in your apartment, so in the cold weather you would wear several layers of clothing. You and your child would have so many layers of clothing on that you would appear to be fat. You would wear these layers of clothing inside your apartment in the winter.

You wouldn't even look up when someone hacked and spat near you. In fact, you probably would hack and spit. too. In the market, you would bargain and argue over prices, sometimes getting very loud and angry.

Your family and friends would be very important to you, and your one child would be very much doted upon. He may be spoiled by all the attention he gets (you would hope that your child would be a boy).

Deb, what do you think? Do you have it too easy? I think everyone should spend time in a foreign country. I read this once and think it is true: "the anecdote to prejudice is traveling."

We look forward to seeing you when we get back there in January.
Love,

Jan (learning about China)

November 11

Dave

Wu Y. wants me to "organize" four films for the CITS people (ticket agents) for December and ask Angela and Pam to help. I'm to show two films and discuss them, after giving a synopsis, and they will show one each on successive weeks. Then, presumably we'd all prepare a test for the students at the end. So, I'm involved in mankind and the Department of English. But maybe there's something in it for me, too, some guanxi, since we need the ticket people to help us get tickets, make reservations, etc. for traveling.

So, yes, I'll do it. That's fine. Let's have at it. I may end up with plenty of guanxi before I fly out of here. My thinking, I suppose, is the same kind that the Chinese do every minute of their lives. Connections, we call them in the U.S. People are the same the world over. It's just that in China there are fewer necessities and goodies, so the connections/backdoor (guanxi) become more intense and more important for survival. To not have guanxi, to reject it, here, would mean making a meager living and being content to just go home after work and wait until the next day's work. Having guanxi means, I think, being able to get around, meet people, make more money, and having things that make your life a little more enjoyable, or maybe a lot more enjoyable.

November 11

Jan

We are all looking much heavier with our extra layers of clothing. Babies especially look fat, like little balls of wool.

...Fred brought no long underwear or warm clothes with him, so Deb and I went with him to help him buy long underwear.

November 11

Jan

Dear Sarah & Chuck,

Help! Someone took two pairs of my underpants and one bra that I left hanging outside on our porch clothesline overnight. Living on the first floor, as we are now, has some disadvantages. At least, living upstairs, I could leave things out overnight without having them stolen. But we are warmer on the ground floor and satisfied that we moved. It all evens out. We also have one more room. Living space is valuable in China, because there is so little of it.

Today I had an unusual experience. We were out walking, as we often are, and we walked by what we now know is a popular money-changing place. A man motioned for us to change money (by rubbing his fingers together). I decided to do it, even if it is illegal, since I had some U.S. dollars with me and felt adventuresome. I was motioned inside of what appeared to be a restaurant (a front, no doubt). I had to walk around a coal burner in the middle of the front room, past people cleaning vegetables in pans of water, and then back into the dingy room where the money changing is done. It felt deliciously sinister. I imagined that at any moment I could be nabbed and thrown in jail. The exchange went smoothly, and I walked away with more money than I would have received at the bank. My life of crime has begun.

We discovered a new restaurant near the foreign students' dormitory about twenty minutes on foot from our apartment. It's in an alley, up a precipitous flight of dimly-lit stairs. Inside, the room was nicely decorated, clean and warm, with Louis Armstrong music playing. I loved it! We ordered Chinese food and enjoyed it; but they had Western, Japanese and Mexican food on the menu also. We've learned from experience that Chinese food is usually the best choice. They know how to cook it. Western food often tastes unlike anything we've ever had.

We saw our California colleague in the restaurant but didn't disturb him, since he seemed to be in deep conversation with an actress he had met. He has asked her to accompany him to Shanghai this weekend. He has probably promised to "take her to Hollywood and make her a star."

Deb, a friend in our apartment complex, brought over some poison for our rodent problem. And today I bought cockroach houses, so now we are "armed." We saw a big cockroach the other night just as we were getting into bed. As it was on its way into our closet, Dave got our fly-swatter and killed it. Deb said she accidentally stepped on a gecko in their apartment and killed it. She felt so bad, she said, that she cried. I felt bad after Dave killed the one we found on our cupboard, but it didn't bring me to tears. I know they are good for insects and shouldn't be killed. I'm learning. But mice, rats, ants and cockroaches have no reason to live as far as I'm concerned, at least not in my apartment.

Dave stopped at a street stand recently to have his shoes, which he just had new soles put on, cleaned and polished. They actually looked worse after the polishing. I think the woman used a dark brown polish on his light brown shoes. The soles he had put on earlier are fairly crude looking, but serviceable. These street vendors are always delighted to have our business. I'm sure they over-charge us, but we don't mind.

Xia Ayi, our cook, came over to cook dinner tonight and as soon as she came in, she broke her glasses. Dave took them out to a street vendor who displays glasses, but he shook his head no. I guess that meant he couldn't fix them or maybe that he wouldn't fix them. I felt sorry for Ayi since she had trouble seeing to cook. She fixed a good meal anyway. After the meal was prepared, she wanted to take a bath. I must have looked puzzled, because Lida (we eat with Mike and Lida on Wednesdays, and the cook prepares their meals several other nights during the week) told her to go up to their apartment to bathe. I guess I wasn't expecting her to bathe here. She always has a bath in their apartment after she cooks for them. That must be part of the deal. She is warm and personable; but when Lida (who speaks Chinese) isn't around, I have trouble communicating with her. We use a lot of gesturing. I like to keep my rice in the refrigerator so the bugs won't get in it, but she doesn't like that. She has motioned to me on several occasions that it shouldn't be kept there, and she always puts it in my bottom cupboard. I move it back to the refrigerator after she leaves. She's from the countryside and can't read or write. I wish I could talk to her about her family, her life. It's frustrating not being able to speak Chinese. She seems to enjoy cooking for us and having dinner with us. She is always animated and expressive. The two of us try hard to communicate with gestures, and I think generally succeed. We try to teach each other words as we point to items and say what they are. She takes great interest in looking at pictures of our family and has brought pictures of her family for me to see.

I guess I've gone on long enough. Write soon.

Love,

Jan (hiding from the authorities)

November 12

Dave

On VOA a report says that China is moving toward private owner-ship, contracts instead of government ownership. There are more and more Chinese law firms and lawyers these days, especially since there are so many joint-ventures with other countries starting up. One lawyer being interviewed said that the government has relaxed controls and people are free to work with private contracts. Another non-Chinese, who works with the Chinese, told us that the Chinese tend to negotiate via bribes, not through legal contracts; that a Chinese may, in exchange for a joint-venture contract with a foreign country, ask that his child be educated in that country.

Dave, Mike, Jan and Xia, our cook

November 12

Jan

Fred came over and we spent the evening drinking—first beer, then wine and then a lot of gin. Fred knows a lot of writers and poets and is intelligent and well read. He said, without emotion, that he would probably die in the next year or so. He has had cancer five times, and says it always comes back. I told him he needs to have a positive attitude, to which he said he does. He's taking an actress he met with him to Shanghai for the weekend. He's meeting a friend from the U.S. there, but he needs her along to help him with his travel arrangements and to interpret for him. I question his motives.

November 13

Jan

Dave was my guest speaker again today (for a different class). He says these lectures are not free, that I must pay him for his services. He's keeping track of my debts to him. I'll have to think of a way to pay him. The class was very appreciative and they want to have him back. It was good practice for them to use their English with another foreigner.

...Parking is a problem on all campuses, and Nanjing University is no exception. The problem is with bike parking. Today, policemen were on guard near the bike-parking area in front of the teaching building, making sure that nobody was parking outside of the lines, so I parked inside the lines, as did everyone else. On other days, bikes are parked everywhere, haphazardly. I've seen them go down like dominoes. They are often so jammed together that it's almost impossible to get them out. One day, I accidentally tore a bike seat on someone's bike that was parked very close to mine. I felt bad but had no way to find the owner. My bike already looks old, dirty and dented. The air and dirty streets make it difficult to keep them clean.

November 14

Dave

Thursday night I got drunk with Fred in our apartment drinking beer, wine and gin—deadly combination—and was hung over most of the next day. I did do a two-hour class for Jan. It was difficult, but I pulled it off. The combining of different kinds of booze is what I need to avoid, and, of course, the quantity. A gloomy hangover, one of my gloomiest ever. And that on top of the realization that I really haven't lost much weight this time in China. Maybe I'm <u>down</u> to 200 pounds, which means I've lost less than 10 in two and a half months. A gloomy fact. I need to get off the sweets, the booze, and avoid the excessive amounts of food; and I need to get back into running.

...Brian strikes me as a contented man. He's in his late 60s, long retired, and he's stored up some money in investments back home. He's done quite a lot of traveling, been in China for 10 years. He seems to take things as they come. He's not afraid to express an opinion even if it goes against the prevailing one. And he has a capacity for leisure, for just wandering off and losing himself in a landscape or city. Maybe the capacity for leisure is what I envy in him the most. He's accomplished things in his life, I'm sure; I imagine he was a diligent, hardworking person at one time. Now he seems to be winding down. He told me that teaching is beginning to bore him after all the years of it. But I watch him walking, looking around. He keeps his youthful curiosity. He told me he enjoys going to Germany and waking up early to go out to talk German to people all morning, and then in the afternoon just going off by himself. He's here without his wife, who is back in England running a bed and breakfast place. She's coming to Nanjing this month, and she and Brian haven't seen each other for months. Jan asked him if he missed his wife; he said yes, but that he has enjoyed his time alone too. I think he really does like to be alone. He handles his solitariness so well. Reminds me of Thoreau in <u>Walden</u>. That book is about, mostly, how one handles solitude. Either you are a good companion to yourself or you aren't.

...I need to find ways to recreate myself; I must learn to enjoy life and not have to always be working or worrying about working: making a story or a poem, or preparing for a class. There is much more to life besides one's work. To only work at something, however successful one becomes at that work, is to waste much of your life. There is so much to see, so many people to talk to and learn from. I must learn to cultivate leisure—being alone and doing nothing but living and enjoying it. Life for its own sake— nothing else.

November 14

Jan

Dave and I were in the store today buying lining for a suit jacket I'm having made. I found some materials that I thought would work and then tried to tell the clerk how much I needed. She seemed to be telling me (in animated Chinese) that I didn't want this material or that I needed more—maybe that this was only lining and that I needed heavier material. Whatever she was saying, I didn't understand. My written instructions, which I'd gotten from Qian, did not satisfy her. Another clerk went to find the person in the store who could speak English. A man came to my rescue, but his English was marginal. Finally, the clerk encouraged me to buy two meters, instead of the 1.7 meters I wanted, as a huge crowd gathered to observe a foreigner making a purchase.

On the way home we bought some pistachios and walked along eating and enjoying the beautiful day. The cold front has passed and we are having warm weather again. Many students are sitting out on the campus grounds. There is a mood of relaxation and contentment. We think about how cold it must be in South Dakota, and feel happy to be in China.

After dinner, walking through campus, we came upon a group of students standing under lighted Christmas bulbs strung around on trees. A big sign said: "Speak English." We decided to stop and were immediately surrounded by students. We talked to them for over an hour under the lights. It was a Saturday night get-together (no beer, no food, no rowdiness), just students who wanted to practice their English in a social setting.

November 15

Dave

Yesterday we walked past a store selling T.V. sets. I looked in the window and to my astonishment saw the Holyfield-Bowe fight for the heavy weight championship of the world. I think it was live; they'd apparently gotten it on a satellite dish. I kept looking, was invited into the store, but stayed only for a couple of rounds because Jan was waiting. She said she could walk home and I could watch the rest, but I decided to walk home with her.

That bothers me now, in retrospect. Never in my life have I passed up an opportunity to see a heavyweight championship fight on T.V. And there I was—and it was a good fight, too—and I left it. What does this mean? Just my mood? I don't want to lose my curiosity about these things; I don't want to quit my interest in the physical life—sports, human beings in battle against each other.

November 15

Jan

Dear Barb & Dana,

How are things in Nebraska? What have you two been doing lately? Our lives are going well in China. I've had a few easy weeks with debates and individual conferences in my classes. Now I have to spend time preparing for new classes. I've sloughed off long enough, but I've enjoyed it a lot. We enjoy our pace of life here. Somehow it seems less desperate and involved. I know it's easier for us being visitors than it is being Chinese in a communist society. We have the best of both worlds.

This morning it was cool and breezy as we walked to the market. We go several times a week. Many people were out on the streets having brunch: parents with their one child, students, teachers, workers. We watched a street vendor prepare something that resembled a burrito in the U.S. She first fried an egg, spreading it out until it was paper thin; then she put a thinly-rolled piece of dough on top and turned it over. On top of this she brushed a hot sauce, sprinkled green chopped onions, and green vegetables, and then some cut-up hot red peppers. She put three or four of what looked like soft bread sticks on it. After that, she rolled the whole thing up and cut it in two and put it in a wrapper. It looked delicious. Other street vendors tried to get us to buy their food. I often do buy baked sweet potatoes on the street, cooked in coals in huge steel barrels. They're handed to me wrapped in a torn piece of newspaper or old pages from books. Most people break them open and eat them right on the street, but I like to take mine home and put butter and brown sugar on it. I think I could make a pie from these sweet potatoes. Thanksgiving is coming up...

The odor permeating the campus has been foul lately. Apparently the grounds are being fertilized. It makes me feel like I'm on a South Dakota farm.

As we walked by the student dining hall today, as we always do on our way to classes, we looked inside and saw the dining tables being mopped with floor mops. These are the dirtiest looking things around. Our apartment floor gets mopped with the same kind of dirty, multi-colored cotton rag mop twice a week. The fuwuyan (maids) use our kitchen sink to rinse the mop out as they slop it around on our floors, pushing the dirt under our shoes, boxes, suitcases, chairs, tables, bed, and still further into the corners and cracks. Some of the foreigners here won't let the maids mop their rooms. They prefer to do it themselves. I don't mind letting them do it (in fact I prefer that they do it); we just don't walk on the floors barefoot or in our socks.

We decided to eat in a noodle shop this evening that was highly recommended by a few of my students. We learned that our standards and our students' standards for a good restaurant are not the same. We went in, after hesitating, and ordered in the best Chinese we knew. We were seated at a small table on two small benches. The waitress came and wiped the table off, brushing the food and other debris onto the floor. We sat and waited for our food, as everyone in the restaurant stared at us. (I got the feeling that few foreigners have eaten here.) We were each served a bowl of noodles with extremely hot sauce on top, and a bowl of soft doughy dumplings in hot water. The dumplings had a sweet bean paste inside, and were served with a bowl of black bean paste on the side. We ate the soup, which was quite good, even though it made our mouths burn. Dave ate one dumpling and I tried a piece of one. They were like eating a glob of uncooked bread dough, but not quite as good. The meal was very cheap, probably the only kind of a meal that students can afford. The filthy decor and the lack of sanitary conditions were difficult for me to overlook.

I told my conversation students to bring topics to class for discussion. One student innocently presented this topic: "What is better, being married or being individual?" What do you think?

We've been upset here about our mail being opened before we get it, especially our bank statements. A letter we got today just had the end completely torn off—no subtlety. It was a letter from the U.S. Embassy. Pam, a foreign teacher here, told us that when she first came, her mail was held up for the first six weeks. It had all been opened. After that it was checked for a while, but she thinks they finally stopped after deciding she was okay. We didn't get mail for a long time, and most of it now comes in bunches. They apparently haven't decided that we are "okay" yet. It's one of the annoyances of living in a communist country.

Write to us. We look forward to mail every day. Have a Happy Thanksgiving! Bye for now.
Love,

Jan (dumpling eater)

November 17

Dave

I bought a tie on the street yesterday. The man who sold it to me tried to get about twice as much money as the tie was worth, but his wife restrained him. Finally I paid Y5 (a buck or so) for a tie that already has a loop, and so I won't have to tie it in front of a mirror, which is always tricky.

...We heard that the universities are losing their younger professors to the market place. The universities can't afford to pay them much more than 200 yuan per month. The low pay forces the professors to moonlight. Who can blame a person who can go into a business venture in a southern city, such as Guangzhou, and make good money and improve their standard of living by about double or triple? "Go South, young man or woman." That's what the young are hearing in China these days.

November 18

Jan

Fred returned from Shanghai with his friend George who is visiting from California. His mood was very somber and he appeared to be sick. He and George must have over-indulged in Shanghai. It was the first time I had seen Fred drink tea.

George asked us what we thought of marriage. We've been married for so long, more than half of our lives, that we can't answer the question with any kind of objectivity. We've never really been single, having been married at 18 and 17. George is in his late 50s and has never been married. He pointed out, immediately, that he is not gay. I told him, in jest, that I was relieved to know that. He's an attractive guy and has chosen to remain single. He says he's actually afraid of the commitment of marriage. George is planning to stay with Fred in his small 1 1/2 room apartment until January 10, when Fred goes home.

November 18

Dave

Dear Friends,

So, you may be curious about our life in China the second time around.

First, living in China is a lot easier this time. We have all the conveniences we need. We can buy everything we need, from prunes to Kleenex to peanut butter to canned tuna to even—get this, this is something new in the last year—fried chicken legs on the street. I mean, we aren't going without as we did in Kunming. Though I must say right away, the food in Kunming was better. Spicy rice noodles we haven't found here. What's good here? Well...the food is "lardy," but we don't mind the chicken-with-peanuts, the egg and tomato and the rice. But you can get all this food anywhere in China. Nothing to distinguish it that we've found yet.

The scenery is excellent. The Sun Yat-Sen mausoleum with its hundreds of steps, its being out of the city in a quiet place (not possible to find a quiet place in Shanghai, our friends from there tell us); the city wall with its defensive fortifications; the bird market close by; the Taiping Museum, where the anti-Christian forces are depicted in pictures as having triumphed over the crazed and so-called "God-Worshipers' Society" led by a rebel Christian named Hong; a restaurant called The Sprite Outlet which has decent fried noodles; and Zhongshan street, the main drag nearby, which is haunted by the two of us, most days a week.

The apartment is more than comfortable. In fact, we have too much heat, and below the Yangtze you aren't supposed to get <u>any</u> heat. The foreign teachers two floors above complained about the cold during a quick cold spell that zipped through two weeks ago, so we have heat: an hour in the morning, an hour at midday, an hour at night. Too hot for us. We have a thick quilt and just simply don't need it, so we fling open the doors and windows whenever the heat comes on. We keep comparing all this with Kunming, where we were cold enough in the cold months to have to keep moving around and stay awake to survive. Here, survival is much easier.

I have only three two-hour classes, so I have plenty of time to hang around my computer and try to make stories and even, occasionally, poems. And the classes are in the middle of the week so Jan and I can travel on the long weekends. We're going by boat to Lushan next month and maybe to Xiamen, both in the south, the latter not far from Hong Kong. I'll be lecturing on recent American poetry and fiction, and Jan about American culture. We might go to Kunming in the spring, and maybe one more place. We want to take advantage of the opportunity to travel, since we may not be back this way for a while.

Tonight we went out to eat at a new noodle-and-dumpling shop. The noodles were okay, the dumplings not great, and the way the waitress wiped off the table just after we sat down was striking. She just wiped everything off onto the filthy floor with a shirt sleeve. We may not go back until we get very hungry. There are joint-venture hotel restaurants here we can go to, but they're obscenely expensive.

My impressions of the Chinese? They are fairly upbeat right now; the market system is in place and doing well. The negative side is that intellectuals are still put down and still don't make a decent living—about a third as much as waitresses (who also get their food). The worst thing, still, is the pitifully small places that most people live in. The most beautiful young women—and by the way, the women are extraordinarily beautiful, and cleanly dressed and sharp—live in hovels, almost without exception. That is one of the fascinating things about China. The discrepancy between beauty and poverty. And the men are in charge. We do see women with bruises and black eyes with some frequency. The culture is still very male-oriented. If I wanted to make a purely sociobiological observation I would say that the women of China have been selected for their beauty and brains and graciousness, and the men, for their deviousness and trickery; but that, I admit, may be an exaggeration.

Are we happy, and doing okay? Yes, we are happy and doing okay. Jan keeps busy with her ten hours of teaching conversation and writing, and she spends a lot of time at the computer on her journal. Is she saying bad things about me? I wonder. I keep saying good things, mostly, about her in _my_ journal.

Clinton is in, which makes us happy. I've been a Populist Democrat all my life and by God I'm not about to change.

That's it for now. We hope to hear from you about what's going on on the other side of the world. Holyfield, I heard, got whupped.

As Ever,

Dave

November 18

Dave

I'm thoroughly disgusted with my slob life. If anything, I have <u>gained</u> a pound or two here, not lost. One of my goals was to come to a place like this, in which the environment forced me to be more resourceful and physical, and get my weight down to a decent 185 or so. I probably weigh around 200. Too much food, too much beer and peanuts. I'm going to do something about it, beginning today. To hell with excess. I will watch myself closely. Doing all this walking and running and not having a car and gaining weight—that shows me I'm a slob. It would help if the living conditions were more like Kunming's. But I remember that there I drank very little beer for the semester stay. And I am backsliding on a big ass. One positive note this morning: I am lifting weights. My arms are still functional.

November 19

Jan

A cold front is moving through. We now need warm coats and gloves to wear even in the classrooms. One student writes in her journal: "When winter really arrives, our limbs are shivering with chilly coldness. However, we still have to sit in the ice-cold classroom to study! What a cruel thing!"

Another student writes: (about walking home from town at lunch time) "I felt hungry. There were many restaurants along the two sides of the street. But I am poor. So I just had a bowl of noodles. It was delicious and I really wanted another bowl. But I couldn't pay for it." They aren't trying to get sympathy, just stating facts about their lives. These things make me feel terrible, however, and I wish I could do something about their situations. They always appear to be upbeat.

November 19

Dave

"Tell me, what's matrimony like?" asks Fred's friend George.

"On what day of the week?" I say. Then: "I don't know what to compare it with, since I've always been married."

What can I say to such a question? "Marriage is great." "Wonderful." "Beautiful." "Blissful." Maybe I should say: "Marriage is relentless. When you are married you are never not married. It doesn't let up." Or, I could say: "When you have a good friend as well as good wife and mother of your children, it's fine, fine. When you grow up together and change together and do almost everything together—well...what can you say to a question like that? Jan and I are always together. We are married. It's impossible to say much about matrimony when you have always been in matrimony. Or, I could've said: "Without this woman I'd have a hard time surviving. I suppose that means that being married to her is a good thing. To not go to bed with her every night, to not wake up with her every morning—that would be a life not easy to get used to. I suppose I could get used to it, if I had to, but after all these years together I don't want to have to."

Am I in love with Jan physically as well as otherwise? Yes, very much so. Am I frustrated sometimes? Yes. Am I happy sometimes? Yes. Does my marriage with Jan for 35 years or so provide something of an equilibrium? Yes. Would I be happy and fulfilled as a bachelor? Probably not. Do I, a solitary person in some ways—an individualist who hates groups (except labor unions) and who needs to be alone to get his work done—do I have, as a married man, enough leeway for aloneness and individuality and solitariness? Yes. The one advantage to the single life, as I see it from the sidelines, is solitariness, being able to pace yourself in such a way as to have almost no interference. Being alone would mean making friends with yourself and even loving yourself at least to the point of tolerance until death do you and your self part. And yet, all of us need companionship too. That is an important part in matrimony. If you can at least live with someone you love you do have a companion, a good friend, a fellow comforter, collaborator, ally against a lot of shit the world kicks up in your face when you are not looking and even when you are looking.

Marriage, then, is a kind of "in-group" that you belong to and that opposes, daily, the slings and arrows of outrageous fortune. "You and me against the world," the song says, and there is something to that.

Matrimony? In general, I have nothing to say about it, really. But specifically, referring to my own life, I prefer it, will take it, will take, that is, this marriage with Jan, any day of the week, knowing that all days of the week will not be blissful. I like the way Howard Nemerov talks about marriage in his short poem, that ends: "One should be watching while the other dies."

I don't believe the essayist Francis Bacon when he says that having a wife and children means giving up "hostages to fortune." I have, on the other hand, been fortunate to have this good person, this sexy, funny, lively, curious, caring, sometimes critical, patient, cool, intuitive, beautiful woman around me most days of my life.

November 20

Jan

We invited Qian, her cousin (a student at Nanjing University) and her mother to our apartment for dinner this evening. Qian's mother, who recently retired, is from Nantong and is visiting for several days. Qian lives with two other women in one room on the sixth floor of a dormitory. At dinner Qian's mother and cousin were slightly nervous because it was their first time eating Western food with Westerners. Qian's mother tried to eat the garlic bread with chopsticks and had some trouble. Chinese people don't consider it proper to pick up food with their hands. Qian's mother said the proper things about not wanting me to fuss very much, about how good the meal was, and then when she was finished eating, she stood up and said she was full and immediately left the table to sit on another chair. I served fried potatoes with pieces of canned ham mixed in, stir-fried vegetables, garlic bread, jello with bananas, rice and tea. They brought along a roasted chicken and some bananas. Qian's mother invited us to come to her home in Nantong.

November 20

Dave

Two things that need to happen in this world rather quickly. One: people need to leave other people alone. Two: people need to be kind to each other.

November 21

Jan

Gao, one of my conversation students, came over today and gave me a brief history of Nanjing. He felt it was his duty as a history major to teach me something about the city, especially since I am his teacher. I took notes as he went through the past 2000 years or so. He also brought up a score I had given him on a recent debate in class. I had written scores for all the students, and his was the lowest. One day when I was taking a break, several students looked through my grade book. (Whatever is sitting out, they feel, is public.) Then they began to tell others in the class what their scores were. Gao's score was low because he had used too much Chinese when he was supposed to use only English. I told him not to worry about the score. They are all worried about what kind of grades they will get for the course. I doubt if I'll flunk any of them, even if their English is poor.

November 21

Dave

Another beautiful day. Cold, cold; but sun, sun! "The sun is a morning star," said Thoreau, at the very end of Walden. Beginnings are better in sunlight, as endings are better in darkness. Sun rhymes with dawn, though I can't remember this rime in any poem. I should write one. I should write more poems, but I don't have the interest these days, or rather, my interest has shifted to story-telling.

November 22

Dave

We took a different street yesterday and came out at a lake and city wall. There is something about coming out at a lake or a river. "Were your Niagara a cataract of sand, would you travel your thousand miles to see it?" asked Melville in <u>Moby Dick</u>. Water. All trails eventually lead to water. Edward Wilson says the same thing. In his essay called "The Right Place" he mentions the importance of a city or stronghold having a body of water near it as a defensive strategy. I suppose it's the moat idea. There is something enchanting about looking out over water, looking beyond. It's similar to looking out over a prairie, your eyes scanning the horizon. Maybe you are looking for enemies? Checking the horizon. Something "out there."

...Everybody has people around them they don't care for. But when somebody does something I don't like, instead of overlooking it I tend to want to even the score, or at least hold a grudge. The books say, "Don't hold a grudge; be on good terms with everybody." Yes, a good idea. If you are on good terms with others, there is some balance in your life between you and the world outside you, the social world you live in. If you are not on good terms, that is an imbalance. But the problem with the "be on good terms" notion is that, while it does make sense and ought to be aspired to, always—what we feel about others is quite often beyond our control. We can make an outward show to get along, and we can be congenial and decent and helpful, but if in our hearts we have enmity and hate, that enmity and hate are also driving our behavior. Emotions are incredibly powerful. I agree with the philosopher Hume: "Reason is the slave of the emotions." If it's adaptive to hate someone else, and to be vindictive toward that person, then your emotions will tell you to be vindictive, to hate.

Maybe the solution is to somehow trick yourself into thinking—and then later, feeling—that it's more adaptive and more productive, expedient, and appropriate to <u>not</u> have these negative feelings and thoughts. Eventually, maybe you can talk yourself into positive feelings, or at least talk yourself into a position or strategy of leaving others alone, of just concentrating on your own work.

Humans have an extremely strong, irreversibly strong predisposition to identify with an in-group against an out-group. I've seen it countless times in my life, I've experienced it personally many, many times. For instance, the way fans identify with athletic teams, and the expression of prejudice by friends I've had.

November 22

Jan

I stayed in my new lounging pajamas all day. My throat is sore. I did manage to work some on my upcoming lecture. Deb stopped by with an orange juicer she bought for us in Chengdu.

November 23

Dave

Sun, sun, sun! Jan wasn't feeling well yesterday, stayed home. Today she seems better, but still has a sore throat. But she's having her class. Moving around helps. I feel optimistic today, as if I'm starting my life over again at this very moment. It's amazing how we intellectualize everything, how we talk ourselves out of things by talking about them, by verbalizing. Words are only approximations. The body never lies. The body, the physical life, is primary; words and the intelligence are secondary by a long ways. The body comes through. "We die, and rise the same, and prove mysterious by this love," says John Donne. Yes. He knew about the physical life. I'll bet he was a physical person—robust, sexual, even athletic. Ministers often are.

...Jan tends to be tentative about taking viewpoints in her classroom. I try to explain that so much of teaching is subjective, and that the best way to handle things daily in the classroom is to rely on your own intuitions. And that you'll never have all the answers to all the questions concerning what is read and discussed, so you might as well try to learn along with the students. But all this is new to her—I'm talking from 20 some years' experience. Sure, for me it's a lot more manageable; and yet it's never easy. As a teacher, I have to keep flexible and alert. I can't assume that my opinions are anything more than opinions, except that they are from someone who has tried to explore ideas for a long time and be articulate about them.

But I am inconsistent. Sometimes I express an opinion and then sit back and watch it move around in the class. Sometimes I refuse to take sides. At other times I express an opinion with the force of a fact. It's something I believe in about people, nations, etc. I say it and then close up to any notions that I could be wrong. I know I'm hypocritical and inconsistent, to say the least. But I am these things, too, because I am human. We all have ideas that we cherish and are even paranoid about. These opinions, ideas, beliefs, and prejudices are a sort of rampart, or wall, around us that keeps us safe from the world "out there." They protect us.

DETAIL OF THE DAY:

On the sports page of the CHINA DAILY, Wednesday, November 25th, the headline reads: BECKER'S PECKER LIFTED BY TRIUMPH

Boris Becker the tennis player has won a tournament. There's nothing else about his pecker in the article, though there is a reference to his girlfriend, an actress, who "would like to see me win again."

November 23

Jan

I woke up again with a sore throat but I made it through both of my Tuesday classes. One of my students called and wanted to come over to ask a few questions and get some help on pronouncing words for a translation job he was asked to do. He brought along a big bag of oranges and ended up staying for several hours. He had me tape my voice, pronouncing some difficult medical/scientific terms. I pronounced some badly, but he didn't seem to mind. I know that his main purpose in coming over was to talk to me. He had been taking another conversation class with a foreigner from a different university in Nanjing. He said she insulted him by putting China down (in his eyes) and he quit the class. He wrote her a note, which, she said, insulted her. I couldn't get it clear what the actual insult was toward him, and I don't know what he said in his letter.

I have the feeling it was a language-related incident and not one that meant any harm. Chinese people are sensitive about being poor and living in a third-world country. They demonstrate a great love and devotion to their country and its people. I see this in their writing, especially.

November 26

Dave

Last night I was embarrassed. The cook prepares meals at our apartment for Lida and Mike and Jan and me, and also herself. She cooks from roughly 4:00 p.m. to 6:00 p.m., Lida and Mike come down, we all sit and eat, while she goes upstairs to Mike and Lida's apartment and takes a shower. Then she comes down and eats with us. Last night I forgot about her coming back down, and went on eating the spicy chicken, which was good, and eating, and eating, until it was gone. Then Mike and Lida left to go upstairs to another apartment to see a tailor, and suddenly it hit me that the cook would be coming back down to eat! I was very embarrassed, and what was especially awkward, as I waited for her to come back—this poor, hard-working, pleasant and enthusiastic woman who can't even afford to get her glasses fixed but instead wears a piece of tape on them to hold the ear piece on—what was really difficult was that I can't speak Chinese and didn't know how to apologize except by pointing to the empty chicken plate and saying, pleadingly: "Duibuqi, duibuqi" (excuse me, excuse me). Which is exactly what I did, as Jan, trying to smooth it over, pointed to my belly and said (she knows more Chinese than I do), something like: "big belly, big eater." But the cook was gracious about it, sitting down to eat. She said, "mei guanxi" many times over, which means (what else could she say?) "never mind." I sat there, feeling like a trapped animal. I wanted to go hide in a closet.

November 26

Jan

Dear Shelly, David, Kari, and all,

Happy Thanksgiving! We opened our door this morning to find a picture of a turkey with the words "Gobble Gobble" written on it. Angela, a young teacher from New York state, had made hand turkeys on sheets of paper and taped them on all the foreigners' doors.

Our day wasn't a very special day, since we had classes. We miss you all, especially on holidays. For our Thanksgiving dinner, we went to the Sprite restaurant and had Chinese food. We found out that the foreigners in the other building (one adjacent to ours) had a Thanksgiving dinner, with turkey from Shanghai, pumpkin pie, etc. We in this building feel left out and are a little miffed about it. Robin, who organized the party, had gone to Shanghai and bought some of the ingredients and a turkey! After the dinner was over, and with no prior notice, she asked everyone there to contribute Y50.00, about $9.00. That gave her over Y500.00, much more than she would have spent for the food and the train ticket. Some of the guests were upset about this, since they had not been told ahead of time; they thought they were being invited for a Thanksgiving dinner, a nice gesture.

Your dad and I were invited by Mr. Xu and a few others in my conversation class to a birthday party last night. They said it was also a celebration of our Thanksgiving Day. When we walked into the huge, cold hall, the students all clapped for us. Mr. Xu introduced us as if we were the honored guests, instead of Zou, who was having the birthday. He then seated everyone and asked me to say a few words. I told them how happy we were to be there, especially since we were in the mood to celebrate because it was our Thanksgiving holiday.

The program then began. Mr. Xu, the organizer of the party, welcomed everyone and acted as the emcee. We were asked to sing a song, which we did—a Simon and Garfunkel favorite. After that, someone played a harmonica, then another couple sang a song. Zou was presented a bouquet of plastic flowers for her birthday (still in the plastic wrap) along with a photo album. She was then asked to have the first dance with her partner. After they danced, everyone else began to dance. Mr. Xu, especially, kept asking me to dance with him. He asked me, as we were dancing, if he could sing a song to me in Chinese. It turned out to be a love song. He then told me how young I looked, how age didn't matter, how he loved the color of my hair. I told him I was "old," old enough to be his mother. He continued the entire evening, making remarks and wanting me to dance with him. He also wanted to have a picture taken of just the two of us so that, as he said, "he would always remember me when he looked at it."

Mr. Xu said—after your dad and I had danced a slow dance, holding each other fairly close (as we normally do)—that in China they are not allowed to do that. They can't dance "face to face." They must turn sideways a little. I said I hoped we had not set a bad example for the others at the party.

The only food served at the party was oranges, hard candy pieces and sunflower seeds. They were just scattered over the several tables in the hall, and the scraps were thrown on the tables and on the floor. We were constantly being handed candy and orange pieces. There was nothing to drink. The room was unheated, so it was very cold. But we warmed up by dancing. Students like to have dances in the winter to warm themselves up (in more ways than one).

At about 10:00 p.m. it was announced that the party was over. Mr. Xu insisted on walking us home even though we were only about half a block from our apartment. I suspect your dad may have been a little jealous of all the attention Xu was giving me, and he didn't seem to like me dancing with Xu as much as I did. I thought it was funny and, of course, it was an ego booster.

These students were all my graduate students. The innocence, the lack of alcohol, the meager party refreshments and the cold dance hall—all seemed very unlike the parties you and most young Americans have attended, wouldn't you agree? It was what you could call "good clean fun," the kind of party that we and most American parents would have approved of for their children.

In class we're talking about American proverbs. One student was comparing American proverbs with Chinese proverbs. His comparison for "When in Rome, do as the Romans do," was, "When you climb the mountain, sing the mountain's song." I'll remember that.

Today, for variety, we went to a different open market to buy food. It wasn't as extensive as the one we usually go to, just a small alleyway with fewer choices, but we bought something from a food vendor that tasted like a hash brown potato patty. I bought a sweet potato for lunch. We walked to yet another new area enjoying the beautiful, sunny, warm day. We feel content and happy here.

You'd like Angela, a young teacher from New York state, about 24 years old. She came over to our apartment and spent a couple of hours today. She wants to buy a snake and take it back to the States with her when she goes home next summer. She says she will keep it in a pillowcase around her waist so nobody will see it. One of her professors back home wants a snake from Asia. She's young, independent and loves to travel alone. One of the good things about being here is getting to know a variety of people.

We want to hear more from all of you. Let us know what is happening in your lives. We miss you all.

Love,

Mom (fending off suitors)

November 27

Dave

Last night we went to a birthday party. Jan's amorous student fell all over her, singing to her as they danced (a love song), and even asking her how much time she spent on "amusement." Jan thought it was a sexual reference; so did I. They had us sing a song. The young women were beautiful and intelligent and sentimental and curious. I was asked to dance quite a number of times and enjoyed it. Though the way Jan and I slow-danced was no doubt too "close" for their comfort. I'm sure Jan's student, a Ph.D. student with a wife and child back home, wanted to dance the same way, but he told her that they "better not." Jan's curious about Chinese sexuality. So am I. Men and women here seem to be more separated than they are in the States. Of course, traditionally, the man/husband was in charge—that still persists. Family cohesion was correlated with national cohesion. Obey your father; obey the Emperor.

...I have to watch my drinking. I've decided, to get my work done and live a better, and I hope long life. I want to wake up sober in the morning. I want to get at my writing in the early hours, which, as Thoreau said, are the best hours for solitude and real work. "Only that day dawns to which we are awake." I want to be awake at dawn, and clearheaded, ready to live in the day, to be happy. "Where can we live but days?" said Philip Larkin. I want to avoid what he calls "the priest and the doctor in the long coats running over the fields." I want to keep them at bay as long as possible with a fresh, sober mind. "Give me," as Whitman says, "the splendid, silent sun."

November 27

Jan

Mr. Xu wasn't in class today.

November 28

Dave

Chinese proverb: "Don't write the book for rice." But Chinese writers these days want changes. Formerly, they wrote for the government. Now, they want to write for rice, for money. There are changes going on, and of course the free market system is having an effect on the arts too.

...Too much wine last night. I need badly to learn when to stop. After dinner I should've gone home with Jan. But I lingered at Fred's place too long.

November 29

Dave

Yesterday when the workmen out back were laying a gas line for the boiler, I was at my desk. I had left the door open because it was so warm. I heard someone on the porch fumbling with the door lock, and walked out of my office into the front room and saw a young worker messing around with the latch. I walked out the door and took hold of the latch, and looked at the young boy, and said, with some force, "Okay?" His eyes increased their size; he knew I didn't like his being that close to our apartment. Actually, the workmen sit on our porch, use the wicker chair and even hang their jackets over our clothesline. They look into the window frequently, sometimes staring with their hands cupped over their eyes. The young man knew my feelings, though I hadn't said anything he understood. And yet, of course, they do have a different sense of privacy. They're not individualistic in the way we are. Ownership too is obviously different. People don't have much in the way of private property. In American, we say, over and over and over again in a million ways: "This is mine." And "hands off." In a collectivistic society the idea of ownership has to be different.

November 30

Dave

Jan had a snappy-looking suit made for herself, and a couple of silk blouses. The bill—which included some altering of pants, mine and hers—came to around Y165. When you include all the material and all the labor involved, it cost around 40 bucks, which is outrageously cheap. The cloth itself is cheaper than what it would be in the U.S. But where you save money—lots of money—is in having a tailor make it for you. This young woman simply copied Jan's blouses and worked from another dress coat of Jan's for the suit. She's very clever.

DECEMBER

December 1

Jan

My dancing partner, Mr. Xu, asked me, after class today, if I had any love poems he could read. I told him I would see what I could find for him.

...The students are doing well with the proverbs assignment I gave them, even with their limited language skills. They love proverbs. One female student asked for my proverb book and copied each proverb by hand (there were hundreds of them). She couldn't afford to make xerox copies.

December 1

Dave

Sometimes I think I'm learning a lot about short story making and then sometimes I don't know. But I should just relax and do it, like the tailor who takes our clothes and copies them. If she can see how a suit is made and then make one herself, I can see how good stories are made and make them myself. That's how all writers and artists work anyway. In the words of Robert Lewis Stevenson, we're all "sedulous apes." The first artist, the first poet, the first story teller—how did he or she begin? Who told the first story? Or was the first story always there, somewhere, in the genes, the human genome? Was it just a matter of someone opening his mouth and having at it? Once upon a time...

A plot is not the same as a story (E.M. Forster). A plot consists of dramatic involvement. The old man died and then his wife died, is not a plot; it's a story. The old man died and then, out of grief, the old woman died. That is a plot. I want to hold onto that distinction. It's the <u>why</u>, the <u>because</u>. Not just the event. And yet the <u>why</u> and the <u>because</u> need not be directly shown or stated, as they are in Stephen Crane's "The Open Boat." Drama, conflict, is everything. I need to drive the story forward just as I drive the poem forward. The story and the poem are different species, maybe, but they belong to the same class. I'm a person with a lot of tension and conflict in my own life. I ought to be able to convey this in stories, and have done so a few times anyway. A sense of urgency. Urgency, a good word. A need to tell a story or write a poem. But a story, unlike most poems, has a plot connection.

December 2

Jan

Dear Pam & Kent,

Your letter was great, Pam. You've had your share of problems with your car. We don't miss having one. Walking or bike riding is fine for us. I know once we're back in the States, we'll probably revert to driving everywhere, but I hope not.

We were asked (told) by our leader to change our classes today to attend an all-day city tour sponsored by CITS (China International Travel Service). The tour guides wanted to practice their English on us, and they did—one by one. One guide told about an American couple who had missed a tour bus that was to take them to the airport for a flight. Because they didn't know much Chinese, they thought they could convey their destination to the cab driver with gestures. They ended up at a duck farm.

On the tour we learned about the "Rape of Nanjing" by the Japanese in 1937. Hundreds of thousands of people were slaughtered in Nanjing during that time when Japan almost conquered China. Many Chinese people remember this and, to this day, have not been able to forgive the Japanese people. We have encountered a lot of anti-Japanese sentiment in Nanjing.

We also got to see the Yangtze River bridge, which is three miles long. Some of the English faculty at Nanjing University had been forced to work on this bridge during the Cultural Revolution.

We had lunch at a Chinese hotel. At the end of the meal a special treat was brought out, which appeared to be beef. Someone thought it might be mutton. The bones were suspiciously tiny. Then we found out it was goh rou, dog! Most of the Chinese were pleased. Our friend Brian, from England, took a bite of it. His wife, who is Chinese Malaysian, became very upset and made quite a scene. I felt bad for the hosts, because they considered it a special treat. It was for the Chinese, since they like to eat dog in the winter; they say it helps keep your body warm. Brian's wife told the hosts they shouldn't ever serve dog to foreigners (which was probably good advice). I didn't eat any of it, by choice. Dog would not be my choice; nor would chicken feet, intestines or eel. Were you served dog meat in China?

At the city gate, there were several beggars from a nearby province. Two of them were little girls. They said their parents weren't with them. One was around 12 or 13 and her little sister was around five. They were experienced at begging and had a way of looking at you that made you want to give them something. Dave and I gave them some food and money. Their faces were beautiful but the clothes they had on were ragged and dirty. The older one was combing her younger sister's hair with a dirty comb with most of its teeth missing. I saw the young girl run up to a man, who had just bought a piece of cooked meat on a stick, and beg for it. She got it from him, but her older sister took it away from her and ate all of it. Did you see many beggars in Kunming when you were there? We didn't.

I have my students keep journals, and one wrote in her journal that she was in a classroom on campus late at night writing a composition (for my class), when she realized it was getting late. She tried to get to her dorm, but found the gates were locked. So she had no choice but to spend the entire night in the cold, dark classroom. She wrote that she was cold and hungry. The next day she had a fever and had to miss class. If the gates are locked around here, there is no way to get in or out. Total control. I know the Kunming apartment complex gates closed at 10:30 p.m. when we were there.

The journals the students write provide good insights into their lives. Generally, they seem to be happy, young adults, although somewhat imma-ture compared to American students. Their innocence is charming. They have serious concerns about their future, as most students do; but in China, as you know, there are fewer options for them.

We ate at our favorite neighborhood restaurant, the Sprite, again today but have decided we're tired of Chinese food. It all tastes the same.

Dave had a dream in which the only thing he had to eat was noodles. We have been eating a lot of noodles lately. We need a break.

Always good to hear from you. Bye for now.
Love,

Jan (rejecting dog meat)

December 2

Dave

What's the best thing I can do for myself? Take care of my health. I haven't been moderate in China this time around. Part of it is the availability of beer and sweets that, in the U.S., cause early death or clog the arteries. It has not been easy. I'm a nervous person, a person given to excess; always have been. I must learn to relax, to push away the beer and food. Running still makes me feel good. My legs are in decent shape, for walking anyway.

Then there's the shortness of breath. The other day, running with Mike, I felt a slight hesitation in my chest, the same kind of hesitation and shortness of breath I'd felt in the last year or two playing racquetball. There doesn't seem to be any pattern. I don't have to be exerting myself to the maximum for the symptom to occur. I can't understand it, but I think it has to do with too much weight, too much beer belly. My father and uncle both died at 52. Is biology destiny? Is it in my genes to keel over sometime in the next two years? Can I avert this by staying in shape, working out and not over-indulging at the table or gulping beers? My father and uncle were in poor physical shape, I know that. I had an EKG test before I came to China. I need to start pacing myself. I need to learn to say "no thank you." Three little words could extend my life. I should never ask myself to do anything contrary to my own interests, should I? Good health is in my own best interest. I have a lot of writing to do, a lot of traveling, a lot of watching my kids and grandkids grow up. When I get home I'll see my doctor about my shortness of breath.

December 3

Dave

Poor Brian. He should've passed on the dog meat when it came around on the turn table. His wife is really on him for it. In their apartment last night, she said she'd <u>never</u> forgive him for that. Brian mumbled, shook his head.

...The food is starting to get to me. It just beats me down, a little every day. My stomach is not right, and I feel generally lousy. Little energy. And we've got to be off on the boat next Monday morning. My face is hot sometimes.

December 4

Dave

Ms. Huang, a graduate student of mine, tells me that the students like my voice when I read aloud in class. So, I'll keep reading aloud. Today I may even sing "Laredo" to them, a cowboy song I love to sing. I couldn't get away with this in the U.S., I told Jan. She agreed and laughed. When you've got an audience, <u>USE</u> it!

As I-I walked out on the streets of Laredo.

As I walked on in Laredo one day...

December 5

Jan

While shopping today, we saw the most pitiful sight I've seen here. A man was walking slowly along the road with his pants partially down and what looked to be a diaper around him. It was wet and dirty, as were the rest of his ragged clothes. His entire appearance was one of extreme poverty and despair—very disturbing to me. And he wasn't begging. I don't think he had the energy to beg.

December 6

Dave

Jan and I saw three boys urinating in a sewer downtown. All were around 12 or 13, and seemed to be enjoying the act, not a single act but a communal one, I remember in my boyhood doing the same thing with friends, except that we were always off by ourselves in some trees or at a lake. In the West with its Christian background, lots of people have a problem with sexuality that the Chinese seem to be free of. There was no need for the boys to hide; they simply unzipped their pants and took a piss together, and enjoyed it.

December 6

Jan

We walked to the post office across town to pick up a package. It had rained during the night and the streets were wet and muddy. I['m fascinated with the little kids with slits in the backs of their pants. Their mothers seem to know when they have to relieve themselves, and the kids just squat down wherever they are and do it. As a result, I doubt if there are any toilet hang-ups later in life. No need for a psychiatrist to delve into their background to find out their problems with "potty training."

...Dave bought two pictures on the street today, one of pheasants, the other a boat scene with a moon shining over it. I teased him about buying something I thought similar in taste to those velvet pictures sold on the sides of roads in the U.S. The ones he bought actually aren't too bad. The boat scene picture brightens our wall when the sunlight comes through the windows and makes the room shine.

...Qian came by to show us how to make tea eggs, since Dave likes them and wanted to know how to prepare them. You boil eggs in tea, soy sauce and special spices. Qian and I bought some <u>baozi</u> (steamed bread with a filling) and noodles, and she prepared dinner for us, using the few vegetables we had on hand. I'm always amazed at how little food it takes for a Chinese person to make a satisfying meal.

December 7

Dave

Soon we'll be going up the Yangtze to Jiujiang, near the mountain called Lushan. We're looking forward to it.

DETAIL OF THE DAY:
A man hauling a cart with 20 barrels in it; I assume they were empty, but I wouldn't bet on it.

...We walked three hours yesterday. That's always good for the body. It leaves me drained in a good way.

...I need to be more flexible, and more open to people. I tend to distrust when Jan tends to trust. I should not be such a Mithridotes, assuming the world has more ill to throw at me than good. That's a cynical attitude. It's very hard to tell, of course, what's coming at you at any given moment. I should take it all in good spirits, sort it out, throw away the bad and keep the other, though it be only half good. I need to assume, more or less, that people are trying to help, not hinder.

December 8

Jan

When I went to see Mr. Z., with a letter of request to go to Jiujiang for a few days next week, and a class make-up schedule, he was a jerk. He said it would be very difficult for the students if I were to be gone then. He said he would approve the request only if we could assure him that we had return boat tickets arranged before we left Nanjing. He knows it's impossible to get round-trip tickets. I was angry at him for giving me a hard time about going, especially after I had made suitable arrangements for my classes. Others around here have gone and and haven't even let people know they were leaving. I had the urge to tell him right then and there that I quit—that he could take this job and shove it, that I don't need it. I felt that he was trying to intimidate me. He brought out a blank contract and wanted to know if I could sign it. He said I would have 60 graduate students next semester, after he had promised me only 40 (I found out later there were actually 68 students.) He wanted to know if I wanted three classes or 60 students in two classes. I told him I wanted only two classes with 20 students each, which was our prior agreement. I've decided I don't like him at all and don't want to teach any graduate students for him. I'll try to teach classes in the English section next semester.

...We went to eat at a new restaurant that looked good from the outside, but found the food to be poor. The pork and vegetable dish consisted of pork fat only; the chicken tasted old' and the green vegetables weren't even good. And it was more expensive than it should have been. The dinner didn't help my bad mood.

...Mr. Ren came by to pick up the "one minute" articles—articles on American life for conversation classes, a project that Dave and I were talked into doing. At first, we were asked to do a few; then it was 70; now he wants 100! We should never have agreed to do any. Dave did about 30, and I've done about 13. Fred was supposed to help, but he's skipped the country—gone back to the U.S. for a visit.

...The stress and tension are getting to us. We're getting on each other's nerves and snapping at each other. We need a break!

December 9

Dave

"Men know men better than women know men," I told Jan. I was right about her boss, Mr. Z. I told her I wanted to go with her when she asked Mr. Z. about going to Jiujiang. I figured he might be nasty, and he was. Jan's fuming; she threatened to quit. Then, last night she asked me to see Wu Y. and ask him if his offer for her to teach in the English Department was still good. I asked him, and he said yes, and that he'd talk to Mr. Z. and get back to me the next day. We'll see. Jan is an excellent, caring person and the students really like her. She spends a great amount of time organizing her classes, and even though she hasn't taught much before, she does a fine job in the classroom. But women still have little status in China. Jan, who came here optimistic and wanting to learn about Chinese culture, and wanting to teach, has to put up with this kind of crap partly because she's a woman. I want to talk to her boss; I want to sit down and say something to him, about insulting my wife, about hypocrisy, about hurting peoples' feelings. But I can't. I won't be able to do much about it because I am a guest and because I have no right to stamp and yell and raise hell. Here it is—the very thing we wanted to avoid: politics, the run-around, administrative bullying. I hate it.

We'll go up the river whether we get confirmation on the return trip or not. We're going, period. If Jan has to quit, she can do that. She doesn't need the money, and she is one who can stay busy; there's plenty to do.

...It seems to me that as China expands at the edges and the market system proliferates, and more people try to start up businesses, the country is at least in some ways tightening at the center. It is caused by the Party, of course, which has its fingers in every rice bowl. Nowadays the Party is not driven forward by ideology as it was in Mao's time. What makes it go is mainly the momentum of the machine already in motion, and the prospect that elite Party members, who run the show, will garnish more and more power and more and more money, even at the expense of the non-elite.

...Feeling a little grim today, waiting to hear about Jan's job next semester.

December 9

Jan

Two of my graduate students came over to take their final exams early, because they'll be gone for the rest of the month. They brought a huge Christmas card for me. Their English skills are so poor that it's difficult to communicate with them. Mr. Wang, one of the two, asked me to give his newly born son a name. He brought a picture of him to show me. I was curious about the red mark in the middle of the baby's forehead, and was told it was where the baby had an injection against infectious diseases. He said it was for hepatitis. I gave the baby the name of Dustin Michael (the name of our oldest grandchild). I told Mr. Wang I was honored to be asked to do this since I know how important the naming of a child is for Chinese people.

...Our cook prepared fish (with lots of bones), spinach and eggs, spinach and egg soup and fried onions with pieces of beef for dinner tonight. Dave didn't eat much at all. He won't eat fish with bones and hates onions. Carp is a popular fish in China, on that we normally throw out in the U.S. (at least in the Midwest). The meal wasn't great, but Ayi tries hard to please us.

December 10

Dave

Food, I figure, is about 85 percent of happiness. I don't like the food in Nanjing, so what does that mean? Last night the cook prepared spinach with egg whites, fish and a bowl of onions. I'm scared of eating fish because of the bones, and I've always hated onions. So I ate very little. I may lose weight yet; I can't eat the damned food! The spinach was okay except for the roots left intact. This is a cultural bias, no doubt.

The other night Jan and I went to a restaurant that Jan thought looked clean; actually it was the YMCA. Nobody else was eating there, which is not a good sign. The pork dish we got had a piece of pork—Jan got it—and the rest was pork fat. I didn't eat that night either. I must've lost about four pounds in the last few days. Good. Usually you have a favorite food you can always get if you need it bad enough. Not so here in Nanjing. We haven't yet found the Korean restaurant and a good noodle shop. We'll keep searching.

December 10

Jan

Wu Y. came over to tell me I could teach in the English section next semester instead of in the graduate school. With me sitting in the room, and with the topic being me, he primarily talked to Dave. He is very male-oriented. He said he had talked to Mr. Z. several times yesterday, once for a half an hour. He said Mr. Z. wanted to apologize to me for his tone, that he wasn't able to express himself clearly in English. I wanted to say that the message he gave me was very clear. But I didn't. I did express to Wu Y. my wish to teach only in the English section, and he agreed that I could. He said the graduate school would still like to have me, but that it was my choice. I chose—teaching only in the English section.

December 11

Jan

Chen Loo, Brian's wife, gave us a home-made Christmas decoration and gave it to us with a Christmas card. Deb also made us a Christmas decoration. I used our computer to make invitations for the Christmas party we're hosting for the English section, and for the Christmas Eve party for the foreigners. I rode my bike to the library to have copies made for distribution. The Christmas season is in full swing. I'm enjoying the relative simplicity of Christmas here. I don't feel overwhelmed by it as I often do in the U.S., the superficiality, the endless shopping for necessary gifts, the expense. Here it is uncomplicated.

December 12

Dave

Mr. Z. had a different attitude yesterday when I accompanied Jan to his office so she could tell him we were leaving for Jiujiang. He was congenial, cooperative. I stood there, right inside the door, close to Jan. He felt my presence. Jan got her signature, and we took it to the Waiban. One reason I came to China was to escape the bureaucracy; it seems sometimes as if we escaped into a much worse bureaucracy.

December 12

Jan

My conversation students came over to the apartment for a class. They presented three-minute talks while I taped their voices. They were nervous about being taped. One student talked about a former teaching job he had in a poor county and told of the bleak conditions. He said he had to walk on a muddy road to get to the classroom, that there often was no electricity or water, that the schoolyard was used to grow crops. They had to get their own water from a well, and it often smelled and tasted vile. The only form of entertainment was "chatting"—no music, no movies, no T.V. Many of the students were malnourished, but they all had one thing in common: the dream of becoming a college student one day.

Another student presented a wonderful talk on a fight he once had in Shanghai. He has studied martial arts and is quite capable of defending himself. In his story he told of being cheated on a hotel room and pedi-cab ride. He and the pedi-cab driver got into a fight over the cost of the ride and the condition of the room he and his wife were taken to. They were led to believe it was a nice place, but it was horrible. I think it's publishable as a short story. The descriptions were vivid and colorful, yet charming, because of his unique use of the English language.

...Our potted Christmas tree was delivered today, for which we paid $6.00 (U.S.). It reminds me of the "Charlie Brown" Christmas tree. I like this tree. And it certainly won't be difficult to decorate.

December 13

Dave

Now, Jiujiang, to the mountain. Up river, up the mountain, toward my "53rd year to heaven," to misquote Dylan Thomas.

December 13

Jan

We spent the day preparing for our trip on the Yangtze to Jiujiang. Qian helped me decorate our Christmas tree with what meager decorations I had. I took some computer paper edging and used it for garland and made a star out of cardboard and colored it with a yellow marker. I made candle holders out of toilet paper holders by covering them with red crepe paper. Qian seemed pleased with the tree. We like it too, even though it doesn't have any lights. This kind of decorating makes me think of how it must have been years ago when people made their own decorations, when Christmas was simpler. People all around, including the Chinese people, seem to have the Christmas spirit. In recent years the Chinese people have become more interested in celebrating Christmas, although it isn't a religious celebration for them. It's more of a time to have parties and exchange greeting cards. Greeting cards are plentiful.

December 15

Dave

We got to Jiujiang and went to Lushan Mountain, which is gorgeous. The streams are as clear as any in Colorado I've seen. Ice hung on the trees, and sometimes chunks of it dropped off at our feet, barely missing us. We visited a Taoist temple, rarer by far than Buddhist tem-

Our Christmas decorations

ples. We saw Chiang Kai-shek's wife's villa, which Mao took over when Chiang fled the country for Taiwan. Mao's bedroom is huge, with reclining, soft sofas where he spent time reading and scheming. One bathroom is luxurious, with two toilets and as much room as anything in the Shangri-La Hotel in Beijing. Another bathroom had a toilet which had been restructured for Mao. The floor was built up to the level of the toilet seat so Mao could use it for squatting, since he was accustomed to that. And then, in the same bathroom, there's a big Western-style bathtub—an incongruous sight, especially if one has seen and smelled a country latrine. The odor itself can knock a big man down.

We saw the exact place where one of Mao's wives took a photo of a mountain scene. Later, Mao wrote a famous poem about the scene, in which he denigrated the past emperors and exalted the present age with its greater leaders. We walked on the same trail that Chiang took the American General Marshall down, as they talked together. Lushan Mountain was a favorite place for poets, and we saw a replica of the great Li Bai's cabin. Another poet, Bai Yi Yu, wrote a famous poem about not finding many flowers in the lowlands, and then, as he reached the top of the mountain, finding thousands of them, hence, the name Flower Path, which we walked on. It's an extraordinary place. Unfortunately, it's been trampled by too many feet in the last half century or so. Yet, according to our guide Mr. Xu, there were tigers in the area as recently as ten years ago.

When I stood beneath one mountain peak and looked up, I thought of the old Chinese saying: "The mountain is high, and the Emperor is far away."

We spent some time in Jiujiang and visited a sort of drinking hall where the poet Po Chu-yi in the eighth century was supposed to have spent some time. We got to see a sequence of paintings depicting his famous poem "The Pipa Player." The speaker in the poem is on a boat, and hears sad music played on a pipa, a harp-like instrument, on the boat next to him. He discovers that the player is a woman who is sad over her loss of youth and beauty. The sorrow in the music parallels the sorrow in her life.

December 18

Dave

We had better weather going down-river back to Nanjing than going up-river to Jiujiang. I was warmer, and there was a beautiful red sun in the morning over the Yangtze fog—two comfortable chairs to sit on, a cleaner cabin. Out on the deck I met a heavy-set Chinese man named Mr. Xiu, who spoke excellent English. He invited me into his quarters and we talked. He's 76 years old and has been working for 40 years on a project having to do with the elimination of a certain deadly parasite that starts its life cycle in a particular kind of snail. Millions are infected with the disease. Apparently, the snail, during its growth, bores into a mammal's skin, shuts down the kidneys and destroys the liver. It's a serious problem in Asia, especially Japan. Mr. Xiu seemed to be well known in his field.

He also was connected with the Three Gorges Dam project, and he said there are many myths about the building of the dam, which, according to him, will only raise the water in the gorges ten percent—it's already a thousand meters high in places. He said there are three reasons for building the dam. One, to control the flooding of the Yangtze, which takes place every ten years and—once every 50 years—can be devastating, and two, to generate millions of watts of electric power from Shanghai to Chengdu. Three, to make the river more navigable, more accessible. Another, secondary reason is to create a huge recreation area, a reservoir, which will mean more tourists. Hotels are going up in the area right now, and some excursion boats cost Y1,000 per night.

Mr. Xiu went on: "The river is terribly polluted."

"Can it ever be cleaned up?" I asked.

"Yes, but it'll take time."

The problem, he said, is not just too many people, it's the industries in China, many of them along the rivers, dumping all sorts of chemicals into the water.

I asked him about the overall ecological effects of the dam project, and he said they were extremely complicated.

"Like this boat trip," he said. "Notice that all the trash is just thrown into the water by the maids. Everything goes into the river." He shook his head. I enjoyed talking to this man. He gave me his card, which is full of appointments and titles.

December 19

Jan

Dear Nan & Gary,

MERRY CHRISTMAS! We hope yours will be good. We still don't have our plane reservations for coming to the States over break, but our travel agent in Brookings is working on it. As soon as we know, we'll let you know. Thanks for offering to let us stay with you while we're in Brookings.

We just took a trip to the city of Jiujiang, up the Yangtze. We left for Jiujiang at 9:00 p.m. on the 13th of this month. If our friend, Qian, hadn't gone with us to the dock, we certainly would have had problems. There were six docks, all completely crowded, with many people sitting on the floor. My first view inside the waiting area was of a peasant woman sitting on the filthy cement floor eating sunflower seeds and spitting the shells out on the floor. She was surrounded by a mound of seeds. It reminded me of the scene in the film <u>Naked Gun</u> where the two men were sitting in a car eating sunflower seeds and spitting the shells out the window. When the car door was opened, one man got out and was almost buried in a pile of shells.

As we entered the waiting area, some beggars came directly to us and were immediately chased away by other Chinese people. Qian advised us to hold on to all of our suitcases while she went to buy a ticket so she could get on the boat with us to help us find our cabin. She was excited for us and animated. We were the only foreigners within sight. There were no luggage carts. People were carrying huge packages onto the boat; some bundles were so large it took several persons to lift them onto the boat. Some passengers used bamboo poles with a load on each end to carry their items.

We were traveling second class (there is no first class), so we had a cabin for two. Third class means you have a cabin with eight bunks, fourth class means a cabin for 12. Fifth class and below means you can have any available floor space. There were hundreds of these fifth-class passengers in the aisles, with their blankets or mats or pieces of cardboard spread out, ready for the night.

This was no "Love Boat," but our room was adequate. It had two wooden bunk beds with curtains to pull around them (like hospital beds), wool blankets folded like fans, a comforter and a hand towel on top of each pillow. A water thermos with two cracked cups was placed near the small sink and a small space heater. Two tiny windows were draped with red velvet curtains, and a pair of plastic slippers was placed under each of our beds for us to use.

We settled in and Dave went out to walk around. He met a couple from Holland who were going to Wuhan. They told us there was an empty cabin on deck-side next to where they were staying. Dave then wanted to change rooms so we'd be able to walk out our door to look at the water. The attendant came and exchanged keys with us for the new room.

The deck-side room was smaller than the first one. The sheets were dirty, and there was no bench, only one folding chair. But we were deck-side! I wasn't very happy with Dave about our move.

We drank some beer, ate some peanuts and candy, and went to bed. It was cold in the room and the heater wasn't working. I slept in my long underwear (two sets, a long-sleeve shirt, a sweater, socks, and a neck scarf, with a comforter and Dave's down coat on top of it. I was warm enough. Dave had two wool blankets, plus a comforter. We slept fairly well, even with the new and various ship sounds—the horn blaring, the water splashing—and the motion of the ship.

When we got up the boat was docked for a while. Dave walked out and watched people buying food from the dock, having it passed over the water to them on long poles with baskets on the end. It was cold and windy—not a good day for sitting on the deck. We were freezing and had no heat. We longed for our other room, since it was inside and not exposed to so much cold air, and it had a bench to sit on.

Dave began to search for the attendant. She kept taking him to rooms already occupied by one person. She just opened the door on them, without knocking, offering the other bed to Dave. He was finally able to tell the attendant that he wanted a cabin for two, not one. (Maybe she thought we were fighting and didn't want to stay together?) Evidently, there were no more cabins-for-two left. A little later, as we were sitting in our cabin freezing, the attendant walked right in without knocking, and motioned for us to come with her and to bring our luggage. She apparently had moved a single guy out of a room so we could move in. We picked up our stuff and moved again to a room that had a working heater and a bench. Since we still had 12 or more hours to go, we were happy. The ceiling light didn't work and the faucet ran continuously, but we didn't care. We were warmer. It was getting colder and colder in the boat. We still had to keep all of our extra clothes on, but we felt comfortable.

The bathrooms on the boat, which were unisex squatters, were vile. The showers had about an inch of standing water in them—and with the cold air I was not tempted.

After a lunch of tea eggs, peanut butter crackers and fruit, we hung the "Do Not Disturb" sign out on our door and had a nice, relaxing nap, swaying to the rhythm of the boat as it made its way up the Yangtze.

We were met at the docks in Jiujiang and taken to a university hotel room. It had twin beds with comforters; the room was freezing. It had a small heater that we turned on immediately, but it didn't throw out much heat. We slept together in a twin bed, with all of our layers of clothing on. Dave even wore his stocking cap. There was no hot water in the morning, so we washed up (even washed our hair) with ice cold water. (We found out later that the hot water is only on at night.) In the bathroom, the broken and unattached toilet seat fell off as I stood up. I did not find this as humorous as Dave did.

At 8:00 a.m. a Mr. Xu came to our room to get us and take us to the school dining hall for breakfast. He left us there to eat rice porridge and steamed buns. The dining hall was unheated, so we could see our breath as we sat there and shivered with our coats and several layers of clothing on, trying to eat.

Later Mr. Xu from the English Department and Mr. Li from the Municipal Waiban came with a driver in a Peugeot to pick us up for our trip to Lushan Mountain. It was a beautiful, crisp day. The ride up the mountain was a bit steep but the mountains were exquisite. Mr. Xu became ill and had to stop to throw up. Dave kept his eyes closed since he had heard it was a dangerous ride. I wasn't bothered much by it since the driver was competent. (I'm usually the one who is afraid of mountain roads not Dave.) It wasn't tourist season so the mountain wasn't very crowded, and some of the tourist places weren't open. We enjoyed the beautiful mountain scenery with all the trees and bushes covered with ice crystals. They sparkled like silver. The over-head wires also were covered with ice, creating a dangerous situation. It was cold, but the sun caused the ice to melt and fall to the ground in huge pieces. We saw a girl holding her eye as if she had been hit by ice or a falling tree branch.

A little later we heard what sounded like parade music. A young man who had just joined the army was being honored. He was wearing his new uniform with a red flower on the lapel, like a pied piper, leading a group of family and friends down the road, playing music. It appeared to be a rite of passage for the young soldier. It was a poignant scene. It must be the same feeling that American parents have when they see their young son or daughter in a military uniform for the first time.

We ate lunch in a Lushan restaurant, upstairs in a cold , unheated room. I was enjoying some noodles when I found a black bug on my chopstick as I was about to put it in my mouth. I didn't feel hungry after that, and I was chilled to the bone from being outside all morning.

Back in Jiujiang we attended a banquet with the vice president of the university and five other people in the unheated university dining hall. There was a huge selection of food and plenty to drink, as has always been the case at any Chinese banquet we have attended. Some of the food was good. The specialty in Jiujiang is fish head soup and, of course, it was served to us.

When we went back to our apartment, we found that the heater had been turned off. It must have been near the freezing point in the room. As we filled a hot water bottle with water from our thermos and took it to bed with us, we spoke longingly of our warm apartment in Nanjing. I wondered about how most Chinese people put up with this kind of cold all the time.

The next morning two young students came in a mini-bus to take us to see the sights of Jiujiang. They were delightful and well informed about the sites we visited. We saw some women washing their clothes against a rock in a city lake. I couldn't imagine how they were able to stand the cold water and the dreary chore of washing clothes by hand.

Dave presented his lecture on American poetry at 2:10 p.m. in a cold classroom, to approximately 200 students and faculty.

We ate dinner in the freezing dining hall with Todd and Jeannette, teachers at Jiujiang College, and the only foreigners living in Jiujiang. I wasn't very hungry, so I didn't eat much. I felt sorry for Todd and Jeannette, who have to eat in this dining hall, but they seemed perfectly happy.

We went to see the movie Raise the Red Lanterns with Miss Tan from the Waiban, and Jeannette and Todd. We enjoyed the movie, but the theater was unheated. When we got home to our apartment, we had some hot water, so we showered. It was the first time I had taken all of my clothes off since we left Nanjing. Todd brought some hot rocks (containers filled with boiling water) for us to use in bed. Have you ever heard of this kind of "hot rocks"?

I gave my talk on American culture the next day to approximately 200 students and faculty. I was terribly nervous at first, since I had never talked to such a large group before, but it went well. The question and answer session went on for almost 45 minutes. Can you imagine me doing that?

We took Miss Tan out to dinner. On the way back to our hotel, all the electricity in the city went out. It was so dark we had trouble making our way to our room. You remember how the electricity in Kunming used to go out.

The night we got to the dock to go back to Nanjing, the boat wasn't in, so we had to wait about an hour. The peasants and poor people standing around in boat and train stations all seem to have a similar look. Their skin is tanned and leathery looking; their clothes are dark blue or drab, dirty and tattered. They have empty looks in their eyes. Yet, when they gather around us to stare, their eyes are penetrating. It's almost as though they think we've just stepped off of another planet. They just can't believe what they are seeing when they look at us.

The boat ride was faster going back to Nanjing. As we were about to dock in Nanjing, the attendant came in with a bowl of water with old bars of soap stuck in it and used an old stiff paint brush to clean out the sink. The garbage they collected from the rooms was just pitched overboard into the Yangtze to float down to Shanghai and then out into the ocean. I understand why the Yangtze is so polluted.

I wore the same under clothes (three shirts and two pairs of long pants) from Sunday night until Friday night, only changing outer clothes. I've never worn the same things for so long or been so cold for an extended period of time. We felt pretty grungy. The key word for this trip is COLD!

We got home to find Qian cooking dinner for us in our apartment. We had left our key with her and told her to use our apartment if she wanted. (She has an unheated room.) It was a nice welcome home. We felt relieved to be back in our apartment with heat, hot water and a regular toilet that isn't broken or dirty. The first thing we did was take hot showers. It's good to have a trip like this to think about when we feel deprived here.

So you can see, we're keeping busy and having many new and unusual kinds of experiences in China. We hope to hear from you all soon. We'll be thinking about you especially on Christmas.
Love,

Jan (thawing out)

December 19

Dave

During our Jiujiang trip, I asked one of our hosts, an attractive young woman teaching at Jiujiang University, what she thought of quanxi (back-door).

"I hate it," she said. "There's so many who are competent and who deserve things, but if you have backdoor you can take things away from those people. So lesser persons often get the job, or a raise or an advantage."

I agreed. But at the Jiujiang dock after waiting about an hour for the boat to take us back to Nanjing, Mr. Li, another of our hosts, started talking to a dock official inside the fence. I saw him hand the man something, maybe a name card, maybe some money, I couldn't see. And after a few minutes, presto!, the gate opened and we went in and down the long ramp and right into the boat before all the others—women, children-in-arms—went in. I didn't mind Mr. Li's exerting some <u>quanxi</u> at that moment.

So I'm ambivalent about backdoor. When it works for me, I'm all for it.

December 19

Jan

We spent the day getting ready for the Christmas party we had been asked to host for the English section and all of the other foreigners in our building. Since it was a potluck, we had a variety of good food. It turned out to be a fun party with everyone bringing a gift to exchange. Chinese people tend to take parties seriously and dress up more than the foreigners do. A few people stayed late and we talked until midnight.

Mike began telling stories about a haunted house in Virginia where he had lived. His description of ghosts and strange events which occurred were so vivid that I was afraid I might have nightmares. Mike also told us about what happened last night outside of his apartment. As he was reading, about midnight, he heard what sounded like a huge, gushing waterfall. He hurried out into the hall to see what had happened, and he saw water pouring through a newly created hole in a wall, flooding the floor and spilling down the steps to the first floor. A serviceman was frantically trying to handle the situation.

Apparently, the water was stopped somehow, but there was a huge, gaping hole in the wall where the water gushed out. He asked today what the problem was, and the girl at the desk said maybe someone had left their sink or tub faucet running. It actually must have been a broken water line. He didn't find out any other details—just another one of the many unexplainable (to us) events that occur in China.

December 20

Jan

Deb is wearing herself out having all of her students over to make cookies, watch videos, play games, plus making plans for entertaining everyone in her department for Christmas. Tom and Deb have a gigantic tree in their apartment and brought all kinds of Christmas decorations and gifts with them from the U.S. Deb had to go to bed yesterday for most of the day, she was so worn out. I have never talked to her when she wasn't totally busy and involved with something related to her students. She has an abundance of energy.

...Zhu, one of my students, brought a sandalwood calendar to us, saying it was a gift from his father. He also brought a book on Confucius for Dave. He stayed for over an hour and seemed to want to talk. He is a traditionalist and has been indoctrinated in pro-government thought. He's sensitive to ancient Chinese poetry and familiar with the works of many poets. Most young Chinese children learn to recite ancient Chinese poems when they are very young. We talked about the films of Zhang Yi Mou—the producer of Ju Dou and Raise the Red Lanterns. He said he didn't like them because they were not pro-government and not in the tradition of most Chinese films. They did not entertain, but left people with a feeling of agitation. He said they did not promote the government. Dave asked why art had to promote the government; Zhu had trouble answering and went on to other topics.

December 21

Dave

Tension rising. Jan irritable. We need to get our tickets taken care of so we can fly home for a break. Mr. D. of the Waiban is balking, and I have to clear coming back late with the department head. But I have a lever: I'll bring a computer back to China for the dean. You scratch my back, I'll scratch yours may be one of the oldest ideas in human relationships. It's also a Confucian idea: don't do unto others what you wouldn't have them do unto you. And, more positively stated, Christian: do onto others... everything involves reciprocity. Every gift ever given, if Darwin makes any sense at all, was given with reciprocity in mind, unconscious or otherwise. You help others so that you may be helped yourself.

Each of us is one little star in the Milky Way. How can we make others see us, let alone help us?

December 21

Jan

As I was riding my bike home from class this morning, I ran into an older man (probably a teacher) who was walking in front of me. My front tire went right between his legs. The walkway was crowded and I wasn't concentrating on riding my bike. He turned around ready to yell at me, I think, but when he saw that I was a foreigner, he didn't. He probably thought, "a foreign bike rider; she doesn't know how to ride a bike." I could only say "Duibuqi" (excuse me). An embarrassing moment.

...I'm feeling like I need a break from teaching and from China. Sometimes, correcting papers and preparing for classes are tedious. I'm looking forward to going back to the U.S. next month. I think Dave is too.

December 22

Dave

Two nights in a row I've dreamed of death. My niece is apparently ill—she's in her early 20s—and my older brother had surgery to remove polyps in his colon. Thank God nothing was malignant. But this does jog my sense of mortality. And Jan's aunt is not well either, and is in and out of the hospital; she weighs only about 94 pounds. I'm the age my dad was when he died. But my brother is approaching 60—did he escape Dad's fatal genes? Uncle Elmer's fatal genes? Did we both? Who can say? Diet enters into it, I suppose, and exercise, and lifestyle and job. Many factors. Yet, after 50, I've found that my body simply doesn't perform the way it could before 50. That 50th year seems to have been the cut-off point. I need to stay in shape, eat right, live right, with moderation in all things except my writing.

December 22

Jan

Dave has a sinus headache and I've developed a head cold. We both feel miserable.

...Dave's graduate students came over to prepare a huge dinner for us for a Christmas party. We had given them money to do the shopping and they seemed to enjoy buying and preparing the food. They don't have much opportunity to do things like this, and most of them dislike the campus dining hall food, which they are forced to eat (typical college students). We gave them each a South Dakota postcard, a South Dakota pin and a scenic picture of a spot in the U.S. with lines of poetry from American poets. They brought us a beautiful calendar and a card. They spent four hours preparing and cooking the food. The apartment was a disaster after it was over.

...When I went to class today, my writing students met me at the door saying "Merry Christmas!" They also had written "Merry Christmas. We want a Party" in huge letters on the board. I read them the story "Twas the Night Before Christmas," and they loved it.

December 23

Jan

Lida's purse was stolen today as she was trying to mail a package in the post office. It was crowded and she must have been a little careless. She had about $60 and all of her identification cards in it. She had to go to the police station to report the loss and to apply for another resident permit card and other necessary identification cards. The purse will most likely never be found.

...Several students stopped over with gifts and cards today. I am touched by their thoughtfulness, especially since I know they don't have much money for such things.

...Angela and some of her students knocked on our door this evening and sang Christmas carols to us. It was the first time for these girls to go Christmas caroling and they were having a great time. I snapped their picture and gave them some M&Ms.

...Angela brought us some of her home-made Christmas cookies. Marianna left a home-made Christmas ornament on our door.

December 25

Dave

Doesn't seem like Christmas, but yet, the advantage of Christmas in China or somewhere out of the U.S. is that there's less, much less, stress. You're just off on your own, away from your family and the commotion and glitter and gift-buying pressures. Of course, you miss your family, but if you're not there, with them, you don't feel as stressed by the season's obligations.

Discovery of the week, the month: the YMCA! I can lift weights for two yuan per day, about 40 cents. Great place, and the young women sometimes come to do aerobics; they can be animated in ways that Western women can't. Tonight, sitting on a bench and rolling a barbell in my hands and looking into the mirror, I noticed how ape-like my hands are: elongated, strong, padded like chimp hands, gorilla hands. I'm a primate!

December 25

Jan

Christmas Day! I spent most of the day in bed while Dave had to go out and find dinner. He first bought something at the university restaurant next to us, but he had to throw it out because it tasted so bad. He then went to the Sprite and tried again, this time with luck. Not a good Christmas dinner, but something to eat. I had stomach problems and a head cold.

...I was scheduled to have two classes today, but since I wasn't feeling well enough to teach, Dave took both. He was going to talk to my writing class anyway, so it worked out fine. I really owe him now, I thought as I crawled under the warm quilt. He won't let me forget.

December 26

Dave

The weather has become warmer; it's almost as if spring were not far away. I need to get back on the track today, too, after laying off because of a sinus headache. The pills seem to have worked. Next week is the last week of classes for the semester. It has gone fast, and I've especially enjoyed working with the graduate students. Most are brilliant and lively. Next semester will be even better, with 20th-century literature, more recent stuff to read and talk about. I'm starting out with Huckleberry Finn. I haven't read it in years, but already I've gone back to it. It's a book of wisdom and innocence. Twain said a lot of what he thought about life in that book, and I intend to find out at the age of 52, by reading it again, what's going on. For one thing Twain talks about lying. I want to know what he really thought about lying, and about honesty. It seems to me you have to be selective about who you're honest with. It's stupid to be honest with everybody all the time. Keep your honesty for the right people. Confucius would have agreed, and also would have agreed that it's not wise to love your enemies, since you should spend your love on your friends and family. After all, a person only has so much love to spend.

December 26

Jan

Chen and Brian invited us and four others for lunch. They've been entertaining all of the foreigners and some of the Chinese teachers with meals for the past week. Chen is noted for her good cooking. She's Chinese Malaysian, but has lived in Britain for a long time and has taken on a British personality. She is very proper and sometimes makes people a bit uncomfortable at her apartment. She watches carefully so nobody puts their glass down and leaves a mark on her "cloths," as she calls them. The apartment is decorated nicely, with new curtains on the windows. All of her decorations are home-made and are quite lovely. George took a book off the shelf when he first came in and Chen admonished him for it. She said he wasn't there to read but to talk and eat. She told George and Fred not to spill the dip she had made for the quail eggs.

She served a duck liver pate with crackers and quail eggs with mustard sauce for appetizers. We had a delicious mulled wine to drink and a rich fruit cake from England for dessert.

Chen talked about what a good cook she is and how she had been on a British television cooking show, and on BBC radio. Brian is with the British Council and has been teaching in China for ten years. This is to be his last year in China. Chen and Brian have two daughters who are married. Chen will not allow her sons-in-law to call her by her first name. They must call her "Mum." She thinks they must show her respect and not feel equal to her. (This comes from her Chinese background.) She also talked about Brian's students and said they could never just come and knock at their door without an appointment. Even if a student calls, and she answers, she requires that they give their name to her and she asks if they have an appointment to talk to Brian. As a result, students don't often knock at their door. We, and most of the foreign teachers, have students coming in our doors at various times without appointments. But I think most of us feel it is okay for them to come. If we don't want to see them, we have the choice of not answering the door or telling them we are busy. The students who come are generally sensitive to us having other things to do and don't stay too long. It can be a hassle sometimes when so many come over in a day, but we feel we are here for the students and we want to help them when we can.

December 27

Jan

Two of Dave's students, Wang and Zhou, came over at 4:00 p.m. and asked if they could take us to dinner this evening. We agreed to go. We went to a restaurant nearby and had a huge dinner ordered completely by them, even down to the Qingdao beer, which they know Dave loves. We had over 15 different items, most of them tasty. We felt guilty letting them pay for the meal and tried to get them to let us pay for at least some of it. They refused and said it wasn't so expensive since we were in the back part of the restaurant where it's cheaper. We had a good time talking

162

with them, and after dinner went to see their dormitory rooms. It was depressing to see where they live. The halls were dimly lit and full of standing water and trash. Inside their room there were three beds and three desks. Graduate dorms house three students per room. The dorms are unheated so they need to wear many layers of clothing. They live on the fifth floor and they must go to the first floor to fetch hot water for drinking or washing. Bathrooms have cold water only. The shower house is in another area of campus and they must pay six <u>jiaos</u> (around five cents U.S.) to shower. I wondered how it would be to live in a place like this. How can they maintain their seemingly positive attitudes and get their work done under these conditions?

December 28

Dave

In a dream last night, I was back at my first college, Augustana, for another football season. I've had this dream many times over the years, a dream of starting over, of having a second chance. The reason for the dream is obvious. I made a mess of it the first time, having to quit football not only because of a bad knee but also because I just couldn't cut it, didn't want to cut it, didn't want to dig in. Here I am in the dream, ready to make amends, as if to say, "This time I'll do it right; I'll show them. Give me the ball!"

Last night I was reading an essay by Lionel Trilling on Freud, in which Trilling says that we dream our worst, scariest moments because, facing them again, even in our unconscious, we assume we can find a way to deal with them. In other words, you keep repeating that which you hate or fear, so that you'll get used to it and be able to handle it. There's a Zen parable about the guy who has an extreme fear of tigers, who goes to the zoo day after day and sits in front of the tiger's cage and studies the animal, get closer and closer, puts out his hand and even, at one point, touches the animal.

Someday, with all these recurring dreams about my failure as a college football player—a failure at something that I was a roaring success at in high school—someday maybe I'll solve the problem, eliminate the nightmare. Maybe I'll be able to cross it off my list of failures, even, and count it as a successful experience because, having failed at one endeavor, I took up another—writing—and became fairly good at it, out of spite or self-venge-ance or whatever. One needs, early in life, a failure, a big one, to send him or in another, firmer direction.

Maybe that was mine.

December 28

Jan

I'm more aware of various customs in China now than I was when we were in Kunming. It is considered rude to call someone by his or her first name. Even faculty colleagues call each other by their complete names. At a dinner table, a younger person is always seated to the left of an older person, and the oldest person at the table is always served first, going on down to the youngest. A Chinese person will almost always refuse an offer of something to eat or drink if he or she is visiting your home. If you continue to ask them three times, they may then accept. If you compliment them, they will almost always belittle the thing you have complimented them on. They don't want to appear boastful or proud.

December 29

Dave

I'm easily irritated this morning, I guess. My electric shaver doesn't work. Jan asks, "Do you ever clean it?" which ticks me off because I always clean it after I use it. So we argue, and I accuse her of being harsh, but she says, all I did is ask if you clean it. And I say no, it's not the question, it's the way the question is asked, and it's the "ever" said in a certain sarcastic way...and I tell her she never admits ("never" is a strong word, I'll admit, but I don't tell her) being wrong or being bitchy; but I, I remind her, am more honest. I honestly think this is a correct and true observation.

The whole point is: we've gone on enough for a time in a small place together, and we need a break. When we fly to the U.S. we'll get more space for a few weeks, and then we'll come back and start over. Life in China will be in two installments—two lives for two semesters.

...We're studying Emily Dickinson in my graduate class. Poetry, after a while, became Emily's only ally. The only thing she could depend on, the only thing that would never betray her. She knew she'd be finally read and appreciated, you can see it in her letters and poems. She would have her summer, she said once. And she's got her summer now.

There's nobody like her in America or anywhere. The most intense, the purest poet we have had so far, in my opinion. Her "slant" strategy was partly playful, and mostly a matter of saying to the reader, do you need to understand this? If so, read on, listen to me, involve yourself in my life. Poetry, she said, is "the house that tries to be haunted," unlike life, which is a haunted house, a real one. Emily, the thin ghost in a white dress, wants to haunt us. "Come on in," she says. "Please sit down. And open my book if you like, 'the valves of my attention.' You can be, reader, the one selected, out of an 'ample nation'—just you and nobody else. The two of us can be alone for a time. But not long. I have more work to do upstairs, you know. The solitude and the work is never-ending. I need to keep moving 'toward eternity,' toward 'that bareheaded life under the grass.'"

December 29

Jan

One of my students left a paper today for me to read and correct and said, as he left, that it contained sensitive material. I assured him that I would keep it confidential. He wrote about his parents' experiences during the Cultural Revolution, about how his father was sent to the countryside to do hard labor and was punished severely. His mother was told to sever all contact with his father because he was a counter-revolutionary—a bad element. He said he missed his father "bitterly" and that other kids said his father was a bad person. He wants to know what happened to his father during that time. But his mother told him that they don't want to talk about what happened, that it is too painful. He wants to know and is driven to find out. It was a very moving piece of writing.

...We went to the bank to get some money and ran into a man from Colorado who was here with a woman from the U.S. who was adopting a Chinese baby. She had gotten a beautiful baby girl yesterday morning and the baby had died last night of pneumonia. She was supposed to get another baby today, but she had run out of money. This man was getting more money to help her out. He said the orphanages here have 99 percent female babies; most of them are left on door steps or at police stations.

December 30

Dave

A student of Jan's wrote a poignant essay without signing his name, and gave it to her, saying he wouldn't want its contents known generally. The essay was about his bitter resentment over what the Party did to his father and others during the Cultural Revolution. First, the government issued a call for criticism ("The Hundred Flowers" incident) in which Mao and others said: "Let a hundred flowers bloom" The idea was to find out what the people were thinking—maybe, promised the Party, the country can learn from this something that will help it. The letters came in, the responses, and then the Party branded all the critics as traitors. Many thousands, millions were persecuted, many even killed, or sent to the country to work with the peasants. This young man's father was sent away and his mother was encouraged to have nothing to do with him.

As a result the young man hates the government. He said in the essay that he hates them because they are hypocritical: they say that what they did was for the good of the country, and yet they themselves, personally, benefited from it. I know what he means. Humans are basically selfish, are selfish more, much more, than selfless. We do things first for ourselves, and then for others. And what the mob fails to realize is that these self-proclaimed altruists are themselves benefiting from their proclamations and promises; benefiting economically as well as in other ways. What is scary is that a lot of these Ollie North types actually believe they are acting out of pure motives. There is nothing more effective than an actor who is not acting, but living the part.

December 30

Jan

I had students in for oral exams all day, one after another. Some reports presented were on: female mosquitoes, cicadas, Chinese education, tea and Chinese medicine. I'm surprised at how nervous most of these students are when they come for their exams. One girl said she was sick and had to take some medicine before she came. Several were literally shaking and sweating. They are under such great pressure to pass this course, as they have been for almost all of their courses during their years of high school and college. I tried to make them feel relaxed. One student who had very poor verbal and comprehension skills wrote me a letter telling me how important it was for him to pass this course. He said if he failed he would be dropped from the Ph.D. program and sent back to his home town, and would be shamed by the school and his wife and son. I hate that.

December 31

Dave

What a privilege it is to be able to discuss Dickinson, Whitman, Hawthorne and others with these Chinese students. They took to Whitman much more than to Dickinson. Mainly because of the simplicity of the language, I suppose.

I've had a good semester here, a good almost half-year. I've managed to write a couple of stories, some poems, and revise some of my stories as well. The fiction is going better and better. When I focus on something and really try to improve my skills, I can do it. I'm not quite an old dog yet, and so the new tricks aren't that difficult to acquire.

...I enjoy the great pressure that Twain exerts on Huck at the opening of <u>Huckleberry Finn</u>. The <u>momentum</u> he creates—the need to escape, to identify closely with someone else, to cling to his past (Jim), the parallel with the runaway slave, the fear of the father—all these things increase my admiration for this book. Reading it at 52 is a different experience than reading it, as I did, at 22 or so. Twain was wise. Huck realizes, right away, that helping others is fine, but it can be taken too far, so far that the helper ceases to benefit from the helping. Twain is quick to point out in the early chapters that Huck is no fool. He may be young but he's not stupid.

I wish I had something large and tangible, like a river, to string chapters on for a novel. I know there is something in my life that will crop up as a setting, a place or an endeavor or an activity that will yield a book in which I can say what I think of this world. I'm doing it right now, of course, in my stories, and have done it for 25 years, to an extent, in my poems. But I need an <u>extended story/plot</u> to get down to the real business. I think, right now, this morning, that the subject/story will have to do in some way with sports.

Whitman: "What is that little black thing far out there in the white?" I like that line, and the opening lines of "Out of the Cradle..." The rest of the poem does not work that well for me; I find it excessive, like Shelly's "I fall upon the thorns of life, I bleed." But the opening lines are from Heaven.

December 31

Jan

We attended a New Year's Eve banquet and party sponsored by the Waiban. It was held in the university dining hall next to our apartment. The evening was pleasant. For one part of the entertainment, we sat in a large circle and a toy was passed around the room to the sound of a drum. When the drum stopped, the person holding the toy had to draw a slip of paper from a box and obey the instructions on it. Dave was chosen to perform, so he sang part of the song "Laredo." He'd had enough beer to do it. Most foreigners had something prepared. Chen Loo and Brian performed a short humorous drama; Kate, John and Kate presented some poetry in Chinese; Fred and George each sang a song; Qian sang; one young American teacher did some juggling; some Chinese people presented a humorous section from a Chinese opera.

Deb was a co-emcee with Mr. D. and, in her exuberant way, seemed to be having a great time. She was given a beautiful whistling teapot for her help. Games were played and prizes were given for winners, and oranges were handed out to everyone. A dance was scheduled for after the entertainment, but everyone was too tired and left when the entertainment was over.

We went to Brian and Chen Loo's apartment for a drink after the party, along with the two Kates and John. Dave had drunk too much beer and wine and developed the hiccups, so he went home. I was disgusted with him.

JANUARY

January 1

Dave

New Year. I'll be 53 this year, beginning to push 60? Well, bring it on. "Live large, and dream small," as the poet says.

I got drunk last night, my second time in China. May it be my last. Actually, I feel decent this morning, and just got through running two miles, so I can't be that bad off, I guess. I've had tougher "next days." Jan was mad. I got the hiccups last night when we were at Brian and Chen Loo's place after the banquet. I had to go home to bed. This morning Jan said, when I got up at the usual time of seven or so, "you'll be back in bed before ten." She was right. I was back in bed about 9:00 a.m. and rested for about half an hour. "I know you like a book," she said when she came into the room and saw me in bed. "I wish you hadn't opened it," I said, which made her madder—madder.

But I'm okay now, having gotten my equilibrium on the running trac.k

January 1

Jan

It's the CHINESE YEAR OF THE ROOSTER. Dave and I didn't even see the new year in. We were too tired to stay up. We went to the Jinling Hotel for our New Year's dinner and had Chinese food. The specialties tonight were dog meat dishes, fish head soup, tripe with vegetables and eel. We didn't indulge in the specialties.

January 2

Dave

Last night I saw as much violence as I want to see in China or anywhere. Jan and I were walking home after dinner. It was getting dark; Zhongshan

169

street was crowded as usual. We came upon a group of people standing around looking at something inside the group. It could have been anything: a hawker, a man playing a game, whatever. It's a common sight in China. But this was different. The street vendors in the area began moving their merchandise away and appeared to be concerned. The closer I got, the more I could sense a serious tone. Then I saw a man leap and kick a man sitting in a chair, a man trying to shield himself with his arms. Was he drunk? He wasn't fighting back at all. Another man kicked him, and he rolled off the chair onto the sidewalk. Then the first man (I think there were a few more who were interested in having at him) picked up a wooden folding chair and lifted it as high as he could over his head, and brought it down on the man's body, which resembled a fetus, as he tried, weakly, to protect himself. The chair broke on his back. Then it was over, the thugs fled. At one moment during the kicking and just before the chair came down on the man, I had the impulse to jump in, but realized simultaneously that the effort would be futile and that the men might attack me, and even Jan, especially because we are foreigners. In a foreign country you can't intervene. You don't have enough information, you don't speak the language, you don't know how to alert the authorities.

This incident was the scariest thing I've seen so far in China. I wonder if the victim was non-Chinese. I hate group violence, hate it when men gang up on someone. Nothing is more cowardly. But I know what it is like to be part of a group that's inflamed over one person. I've been part of such a mob, though there was no violence in my case. I was a teenager. My friends and I, maybe four or five of us, were pursuing a drunken man up the street just to see him reel and stumble. Nothing came of it. But it's a strange feeling—on the one hand, a positive sense of power over someone, and on the other hand, knowledge that your power is the result of exploitation. Safety in numbers must be part of it. Humans, I believe, have a built-in, genetic behavior that was selected for killing enemies. In a group situation, the hormones mobilize as one big, collective hormone, one big machine that won't stop until it destroys the enemy. Arthur Koesler thought that this natural impulse/instinct was the key to our success as a species, as well as ultimate destruction, if we don't find a way to eliminate it or override it.

January 2

Jan

The weather was perfect today, so we took a bike ride to a Buddhist temple in the southern part of the city. It was still considered a holiday, so the streets were unbearably crowded. We could barely squeeze through the crowds. We did find the new Kentucky Fried Chicken restaurant and had a tasty chicken dinner. I wonder if the next thing to show up in Nanjing will be the Golden Arches? I hope not. I think all of these Western-type facilities will ruin the flavor of China.

January 3

Dave

DETAIL OF THE DAY:
The waitress at the Jinling Hotel poured the rest of Jan's beer not into Jan's glass, but into mine. We shared the beer, even though that was not necessarily our intention.

January 3

Jan

The weather was cold and rainy, a perfect opportunity to stay in and concentrate on correcting papers and assigning final grades to my 98 students. I was surprised to discover that a couple of my writing students had copied, verbatim, essays from a book I've been using in my conversation classes. I gave them zeros and wrote notes explaining why. One of them was a top student and the other has trouble with her writing. In China students don't feel it's a bad thing to copy something that is written well, and pass it off as their own writing. They need to learn that this is not acceptable to American teachers and certainly couldn't be done if they went to America.

January 4

Dave

Dreams, dreams. I was restless, woke up at about 4:00 a.m., then slept, and dreamed again. I was back in my youth, in what seemed like both my first and second neighborhoods. I was both a man and a boy. I could fly; I flew, flapping my arms, and Deb (a friend here in China) asked which one, my older brother or I, flew first, and which of our wives was pregnant first? I performed, flew over a stream on a small bike. Then a young girl recognized me. She said she remembered me from when I used to live there, remembered me swinging in the park on the huge swings. It was wonderful to be remembered! I think that's what the dream was about. Who doesn't want to be remembered? Who doesn't want their place in the sun? I want to do something people will remember me for. I'm evidently a performer of some kind. I have a talent; I perform for people. An artist, a writer. How delicious it was to go back and to have someone in my home town recognize me!

What a feeling to be buoyant, to flap my hands, wave my arms and lift off the ground, to soar as high as I wanted. Everybody looking up, wondering how I did it. "It's easy," I say, "Just move your arms and hands, like a bird."

January 4

Jan

Mr. D. from the Waiban called and said he thought we had a FAX. It had actually come on January 1, and he was just getting around to calling us. The message informed us that our airline tickets from Beijing to San Francisco in January had been mailed Federal Express from South Dakota. We have been anxious about getting them. Express mail does not necessarily mean "express" in China.

January 5

Jan

Our daughter Shelly's birthday is today. We miss her a lot and the family gatherings for birthdays and other special events. We thought about her today and about the day she was born. It was snowing then and our old beat-up car almost wouldn't start. After repeated attempts, and much anguish, it finally turned over. We were living the poverty-stricken lives of college students. She was tiny, 6 lbs. 1 oz., and had very dark skin. In fact, we thought she had been mixed up with a baby of a darker-skinned couple. She was adorable.

...Three students, whom I didn't recognize, knocked on the door today. They told me they were sorry but they hadn't known they were required to take the conversation class I had just finished teaching, and asked if I could give them the examination so they could get a grade. I sent them to Mr. Z. in the graduate school. A little later they came back, full of apologies again, and said Mr. Z. had sent them back to me. I realized he was leaving it up to me, so I told them no. It wouldn't be fair to those students who had attended classes for 18 weeks and had taken part in all of the activities, that my grades were based on class participation, that if I let them take the exam it would make the classroom activities meaningless. They were not happy about my decision, but I couldn't let them get by without attending class. Mr. Z. should have told them that they couldn't get a grade without attending class. The Chinese have always placed great importance on the "examination," and not much on the work it took to prepare for the test. If you can pass the examination, that is sufficient. I'm feeling a bit guilty and worried that these students may be sent back home in shame for failing to pass their English conversation class. I hope that won't happen.

January 6

Dave

"Do you think I'm super sexual?" I ask Jan.
"Yes."
"Do you think I'm abnormally sexual?"
"No."
"Do you think I'm hyper-supersexual?"
"Yes."

George's question about what I thought of matrimony still intrigues me. A heterosexual man needs a woman or many women, more or less all the time. If a man has access to one woman he truly loves and enjoys being around—who is a companion and buddy as well as a wife—if that woman reciprocates and needs him in the same ways, then that can be a successful marriage. To be a bachelor, unless one has a great deal of money or is extremely resourceful, means to sleep alone most nights. Of course, some bachelors have steady dates or live with one woman—that is a different matter. A man may even be happily "married" as a bachelor, to one woman, the way a married man (officially) may be happy. Maybe the crucial question is, how often do you sleep alone? In my case, never. Therefore, I'm more contented, all things considered, than most bachelors. Then the question comes up: what about variety? That, of course, is a potential advantage of bachelorhood. On the other hand, frequency of sleeping with a woman is probably more important. Variety can be achieved within the monogamous marriage. A woman can become newer as she matures. She can be familiar and strange at the same time. I don't understand that paradox, but it may have a biological origin. A woman can continue to appeal to a man as the same woman and yet as another woman simultaneously. We see it in expressions like "she keeps you guessing." A wife can be as fickle as a lover, even more fickle, since she can use her accessibility to her husband in creative ways; she can play with it, withhold it, offer it, take it back just as she's offering it. The close becomes the far away. You have to court a wife just as you do a lover.

January 6

Jan

Several students stopped over; one stayed for over an hour. She told me about some of the experiences she and her roommates have had recently. She said they have mice in their room. Recently, when she picked her shoes up from under her bed, she found that mice had built a home in one of them. She and the rest of the girls screamed wildly as she threw the shoes out the door. When she reported it to the dormitory manager, he just told her not to pay any attention to the mice. I can't imagine that. I would no doubt have a panic attack if I found a mouse in my shoe.

... After lunch, Qian accompanied me to the best hotel in town to get my hair permed. They only charged me Y30, probably because Qian was with me. Others have paid Y30 just to have their hair cut. The perm process involved several steps with many different operators. One male stylist was responsible for looking at my hair and deciding what kind of perm to use; one woman washed it; another one rolled it up; another one rinsed it and put neutralizer on; another one rinsed and washed it again; and yet another male hair stylist cut and styled it. It turned out curlier than I had wanted (I have the Little LuLu look), but it will be okay after a while. The service was good and the beauty shop personnel were friendly. This was a modern shop, but they used rubber wraps (which are re-used) and tiny plastic rollers with rubber bands to hold the rods on. A little bamboo stick (re-used) with bristles was used to put the perm solution on. A hot towel and a plastic bag were put around my head for the processing. I had to keep track of the timing myself (they gave me a small clock to watch). The towels and the cape were wet and were used for several customers before being thrown in the wash bin.

January 7

Dave

A student came yesterday and asked us to help her write a letter to Berkeley for an application. Her letter was seven pages, and she was mainly arguing that her application fee should be waived because she didn't have the money to pay it. How many students are there out there in this same situation? She was desperate; probably never will get out of China, will settle in as an engineer at Y300 per month more or less for the rest of her life. Her English skills, both oral and written, were not good enough for a decent TOFEL score either. I feel bad that she is going through this much work and most likely will not be successful.

January 7

Jan

One of my students came over this morning to tell me he will study mycology and do research on DNA structures next semester in Shanghai. He talked about living in Shanghai, his research, and about how he will miss Nanjing and his friends. He was then in a story-telling mood. He began as if these were true stories. He said he was on his way home to his dorm after studying one night, and he was following what appeared to be a beautiful woman, dressed in a flowing white dress, with long silky black hair and a lovely figure, in high-heeled shoes. Because he wanted to talk to her, he hurried along to catch up to her. When he finally caught up and she turned around, he said, she had no face! I was shocked—the reaction I'm sure he wanted.

Another story he told me (this time I was prepared for anything) was about a new-born baby. The mother had delivered the baby normally in a hospital. The baby had an large amount of thick black hair, but nobody seemed bothered by it. A week or so later, after the mother and baby were at home, the mother was giving the baby a bath. As she began washing his hair, she was horrified as thousands of eyes suddenly appeared throughout the thick hair, each of them staring wildly at her. His stories reminded me of the ghost stories adolescents tell to one another at Halloween or slumber parties.

He talked further about his research work, which he thinks is immoral since knowing the DNA patterns of humans will allow scientists to be able to predict who will develop certain diseases and who will have mental problems and certain behavior characteristics. He thinks the work itself is not immoral, but the way in which it could be used would be immoral. I told him that I understood his feelings and his reluctance. I wouldn't want to know if I were going to get a horrible disease and certainly wouldn't want it used against me. His main goal in life is to finish his Ph.D. and then go to the U.S. to do post-doctoral research. I like to talk with him; he's intelligent, sensitive, considerate, and one of my best conversation students.

...Fred and George left for the U.S. today at noon. We went over to their apartment to tell them goodbye and then went to see them off in the cab. We'll miss them and their eccentricities. China seems to be a magnet for unusual people (including us?).

January 8

Dave

I yearn for, crave, American food. Can't wait until I hit the San Fran airport in a couple of weeks. Hamburgers, fries, pizza—the works. And, the best part of it is, I won't care about the calories and the fat.

...Glym's Key to Success: "Sincerity. Once you can fake that, you've got it made."

January 8

Jan

It has rained for the past two days and has been dreary and cold. We went out to buy some food and then holed up in our apartment for the rest of the day. It was the first day I've felt a little bored since we've been here. I read and did crossword puzzles. Dave read and was a crab.

January 9

Dave

What a great book, <u>Huckleberry Finn</u>; what great characters, Huck and Jim. They're equals in all ways. But Huck is patient. He rides things out. He is taken, on his raft, literally and symbolically, through all sorts of dilemmas and experiences. And he doesn't buckle. He's a great liar but a liar for the sake of his own survival. He's marvelously tolerant. He forgives, he's sympathetic. Empathetic. And he's wise, sometimes on the verge of a cynic, which Twain became in his later bitter years. But Huck is wise enough to know that cynicism is destructive and self-defeating. He can humble himself before a man he believes to be inferior to him—Jim— because he does not put himself above anybody. He knows that the duke and king are frauds, comes to despise them, but he feels genuinely sorry for them when they're ridden out of town on the rails, tarred and feathered.

At the end of the book he strikes out for "the Territory" because he won't, finally, be tamed by anybody. He's a young man who truly goes with the flow, who is "in it" for the experience, for what he can learn. And he's a responsible person. He's not just for himself, but he helps others too.

I am humble before Huck Finn.

January 9

Jan

Qian came over to cook for us and brought me a lacquerware plate for my upcoming birthday. She was given the plate as a gift for some translation she had done, and she wanted me to have it. I was touched by this gesture. Earlier she had asked us to give her an English name, and when we told her we had chosen Catherine Ann, which means "pure and full of grace," she was pleased. She was also pleased when we said we would call her Cathy for short. After dinner, we watched the video <u>Pretty Woman</u>. Qian said videos on campus are often censored, with the explicit parts edited out. This video was one from Tom and Deb, uncensored.

January 10

Dave

David Jr. says in a FAX that he's worried about his confidence in his writing. I must write to let him know that confidence comes with time and with work, and that good things, major things, come out of self-doubt.

January 10

Jan

Rain again today, and some sleet. We had dinner at Deb and Tom's. We had looked forward to having pizza, but had left-overs instead.

After dinner we went to tell Pam good-bye. She and Angela left for Beijing at midnight. We took them some snacks to eat on the train. We heard fireworks around 10:30 p.m. and found out it was Tom, Deb and others shooting them off for Pam. Qian said it was not good, according to Chinese customs, to shoot off fireworks when someone is leaving—only to celebrate some happy event. A person's departure is not necessarily a happy event for those left behind (or shouldn't be).

January 11

Dave

This is my last entry in my journal until I get back to China in February (on Feb. 20th).

Today we may even see some sun! After going about a week without it. That'll make my life here this last day of the semester much easier. Tomorrow, off to Beijing at about 10:00 a.m., four or five days in Beijing, and then to the U.S. We're looking forward to seeing the kids. I worry about them too much, probably, but I can't help it. And a whole year without seeing them would be intolerable.

January 11

Jan

Today we finally have sun. We feel great. Tomorrow Beijing! Dave took our computer to Wu K.'s apartment where it will stay while we're gone. Wu K. lives on the 5th floor in an apartment building on campus. When Dave got there, Wu's wife was sitting in the apartment with a heavy coat, scarf and gloves on. We wonder if our computer will freeze.

January 12

Jan

We got up this morning to snow and sleet—the day of our Beijing flight. A cause for concern. The plane was four hours late because of the weather, so we had to sit in the airport and wait. The airport personnel gave us a box lunch of tofu, mushrooms, rice, two meat sticks and mango juice. We met a man from Beijing who helped us with translating the airline messages which were blaring out over the loudspeakers. The wait was boring.

In BEIJING:

Our hotel room is wonderful! We are on the 20th floor with a great view of Beijing. We have a queen-size bed, four pillows and two night stands with a T.V., radio and light and heat control, and a bar and refrigerator stocked with drinks. Complimentary supplies of shampoo, conditioner, lotion bath foam, Q-tips, a shower hat, clothes soap, tooth brushes, toothpaste, tissue, slippers and plush terry cloth robes are included with the room. The T.V. has CNN and the Star channel in English. We feel like we have returned to civilization after a long spell in the woods. This kind of living is decadent after our apartment in Nanjing. The hotel has a great swimming pool, a health club, beauty shop, many restaurants, bars, function rooms, lobbies, a bakery, shopping arcade and beautiful Chinese carpets.

Dave bought me a cloisonne bracelet in the airport for my birthday (on the 14th) but gave it to me now. He never can wait. He's worse than a little kid when he has a gift for me.

January 13

Jan

The Fulbright meetings began at 8:30 a.m. We greeted everyone and compared experiences. Many had put in difficult semesters. We feel lucky because our semester was relatively easy and enjoyable. One scholar's wife and child went home because living in China was too difficult for them. I remember the woman had been quite ill during our first meeting in Beijing in August. Evidently, the couples' son was the focus of so much attention that he had nightmares and couldn't cope with it. He is a blond, blue-eyed, five-year-old. Later in the semester, the husband was sick and was told by a Chinese doctor that he had a heart problem. His father and brother had both died of heart disease in their 40s, so he was extremely worried. He said it turned out to be a nightmare and that the doctors had even taken the EKG wrong. Everything seems to be okay now.

...Beijing is a modern, livable city—Western in many ways; yet, it is traditional if you get away from the center of the city.

We feel happy and relaxed here.

January 14

Jan

My birthday! Deb and I left at 10:00 a.m. on the bus shuttle to go shopping. We ate a great lunch at the new Beijing McDonald's restaurant. The food tasted so wonderful to us we had trouble containing our joy. We heard that the employees think they are working too hard for too little money. Sounds familiar.

After an enjoyable all-day shopping spree, we decided to walk the fairly long distance back to the hotel instead of catching a bus or a cab. It was so cold our feet began to feel numb (we had tennis shoes on). We stopped in a little store on the way home to pick up some beer and thaw out our feet.

January 16

Jan

We boarded a shuttle to go to the United Airlines office to arrange the boarding passes for our trip to the U.S. We had to wait in a line for 1 1/2 hours because they were so busy and each transaction seemed to take an incredibly long time. While waiting, we met some people from the U.S. who had been teaching in Tianjin. One woman's health had been getting progressively worse over the past three months and she was going home to find out what was wrong with her. Another woman was pregnant and was going home to have her baby. We wondered if the father was Chinese. She appeared to be without a husband and had been in China for the past year. A man with them was going home to get his wife and bring her back to China with him for the next semester.

...We called our daughter in Reno and found out that the mountain passes from Reno to San Francisco were closed because of the snow, so they can't get there to pick us up. We'll need to catch a plane when we get to San Francisco—not something we want to do.

...We shopped for a while and caught a pedi-cab home because it was so terribly cold. The pedi-cab driver was not wearing a hat and looked miserable. When we got to the hotel, Dave paid him and then spontaneously gave him the stocking cap he was wearing. The driver put it right on, took Dave's money and peddled away—a little happier and a lot warmer.

January 17

Jan

Flight to the U.S:
The Western food on the plane was a nice change for us. The flight was rough, and I couldn't get comfortable enough to sleep. Dave can usually sleep anywhere, anytime. He's lucky, I thought, as I watched him nodding off.

January 18

Jan

Back in the U.S:
How great to see Kari, Jef, Justine and Josh again. It feels familiar and yet strange to be in America. Greatest pleasures: to be able to drink water out of a fountain, to have endless food choices, to understand the language. I watched some of the upcoming inaugural activities with renewed interest. Democracy is not perfect, but it's much superior to Communism. An extended stay in a communist country is one way to build good feelings about America.

January 19

Jan

Kari has a teaching assistantship and had to teach her first college class today. She was visibly nervous about teaching. The first day is scary. I know now, first hand.

January 20

Jan

We couldn't sleep last night, probably from drinking too much coffee and jet lag. I was awake until 3:30 a.m. and got up at 7:30 a.m. Kari and Dave had nightmares.
Dave won some money on the slot machines and bought Kari a jacket. It rained all day, melting the snow.

January 25

Jan

We left early for Sioux City, but didn't get there until after 10:00 p.m. because of lay-overs and bad connections. My sister's home is always comfortable, clean and warm. I feel happy just being here.

January 29

Jan

We had lunch with friends Dean and Harriet, who will be leaving soon to teach in Kunming, China. We drank lots of coffee and made plans for getting together in China. After lunch, Dave and my brother-in-law Larry went to a bar and drank some beer. For dinner we all had more beer.

At 12:30 a.m. Dave woke up with a very rapid heart beat. I felt it as I lay next to him and became alarmed. He was worried and thought he should go to the hospital to be checked. I was shaken as I drove Dave to the nearest emergency room. The testing began without delay. He had what they call atrial fibrillation—an irregular heartbeat. I sat near Dave's bed all night and waited for the heart specialist to arrive in the morning. After examining Dave, the doctor said he would put him under and shock his heart back into normal rhythm. But I consulted with my heart specialist in Sioux Falls, and we decided to wait to see if the problem would correct itself.

As I stepped out into the hall from Dave's room this morning, I saw an old man with a cane walking slowly down the hall. It was my uncle. He looked sad. I knew my aunt was in this hospital. He didn't think Emma was going to make it because her cancer had gotten worse and she didn't weigh much more than 70 pounds. She didn't want to see anyone, but asked to see me when she was told that I was there. Emma is my favorite aunt. When I saw her, I could tell by the look in her eyes that she would not live much longer. What will Lee, her husband of 68 years, do without her? The two of them have always been able to take care of themselves and get around in their own car. Their relationship seemed so special. They were great story tellers and each had a keen sense of humor. Most of all, they seemed to like each other.

In the afternoon, while I was in the maternity ward of the same hospital visiting my niece who had just had a baby, my aunt died. I went up to her room to tell her and her family goodbye, but the family had all gone home. My aunt's body was still in a hospital bed with the curtain drawn around her. There are now only two members of my dad's family left. That realization made me sad. I thought about how much I miss my dad and the others of his family who have died.

By afternoon, Dave's heartbeat was back to normal and he was released with a new kind of medicine, and was told to avoid caffeine and alcohol. I don't think he had any plans to have either. This experience has frightened him.

FEBRUARY

February 1

Jan

We arrived in Madison, Wisconsin for a visit with Shelly, her husband and four boys. Dave and Shelly went to the gym to work out and, afterward, Dave felt weak and nauseous. Shelly, a nurse, thought his heart rate was faster than it should be on the medication he was taking. So we went to the emergency room at the University of Wisconsin hospital where Dave was admitted, checked over, and put into the intensive care unit for the night. Shelly and I left at 4:00 a.m.

February 2

Jan

Doctors performed several tests on Dave this morning, including a thallium/stress test, and they all turned out good, especially the tread-mill test. The doctors called his fibrillation incident "holiday heart," and said it was fairly common after overindulging in caffeine or alcohol. There was some mention, however, of a slightly questionable area in the heart, based on the thallium test. The head doctor on the team said that Dave may have moved to cause this glitch, and said not to worry about it. Dave was released and felt good.

February 3

Jan

The doctors met again and decided the glitch on the x-ray was, in their opinion, a slight defect, but that nothing had to be done and that Dave shouldn't worry about it. They gave him no restrictions, and said he could go on with his exercise, but told him to avoid caffeine and alcohol in excess. They also gave him a different blood pressure pill, a beta blocker. Dave thought

185

the medication he had taken for so long was causing him to itch.

Dave is experiencing quite a bit of anxiety over the slight defect.

February 5

Jan

We're happy to be in Carbondale visiting David and Karen, although Dave's temperament is not good. I think it might be the blood pressure medicine. He couldn't take a beta blocker previously, and may not be able to now. He's like a zombie. He's worried about his heart. His Dad died at age 52. Dave is 52.

February 9

Jan

We're back in Sioux City. Dave is still not himself.

February 10

Jan

We learned that Karen had a miscarriage. Dave feels guilty and possibly responsible for creating stress for Karen by being there. He's become somewhat paranoid.

February 12

Jan

Back at home in Brookings. We are seeing friends, sorting through third-class mail and cleaning our house—our renter moved out. I had a doctor's appointment, and Dave, who was there waiting for me, asked if he could see the doctor, because he was feeling terrible. The doctor decided to take him off the beta blocker and put him on yet another blood pressure pill.

February 13

Jan

Dave still isn't himself. He is constantly worried about his heart.

February 15

Jan

We went to the doctor for some gamma globulin shots, and Dave asked the doctor for some pills to help him relax. He's having anxiety attacks and is not doing well.

February 15

Dave

What Do I Enjoy?

1. Floating in a boat in calm water—just floating, relaxing, letting the boat take me, drifting, drifting.
2. Working out—jogging, racquetball—feeling, just afterward, the blood moving through my body—relaxed, lying on a couch or in bed.
3. Watching the sun come up over a hill—just sitting and noticing how it comes up, minute by minute, bigger and bigger.
4. Watching the grandkids play—playing with them—pushing them on a swing, pulling them in a wagon...listening to them talking, laughing, running, jumping, skipping.
5. Loving Jan—feeling all of her—holding her, feeling her feeling me—building up to love—the tender, close embrace, the terrific give and take of love— the exquisite release.
6. Drinking cold water after a workout on a hot day—or 7-UP.
7. Watching son David hit a racquetball—he is so strong and his arms are so hard—he connects so perfectly with the ball I can hardly see it—watching him throw a frisbee, which is the same motion as his backhand in racquetball.

8. Waking in sunlight—in snow or any time of the year—sun, sun: the great healer.

9. "If you want to know how strong the pine limbs are, wait until the snow melts," by an ancient Chinese poet.

10. Patience—being patient—waiting—emulating Jan's patience—watching her—she is not self-indulgent, but sociable, caring—she is genuinely interested in the feelings and thoughts of others—she does not need to dwell on her own ideas and feelings—she just naturally is and naturally does—and that is health—if she is warm she takes off a shirt; if she is cold she puts another shirt on—she does what she needs to do to maintain her equilibrium—she is a survivor—she loves China—she has an abiding, healthy interest in the Chinese: their habits, their peculiar situation, life-style. Jan believes—and she is right—that she is needed—that what she does and knows and feels, who she is, is important and useful to others—I watch her—I am astonished by her—I love her—I want to put down my love and my need on paper—I will be with her, observing, following her intuition, which is usually reliable—Jan—she is instinctive, intuitive—I watch her, take all of her in—absorb her insights, in words or gestures— I need this woman more than ever.

11. Making poems and stories—I like getting into a character in a story and making an interesting plot/situation, showing how people deal with crises.

12. Just sitting still, reading a good book—just doing nothing.

February 17

Dave

I had a good walk in the cold, in the sun—there's snow here in Sioux City, lots of it, in February—and it's cold—but I love to walk in the sun—feel and hear my shoes crunching the snow/ice beneath my feet.

...Last night I was feeling anxious, so I took a Xanax and felt better. I'm anxious about the flight more than anything—once I get through that I'll be able to settle down, I'm sure, especially when we get back to Nanjing to our apartment. We have a good life there. Friends, students we enjoy and who I believe enjoy us.

We'll be back in China in a couple of days. It will take a few more days to settle into our class schedule—then I'll be fine. I no longer have a great fear of my heart acting up—it's been steady and strong, and my heart doctors in Wisconsin told me my problem is very minor, will not require any change of habits—can be controlled by blood pressure medicine.

I'm not drinking caffeine anymore, or beer. I will, when I get settled, drink no more than one or two beers on any given day for the rest of my life—no more binges, they're hard on the heart rate, the heart in general. I can live with these restrictions if that means a healthier life, a longer life.

I've also lost weight—down from over 200 to around 190. I want to get to 182-185 and stay there—what I weighed in my second year of college.

The Xanax made me realize that my "symptoms" were imaginary—it was a panic attack I was having, anticipating the plane ride. Plane rides do make me nervous, but I'll be okay.

February 18

Jan

Dave had to take a pill for anxiety before we went out to eat with family and friends. A friend we were with had recently cut the end of her ring finger off and still had it wrapped. She was upset that people didn't take the loss of her finger more seriously. She says people laugh about it. She also said she was "ugly and fat and didn't need to have another ugly thing on my body." I wondered why and how people could laugh about a severed finger.

February 19-21

Jan

On Our Way Back to China:

We left at 4:30 a.m. for the airport for our return trip to China. Dave has been extremely apprehensive, even to the point of thinking we should not go back. Neither of us could sleep.

We boarded the plane in Chicago to fly to San Francisco, and after an hour or so of sitting in the plane we had to de-plane. There were hydraulic problems and the plane had to go to the hangar for repair. That meant we had to re-schedule our flight to China. We spent much of the day standing in various lines. We were frustrated. Our new flight would go directly from Chicago to Tokyo with no stop in San Francisco. This created considerable stress for Dave, so he took a Xanax.

We had people meeting us in San Francisco, so we had to get a message sent to tell them we wouldn't be there. The flight finally left about 6:30 p.m., which meant we would miss our Tokyo flight to Shanghai. United put us up in a hotel in Tokyo and we sent a FAX to China for the person who was to pick us up on the 20th in Shanghai. We would now arrive on the 21st. The hotel was great, and we had a delicious dinner and buffet breakfast the next morning before leaving for China.

...Japanese airplanes are the most comfortable planes we've been in, with roomy seats and ample leg space. When we got to Shanghai, we realized that our FAX to Nanjing must not have been received because no one was there to meet us. We were on our own. We struggled with all of our heavy luggage and got a station wagon cab to the train station to book train tickets to Nanjing. Dave was full of anxiety. Since the plane only flies to Nanjing in the mornings, we were too late to catch a plane today. It was now afternoon.

...We were surrounded at the train station by people who looked like they wanted our money and our luggage, but we managed to find some train personnel to help us—"Red Hats," they are called. I bought what I thought were "soft seat" tickets, but when we got on the train we realized we had "soft sleeper" tickets. This meant there were two sets of bunk beds in an enclosed room with six people to share the two bottom bunk beds for seats. The top bunks were used for luggage, but all of our luggage would not fit and had to be left in the hall. We had to check on it often, to make sure nobody walked off with it at the various train stops. The seats were uncomfortable and the room was stuffy. We were exhausted and uncomfortable for the six-hour ride to Nanjing.

In Nanjing we caught a cab and got to our apartment around 9:30 p.m. It was good to be "home." Our apartment looked familiar, comfortable. Qian came over to greet us.

Dave is still anxious; he needs to find a way to deal with his anxiety. Being back in the U.S. would make it easier for him. Should we have stayed?

February 19

Dave

In the Chicago airport, on the way to China:

Delay—sitting in Chicago airport waiting for flight to San Francisco. Earlier flight scrapped because of faulty hydraulic valve.

...Last night my left arm burned and stung. I took a Xanax. Jan says it's nerves. I hope it is nerves and not my heart.

I called my main cardiac doctor at the University of Wisconsin hospital yesterday before we left Sioux City and he assured me that I have a "good, strong heart"..."absolutely." When I asked him about the test, he said the "defect," if it is a defect and not a machine error, is a "tiny" one, as he called it in his written report. He told me that the thallium scanner is so sensitive that many individuals, if they took the same test I took, would show defects. I want to believe Dr. D. I do believe him. It made my day—most of it—to hear him say what he said.

I think I'm jittery about several things: the flight itself—long, cooped-up feeling; going back to China, a third-world country; my heart.

I need to work on eliminating these negative feelings.

I know that when I get back to China I'll settle into my usual, comfortable routine and start feeling better. Part of our stress these last several weeks is that we went home and lived out of our car/suit-cases while visiting the kids. And the kids have their stresses as well. We had two kinds of stress. Our own, being more or less homeless, floating, and theirs—a double dose. We should have stayed in China and kept our home base, traveled leisurely. We did learn from this experience. We have our own life, a life together. And it's time we accept that fact and live. Our kids have their lives, their work, their friends. It is theirs, no longer ours. Never has been ours.

...Took a Xanax after an incredibly uneasy feeling came over me, a panic attack. When we had to get off the plane to San Francisco because of mechanical problems and had to reschedule our flight to China, I became stressed. As did Jan, who has a class on Monday, and we're already a week late for classes. I felt the change all over my body. I had taken two aspirin about a half-hour before.

Panic is the only word that works here. Then I tried to calm Jan—said it really didn't matter, we'd get there. The people we work for are flexible. I kept fairly good control of myself.

We had dinner, and I settled down somewhat. Then, about two hours later, I felt a slight pain in my left arm—a warmness, a stinging—just as I was about to look for a FAX machine to send a message to Nanjing. I felt spacey, scared. Thought I wouldn't make it back in time for the flight to Tokyo. At one point I doubted my ability to do this task. But I got it done, though I wasn't sure if I'd read the instructions on the machine correctly.

Ink drawing by Dave

I went back to Jan still feeling uneasy—had thoughts of suicide, insanity, paranoia—was everybody looking at me?

Then, as I was sitting near Jan waiting for the plane to get in, gradually the calm feelings of normalcy came back. She felt my back, my hands, she talked to me and calmed me down.

Is there some chemical reaction between the two of us going on here? Is Jan a sort of catalyst of good feelings for me—giving me a sense of well-being, a calmness? Or was the Xanax just now, after five hours or so, kicking in?

Right now, two hours later, I feel good—calm as I write these words. My arm is okay. Is it arthritis that gives me pain when I'm stressed?

On the plane to Tokyo:

Am I getting control, finally, in general? I don't want to use Xanax if I can help it—maybe it does weird things to me. I don't want to have to rely on drugs to calm down. I know that the brain, like the heart, is a physical thing.

I'm reading a book on the brain, The Evolution of Consciousness by R. Ornstein. He says we must control the little things all along, so that, having mastered some problems, we can master the bigger problems when they come up. His idea is that by doing this we "trick" the brain by being in a good, positive mood when trouble comes knocking. Keep control of little things— since that control enables us to be optimistic. He also says that people differ as to what they remember—their successes or their failures.

I believe, as Ornstein says, there are many different "selves" inside our mind. The mind shifts, and therefore selves change. Right now as I speak, my mind's self is the one I like best, trust most. He/it is the one I want to be "in charge." I can write stories, make love, teach with passion and compassion when that self is present—the question is: how can I get him to take up permanent residence?

February 20

Dave

Woke up in the plane after sleeping fairly well, and feel good. I feel like Alice must've felt after her fall through the rabbit's hole—the fall was giddy, unpredictable—but now, at the bottom, having landed on both feet, I'm here in the East, for whatever it's worth, for the next four and a half months. Here we are—let's make the best of it.

I don't want to take any more pills—either I'm healthy or I'm not. I choose to be healthy! What my doctor said is good enough news for me. I have a very good heart—"absolutely."

Right now we're about a half hour from Japan, where we'll spend the night; thence, into Shanghai.

February 21

Dave

Woke up early. The pessimist, but a weakened one, is back inside my head. I need to keep a positive attitude. Lots to do today—need to get back to Nanjing, to our friends and our home.

I know I'm strong, confident; that came out on the 13-hour flight to Tokyo—I felt calmed, strong. This is one of those moments of unease I'll have to suffer to get through to the normal, the equilibrium.

I know I can do this—I intend to stay calm—concentrate on small victories, small goals—the moment, the present moment, which is everything.

Put one foot down and start your journey. It's that simple. I was very close to Jan last night. The closeness is important to me. And I know to her, too. I need her. I need her to need me. The key word is RELAX. Don't get excited—the world is not ending today. I am healthy, vigorous, strong.

February 22

Jan

It is good to be back among our friends in China.

...Dave went to see the new physician's assistant, who replaced Dr. Steve at the Hopkins Center, to talk to him about his heart. He came back feeling reassured.

February 23

Jan

It was a beautiful sunny day, so we went for a walk. Getting back into the routine we had before has helped, but Dave is not himself.

February 24

Jan

We're not sleeping well at night. Jet lag has been more difficult this time. Dave had to take a Xanax again. It was terribly cold in class today, what I think could be considered "ass-freezing cold."

February 24

Dave

I've been having anxiety attacks. Something is wrong, I'm not sure what. I get extremely anxious, and feel pain in my chest, a sort of indigestion. It's difficult to concentrate. I can't sleep, but that may also be jet lag. The doctor in Wisconsin assured me that my heart is fine, that if I do have a "tiny defect," it doesn't mean changing anything, that it can be controlled with medication. The physician's assistant here also assured me, and he says I need to get my exercise up to the level I'm used to. That makes sense. This morning before class I walked for about a half-hour and felt better. I was terribly anxious about class, thinking that maybe I haven't been doing a good enough job with these bright students. And yet, just as I know in my mind that I'm physically okay, I know that I do a good job. But something is pulling me away from confidence. Something is threatening my equilibrium.

One day at a time. I need to get both feet on the ground. I need to work out, really air out the heart and body. I know I can turn this around. I will.

February 25

Jan

Dave went to see David P. again and took along his health records from his tests in the U.S. David P. is understanding and seems to have instilled some confidence in Dave. I don't know how much time it will take for him to feel like himself. He and Mike have been jogging at noon. Dave needs to stay busy and learn to not worry about a health problem that is non-existent.

February 25

Dave

Better, by degrees, better. I need to emphasize my victories. And one of them was meeting my first class yesterday and doing very well. I had taken a Xanax the night before, a big mistake. I was paranoid, scared that I haven't been doing a good enough job of teaching. Jan thought I was going crazy; I tossed and turned and fidgeted all night, and had another ugly dream. The stress lingers, but I'm getting it under control. Control is the key. Either you have it or something else is in control of you, and then you're done. I think of Stafford's poem, which begins:

> Every night in my sleep
> a little voice cries out, "Faker, you Faker!"

That's a scary dream, but I've had some myself. I wonder if some of this isn't withdrawal from beer, which I've drunk for years. Maybe so. The heart expects it? The heart, said Emily D., "asks pleasure first,/ and then excuse from pain."

I don't agree. It asks excuse from pain first. It asks for equilibrium, stasis, evenness, levelness, peace, comfort, the status quo.

February 26

Jan

We walked to the bank and had to wait in line for what seemed like an unusually long time. Dave was uncomfortable and more impatient with waiting and the crowds than usual. He has become paranoid and depressed about his health. It's wearing on me as well.

...We tried to watch a movie, but we were both asleep by 8:00 p.m. Jet lag is still with us. Maybe it's because of all the emotional trauma we've been through. Sleeping during the night has been a terrible problem for us. We get tired in the late afternoon and early evening and then wake up at midnight or so.

February 27

Jan

If we had to do it over again, I don't think we would have gone to the U.S. for our spring break. It was emotionally and physically exhausting for us and it has been difficult to get back into our routine.

February 28

Dave

Still struggling, can't get bad thoughts out of my mind. But yesterday, and at other times, I felt perfectly normal. My chest is tight, and I know it's stress. I need to learn to think myself out of worrying. It'll be hard to learn, but I need to learn it. At times my deep breathing exercise seems to help. This morning I felt a mood change in my room, breathing deliberately in through my nose and out through my mouth. I think there are different "characters" or dictators in my brain, and I need to bring out the mature one, the one who can relax and have a good laugh at the world and not be intimidated by bad thoughts. I know he's in there; I've got to invoke him, somehow.

...My running yesterday also helped me; I think I released some endorphins after that run, I felt so good (2 1/4 miles is the point at which I get my "high").

February 28

Jan

Today was a better day for us. Dave seemed less anxious. It was also a sunny day and our moods seem to be governed by the sun. We've been isolated in our apartment for a few days, which has been good for us. We haven't even seen much activity around here with the other foreigners. Maybe we're all feeling the need for a little solitude and some time to prepare for this semester—time to reflect.

MARCH

March 1

Jan

Spring has arrived. Students are sitting out on the campus grounds. Heavy coats are no longer needed, except for in the classrooms. They are still cold, since it takes a while for the sun to warm up the cement walls.

...Dave is having better days and is more like himself.

...While walking home after our dinner at the Sprite, I turned my ankle when I accidentally stepped in a ditch. It hurt so much I was in tears. Dave was sympathetic and then was angry about the lack of lighting on the streets. The irony of this was that we had moved to the sidewalk from the street, so we would be safer.

Nanjing University: main campus building

March 1

Dave

In a better mode/mood this morning. Amazing how the mind shifts from one mode to another. Unpredictable, mostly, though I am beginning to understand how it can be a matter of conscious manipulation on the part of the "owner." Yesterday, breathing quietly in my office, I was able to shift my mood ever so

199

slightly. I actually <u>felt</u> better after the breathing exercise. I will try to find a yoga instructor; not sure what I can find in China, though one would think it would be easy to find equivalents. I know now that it's up to me and up to no one else to make my life better, happier, more livable and longer. My health will not suddenly change when I leave China. I will still have the same body/mind, the same problems, the same character with its positive and negative modes and states of mind.

...Sooner or later in life, we realize we are not forever, that eventually we will die. The point is that the adult accepts this fact and goes on. The whole tendency of the healthy person, as he or she gets older, is to settle down and grow up. And take the givens of life as they come, and not be crushed by them. Depression, grief, loss of this and that—all these things can be, must be endured, accepted, lived through. The child in us keeps rebelling and refusing to accept. The emerging adult calmly accepts, and goes on, and does what is necessary.

I envy the unconscious life, the life of animals, "so placid and self-contained," as Whitman said. I wish I could, if I were tired, just lie down in ashes like the man we saw at the train station the night we got back to Nanjing. He was only sleeping, and trying to stay warm.

I like Jan's simplicity and wisdom. If you're tired, she says, sleep. She is a mature woman. She can handle a lot of stress—for instance, living with me. I love her and need her almost too much. I told her I don't want to become too dependent on her. I told her I would try as hard as I can to adjust to life in China again, in spite of my fears and anxiety. I told her I'll have setbacks, but that I know I can adjust. We've found some humor again—we never have lacked humor between us, really. If we can laugh together, that will be good; and we can, and we do.

I'm feeling a little better today. Yesterday, I was apprehensive at the crowded market. I deliberately tried to calm down and it seemed to work. Aspirin helps. I've been avoiding Xanax, which I know can be addictive and I don't need the problem.

March 2

Jan

I scheduled my office hours for Tuesday evenings from 7:00 p.m. to 9:00 p.m. One male student seemed surprised that I didn't remember his name. I've only seen him one time, but I'm sure I'll remember it from now on—it's Glenn (his English name). As a result of having students here most of the evening, I didn't have enough time or energy to prepare for my Wednesday writing class.

March 2

Dave

Had my best day in China (this semester) yesterday. Felt good, ran 2 1/2 miles, did a lot of class reading. A good day. This morning I get up and feel a pain in my back. I hope it isn't a kidney stone. I think it may be the aspirin I'm taking. Seemed to bother my stomach a little yesterday when I took some. Or am I a hypochondriac? Or, a hypochondriac with a kidney stone? What I am I sometimes don't exactly know. But I do know this: that I will get squared away, as they say, in China this second and final time around, when I get back to my writing. That's my next goal, to get into the writing, to start a yarn.

...I'm back to dreaming, which means, finally, I'm starting to sleep better, in sync with the day's rhythm. But guess what I dreamed about? Talking to several heart specialists and getting a less than perfect report.

I'm still a little shell shocked. The old hurt comes back. When it comes to the matter of the coronary arteries, once stung is a thousand times warned. I need to watch my intake of fat and sugar. Eating too many cookies lately. I intend to cool it. And my arms are turning into dowels. I need to start going over to the "Y" for 20 minutes several times a week for lifting.

The running felt glorious yesterday, even if I was tired. The endorphins kicked in at about 2 1/4 miles. I want to get up to three miles and level out—get the weight to an even 183-186. Right now I'm probably around 188.

Alright, what will the day bring?—the bright, blue-sky Nanjing day?

March 3

Jan

Dave had a difficult day. He is now worried that he has had angina, that he didn't tell the doctor about it because he didn't want to believe he had it. I think he is imagining it. He has been reading a book about the heart that Shelly gave him when we were in the States, and his imagination is running wild. He is genuinely frightened, as I would be if I had a serious health problem in China. It is scary to think of various scenarios of getting sick and needing emergency care here. But I think we are both healthy and don't need to worry.

...We attended a "working lunch" today with the English section. We were told to take roll in classes and to report absences to the department chairman at the end of each month. Dave seemed detached.

...I noticed tonight that the cook has pierced ears, so I gave her a pair of gold earrings I had brought from the States. She was visibly excited and appreciative. A lot can be communicated through body language after all.

March 3

Dave

Last night was awful. I remembered feeling pain in my face (left side) after my thallium/stress test in Wisconsin, while lying in the scanning tube, and so I concluded, suddenly, that it was angina. When am I going to forget all this and just go on with my life, and accept what I have for a body—just LIVE MY LIFE! I'm tired of all the depression and anxiety this has caused me. And it may be over nothing more than a mistake made by the thallium machine/scanner, a "movement artifact," or machine error. Shit. I'm not ill. My heart is strong, I can still run two or three miles without pain and with plenty of wind. I need to accept my life as it is, and just live—love, write, teach, socialize—whatever.

One of these days I'll wake up—I notice that I _do_ wake up every morning! that's my habit—and realize that it's not worth it to worry about what happened in the past. It'll dawn on me that what is important is the present moment, the one I'm breathing and living in <u>right now</u>, that counts. I'll realize, in Allan Watts' phrase, "the wisdom of insecurity." We never have complete security unless we are children and can crawl back into our parents' laps or snuggle in bed, feeling safe, as the bad world rages outside the windows. When we grow up we do just that: we grow up, we settle down and accept what comes and what happens. Then, having accepted all this—dealing with the momentary, day-to-day tasks of life—we can relax. We can smile. We can kick back and have fun, even. When we really in our guts know that there is no total security in this world, that we are mortal, then that fact should make us more inclined to value the moment, the little time we have with ourselves, with others. Our little allotted time. The wisdom of insecurity. Only when you know you are going to die, only when you accept that fact in every way, can you begin to really live and appreciate the living.

And I agree with the poet, Theodore Roethke: "In a dark time the eye begins to see."

March 3

Dave

Dear Phil:

Well, how are you? I've been thinking about you. I've been sort of out of sorts lately. Long story, but basically, this. Jan and I went back to the States for a hectic break (driving to see the kids spread out all over the country—and not having a real base). I ended up in the emergency room of a hospital with atrial fibrillation, which means my heart was pounding damn near out'n my chest. What they call "holiday heart," which means too many beers and coffee (which I had over-indulged in the night before). Anyway, that scared the holy hell out of me. The heart was out of sync, they were going to shock it back with those god-awful shocking paddles, but luckily, it slipped back into rhythm. I recovered, no big deal. I ended up a few days later in another emergency room in Madison, Wisconsin with shortness of breath. They did a stress test on me and I came out okay. Said I had a strong heart. But then, different pills, different side effects, and all this as we're getting ready to go back to China, of all places to have something bad happen.

So, here I am, shaky, but, recov-er-ing. Slow-ly. Shak-i-ly. I'm off booze and coffee, which also involved some withdrawal symptoms. All this has affected me rather traumatically. Hard to sleep. Jan is so marvelously understanding and patient. Only she can calm me down, it seems. She is a person who can put the past in a box, wrap it up and send it away. That is a wonderful characteristic, one that makes for longevity, seems to me. But I am doing better, trying to put it all behind me and get down to work here.

What else? Jeeeeeez, this is a self-indulgent letter, full of self pity and all. I need to get out of myself and back to my writing and will, and when I do I will know I'm okay.

By the way, I keep thinking of baseball season, the fact that I won't be in the U.S. on opening day. But I do have your "Mystery Baseball," the next best thing. I believe it's the best damn baseball poem ever written, and one of the very best poems on sports, period, period. And there you have it. I wanted to write to you and tell you this and that, and especially that.

So, my friend, stay in there, let us hear from you. How goes the writing? Send me some stuff you've done lately. And let me know what goes on in Marshall and surrounding environs. It seems that you are teaching less and less and writing more and more. That's good. Dip him in the river who loves water, as Mr. Blake would say. I envy your lifestyle, your quiet seclusion. I keep thinking of Stafford's line: "Wealth is nothing but lack of people." In China you understand that. It makes pure, unadulterated, genuine horse sense.

Take care and let us know how you are.
As ever,

Dave

March 4

Jan

After I finished baking some muffins, Angela came to borrow our

Rainy Day in Nanjing

portable oven to bake chocolate chip cookies. We shared each other's goodies. She stayed for almost three hours. She told about a foreigner who had been pick-pocketed last year in northern China. The foreigner chased the thief down and reported him to the police. He was asked later to identify this person. After he identified the man, the policeman pointed a gun at the back of the man's head and shot him on the spot. There is no mercy when a Chinese person is caught violating a foreigner. They want foreigners to come to China and spend their money. And they want them to feel safe.

...Xia Ayi, our cook, came to our door at about 7:30 p.m. with a bowlful of jaozi (filled dumplings). We were delighted since we hadn't gotten around to fixing anything for dinner.

...Dave and I played Scrabble for the second time this week. I won again. I can usually beat him, but I don't think he's concentrating very well.

March 4

Dave

Thoreau was right. Why didn't I listen to him when I taught Walden last semester? " If we are dying, let us feel the death rattle in our throats. If we are not, let us get on with our business."

Better day. I taught my classes, didn't feel too bad. Slowly, slowly, the stress is diminishing. The ache in the right side of the face still persists, off and on, as in the left arm. It bothers me. It must be stress. My chest feels better.

I think I'll become more domestic here in China. Mike gave us a recipe for scones. I think I'll try to do some cooking with our new oven. But I don't want to sit around and get fat eating scones and muffins, for God's sake!

March 5

Jan

Dave went to see David P. and said he wants to set up regular appointments with him. That may be a good idea. He's having too many anxious moments.

...Our dinner party was a failure. We had Wu Y. and Wu K. and his wife for a "Western" dinner tonight—spaghetti, soup, carrots and onions, garlic bread and chocolate cake. We thought it was good, but Wu K.'s wife didn't like most of it, and wouldn't eat it. She ate a little bit of chocolate cake and drank some tea. Wu K. ate a little more than she did, but not much. Wu Y. ate two helpings of everything. They left by 8:00 p.m. I felt bad about it, but we had good intentions. They brought us some coffee and biscuits (cookies). I've decided to save our valuable "Western" food for us foreigners, and hire a Chinese cook for my next dinner with Chinese friends. Who could not like spaghetti? And, does she think it's not safe to eat food that foreigners have fixed?

March 5

Dave

Another day of sun! The days are merciful here. Yesterday I ran two miles in a T-shirt, it must've been 65 degrees out. Brian says he's like me; he needs sunlight. Without sun I feel closed in by the clouds; I want to sleep the day away, my head under a pillow.

I'll be seeing David P. this morning. Maybe he can give me some ideas on how to avoid stress, how not to worry so much. I am getting better. I feel stronger when I'm in crowds; my stomach is holding up better. I'm too self-conscious—too into myself. I need to be like Jan. She can just listen to others and forget herself. She's tough, tough, resilient. I want to do more real listening to others. I should be interested in them. Reciprocity is very important. Humans are social animals. I can't exist alone.

March 6

Jan

Mike told us about a friend of Lida's who is doing research on ancient medical history of the Qing Dynasty. She is also interested in current medical care and has found many back-alley clinics in China for treating venereal diseases. These clinics are often set up in an individual's one- or two-room home. There is no privacy; other family members may be there during the consultations. They tend to be expensive and don't always have adequate medication. Since there is a stigma associated with premarital sex, people don't want to visit a regular doctor with these problems.

... Dave is preoccupied with the idea of having a heart attack. I told him that he sounds like an old person, one who often sits around worrying about his health and the weather. I'm weary of hearing about his unfounded health concerns. I sympathize with him, but want to get him to think positively and to believe that he is healthier than most men his age. I'm not used to his anxiety and feel like I'm becoming anxious because of him.

...We had dinner in the apartment of a Japanese couple tonight. I was fifteen minutes late because I had gone to a film with a friend. The film, which was shot in Hong Kong, was full of violence and kungfu fighting. It had English sub-titles, but they were not always visible on the screen or easy to read. Our seats were next to a young Chinese couple. Liu whispered in my ear that the girl next to me was her cousin and that she had given her two tickets for this film. She then said we should not talk to her or act like we know her. She apparently was not supposed to give the tickets to anyone other than departmental people. So we ignored the couple during the entire movie. Before we went into the movie, Liu had four extra tickets and was able to sell them to some people outside of the theater. She said she should have gotten Y10, but she got only Y7 because she didn't want to spend any more time negotiating.

...Brian and Chen were also at dinner. Chen is going to be directing some upcoming plays and asked the Japanese couple if she could borrow their small table for the plays. They told her no, she couldn't borrow it, which offended her. Maybe the Japanese couple didn't understand the request. Their English is not good, and we had some trouble communicating throughout the evening. The dinner consisted of ten different exotic Japanese dishes. I'm sure it took Mrs. K. the entire day to prepare the meal.

Mr. K. is a novelist and Mrs. K. is an artist. They have their own automobile here, and they are good friends with the university president and vice president. They have guanxi.

...Dave went to Mike's apartment for a lesson in making scones and came back with a look of confusion on his face. He has never even separated an egg. We'll make scones together as soon as we find all of the ingredients. We had gone out to find butter earlier, but couldn't find the right store. We now have better directions from Mike.

March 6

Dave

Slept the best last night I've slept so far this semester. I didn't think it was possible to have a normal night's sleep, but I nearly did just that, which makes an enormous difference, psychologically as well as physically.

...I have a huge gripe with Western and American medicine. It's far too scientific. The mind, I've found—by which I mean the emotions especially—is involved in health just as much as the organs, the body. Physicians in the U.S. tend to forget that fact. They treat only the body, which is not enough. One doctor told me, after an evaluation: "It's no use telling you not to worry, because I know you will." Why didn't he give me some ideas about how to deal with my anxiety? He has confidence in his machinery, in his knowledge of the body and its workings, but he doesn't seem to understand that the mind is also included in matters of health.

I told Jan yesterday, walking downtown, that I refuse to get bent out of shape about my heart when the tests were essentially inconclusive. And even if they did show something, I'll go with what the Wisconsin doctor told me: it's a "tiny defect," and shouldn't mean any change in my lifestyle; that it can be controlled well with medicine, meaning blood-pressure pills, and an aspirin a day. The only lifestyle change I got from the Wisconsin doctors has to do with drinking, and I'm the one who asked for the advice on it. They said I should drink moderately, which means no more than a beer or two on any given day. I've held to that quota well since my fibrillation incident. I knew that I was drinking too much, and Jan knew it, and she had mentioned it to me a number of times.

March 7

Jan

Dave says his pulse rate is too low. It's 48 or 52—maybe a little low. I told him that he was either in really good shape, or he might be dying. Maybe he's so tired because his blood pressure pills are too strong. Every medical problem Dave reads about in the medical book, he seems to think he has. A little medical knowledge is turning out to be a dangerous thing for him. I asked him if he was familiar with the word hypochondriac.

...For variety, we changed our livingroom around today. A new semester—a new look.

March 7

Dave

At last, sleep. Gentle sleep. Sleep that knits up the ravelled sleeve of care, to quote Shakespeare. Last night I slept from seven to eight hours. Glory. Two weeks, exactly, after we get here, and finally I'm sleeping normally. Without the stress, it would've been much earlier. But I'll take it. I feel much more rested. Confident. Strong.

...The Japanese man, Mr. K., an historical novelist, is about 65 years old. He's been told to stop drinking because of his high blood pressure. He also has diabetes, and says he can't sleep. And yet, he and his wife recently spent about a week on a train traveling in China. And I'm complaining?

...I stayed home yesterday while Jan went to a movie, which turned out to be a bad one, celebrating Women's Day. I think she's ticked at me for not going. She doesn't think I've been very talkative in company, and maybe I haven't been, without beer anymore. But I try to be outgoing, I try to mix. It angers me when she says that, and I told her that last night. This morning she's quiet. Oh, well. Two steps ahead, or one, or none.

March 8

Jan

Dear Kari, Shelly, David, and all,

It was good to see all of you, even though it was a whirlwind of a trip. Although I think there is nothing wrong with your dad, he is imagining that he has some health problems. The experience he had while we were there has had an effect on him. You shouldn't worry about him, though, because I'm sure he is healthy. There is a competent and helpful American physician's assistant available for us should we need medical care.

Today is International Women's Day in China. I think to celebrate this day properly, all women should get the day off.

Angela, a colleague, just returned from a city not too far away called Hefei. She went by bus for the weekend. Her two young friends who are teaching there don't like being in China and can't wait to go home. Angela says that Hefei is a remote, polluted, dirty factory town. Her friends' living conditions sound bleak. They have electricity and water only about four times a week. Their students are unmotivated and not very knowledgeable. It has been a bad experience for them. They plan to visit Nanjing before they go to the U.S., and maybe that will help to change their views of China.

We rode our bikes to the Jinling Hotel for a Chinese dinner tonight. The waitresses hovered over us so much we felt like we were on display.

They brought us a wet wash rag before dinner and another one after dinner. They placed the napkins around our waists before we ate. They watched us take each bite and gave us clean plates when we had finished each entree. Our tea cups were refilled as soon as we had taken one sip. The noodles we ordered were brought on a large plate and the waiters cut them up and gave us each half a serving. They kept asking how we liked the food. Their intentions were good, but we felt conspicuous and wanted to eat in peace.

This made us think about the kind of service we used to get at a nice hotel restaurant in Kunming in 1988. We often had to wait an hour just to have our order taken. And then it was taken without enthusiasm, and the food was brought without enthusiasm or a smile. Quite a contrast.

Today on the street, I watched a little boy, who was probably 1 1/2 years old, squat down and poop. He looked like a little ball of wool with all of his layers of clothing. After he finished, he bent over and looked at what he had done and smiled at his mother. A woman with a "pooper scooper" came along and scooped it up.

Better prepare for classes. Again, don't worry about us. We're doing fine and will return home, no doubt, stronger than ever. Write.
We love you,

Mom (readjusting)

March 8

Dave

Woke up worrying. I have to stop worrying and just get on with my life. What I should remember above all is: I can lead a normal, healthy life as is. Carry on, should be my charge to myself. I need to get to work and just do what I've always done. In that way, day by day, the bad memories fade, gradually.

Jan is so right about this. She has the ability or talent—God given?—to put things out of her mind. I would like to be like that.

March 9

Dave

Still struggling, but had a decent day yesterday. The key is to have something to do. I had my British Council class to organize, and I did it. Then I lifted weights and went for a walk alone for about an hour. I was proud of myself for taking off alone and mixing in that big crowd down by the Jinling Hotel. Last night I didn't feel so good. I wasn't in a good mood when Jan turned off the TV when two former students came to visit. They stayed for about an hour, and I moped. Jan was mad, I suppose, because I wasn't all that friendly. I felt sorry for myself, and wanted to just lie around and watch a movie. Jan welcomes everybody who comes to the door. That is her way. I'm not as outgoing and sociable. So conflict sometimes arises. We need to talk about that one of these days. I need to bend a little, and so does she. You don't turn people away from your door; on the other hand, there are distinctions to be made. Tonight, Jan has an office hour (two hours, from 7:00 to 9:00). Last week she had a houseful of students. I wonder what tonight will bring...

...Stopped at the Jinling and checked out flights to Kunming and Xiamen. The beautiful woman who waited on me was so pleasant, so efficient. The beautiful Chinese women do make a difference. What a diversion from the disease of too much self-consciousness.

I've got to turn this thing around, somehow. If the body feels okay—I feel okay, basically, though every little discomfort is magnified into chest pain—eventually my mind will find a way of smoothing things over. I have to learn to be cheerful and healthy sounding. I look around me and see all the other healthy people coming and going, shouting, smiling, laughing, cursing, hurrying through life more or less unconscious and unselfaware. That's the kind of person I want to be. I want to just live, to get on with all the things I need to do to stay healthy and to do my work—to the very end.

March 9

Jan

Today it was "Sports Days" on campus. Morning classes were canceled, and, as is often the case when holidays or days off occur, we were not told about it in advance. I only have an afternoon class on Tuesdays, so I didn't get a break. The weather has turned colder and it rained during the night. Spring isn't here after all.

I stayed in this morning and made granola, a "tried and true" recipe from another foreigner here. It tastes great, so we won't be eating Heinz high-protein baby cereal for breakfast anymore. We haven't been able to find regular cereal here like we're used to eating at home, and we don't eat a lot of protein, so we thought this Heinz high-protein cereal would be healthy for us. Besides, I've liked the taste of it since I first fed it to our kids. Our diets here in China probably lack protein, but we get plenty of vegetables and rice.

...Dave had a good day today. He is improving and has even started writing again, something he hasn't been able to do for a while.

March 10

Jan

Mike, Lida and the cook all have colds. I wondered, when I heard the cook sneezing in the kitchen, and after we shared dinner by helping ourselves to the communal food with our chopsticks, if we would be next.

When the cook was leaving this evening, I offered her a cookie from a box of delicious cookies we had been given as a gift. She thought I meant to give her the whole box, and she took it. I didn't have the heart to take it back from her. And we loved those cookies.

At dinner, we talked about the two desk clerks in our apartment complex—how they don't get any time off. They have worked seven days a week since the first of January, with the exception of Julia, who got married and had two days off. They are good workers—pleasant and efficient while dealing with so many different kinds of foreigners. Dave often gives Helen, one of the two clerks, videos to watch. She appreciates this and likes to discuss the movies with him.

March 10

Dave

Last night I felt the best I've felt since returning to China. I don't understand it, but something clicked in my brain and I no longer felt anxious. My body was relaxed; I was watching a <u>Star Trek</u> movie with Jan. I felt absolutely normal. This morning I feel fine, and I finally had a normal dream, with some confidence in it. It's all a matter of confidence, I think. And this, after not running for two days. I want to feel this way all the time.

I've lost some weight, probably down to 185, which is a good weight. Blood pressure down, pulse down to around 50 and even below. May have to cut back on the blood pressure pills.

...Jan had three students over last night, all women. They are so smart, so young and so immature by American standards. What they lack in maturity they make up for in brains.

DETAIL OF THE DAY:
I swear—98 percent of the Chinese wear glasses. A much higher percentage, I think, than in the U.S. Why? Genetic deficiency? Diet?

March 11

Jan

One of Dave's students brought us a piece of "artwork." It is a brown and tan sculpture with three lotus flowers, a crab sitting on a seashell and two crayfish with long antennae. It may not be something I would have chosen, but I appreciated the gesture.

...Zhang came over to spend the evening. He brought us some coffee and some fish cakes his wife had made. He told us we should slice them and fry them in oil for our breakfast tomorrow. We gave him a snow globe (he said he wanted one after reading about one in a story of Dave's), a U.S. calendar and a date book. He said he would like to have us come to his home for dinner, but it would be too difficult. He lives in two rooms with four other people: his wife, her mother and his two daughters. He said it would take more than one week just to clean his flat and also at least that much time to prepare the food. His wife is traditional and would feel the need to have 10 or more Chinese dishes for us, each elaborately prepared. He said his mother-in-law saves everything, so their apartment is full of things that are never used. We agreed to have him and his wife over to our apartment for a dinner for which they will bring part of the food. I wouldn't want to attempt to fix everything, especially after our last disaster of a dinner for Chinese people.

Zhang has many connections all over China. He said he will help us introduce Barbara, our artist friend from Iowa who is coming to China, to some famous Chinese artists, and will help her get an art showing in a gallery.

We served him some chocolate chip cookies I had just baked, and he wanted to take some home for his wife. He said they tasted "so American." He said, as I got out a zip-lock bag, that I should give him <u>six</u> cookies.

...Qian came over, bursting with excitement. She is leaving tomorrow for a seven-day trip to Shanghai and Hangzhou, where she will present a paper for a translation society conference. We gave her some chocolate chip cookies and a scone, which she said she would eat for breakfast. She loves the toaster we gave her.

...Dave is having chest pains and jaw pains again. Is he actually <u>having</u> them or is he <u>imagining</u> that he is having them?

March 11

Dave

The drama continues. Yesterday, after I ran, I thought I felt a minor twinge close to my left nipple. It scared me, of course. Then I figured it out, after Cathy (David P.'s wife, and a P.A. herself) told me it probably was muscular. I'm pretty sure it has to do with my bench pressing. I went over to the "Y" and lifted the other day, and I'm not in lifting shape yet. I think I took on too much weight, trying to get instantly back into shape. So, my pectorals ache a little. This morning I had the same faint pain in my right pectorals, so that confirms it. It's not a heart attack. To think that I had such a wonderful Tuesday evening, and then Wednesday, after a 2 1/2 mile jog, pain. But the pain is muscular.

...I am writing some—got into a short story on Tuesday, continued yesterday, and continuing today. I may get a hook on this one, about an aging professor who takes up karate.

DETAIL OF THE DAY:

I saw a man on a bike parked on the side of a busy lane, his legs spread-eagled for balance, his head resting on the handlebars, sleeping. Maybe he was sick. But he looked perfectly relaxed. It's interesting how people can be seen lying around on carts or just on cardboard on the busy sidewalks in the middle of the day. I don't think that could happen in most U.S. cities. Maybe it's easier in a socialist country.

March 12

Jan

We didn't sleep well last night. I think we drank too much tea. Dave got up early and went for an appointment with David P. He had a good talk with him, and once again feels better.

...Zhou, a young teacher in the English section, came over to have us help her with her pronunciation for some news material she is going to present on a television English newscast this weekend. She was chosen from the English section to do this. Being attractive, I'm afraid, was a pre-requisite, since her English isn't so good, especially for a TV announcer. There are others, less attractive, who have better English language skills.

...I'm getting a cold and feel awful.

March 12

Dave

Got a glimpse into the younger generation last night talking with Jan's student, Zhou. He said that students in their teens and early 20s are now confused. They can't rely on the past, on the socialist system—on Confucian ideas, etc.—and they don't know what is in their future. They are in limbo. Mr. Zhang, earlier in the evening, told us that the young no longer believe in anything, no longer have an anchor: God, the State, Confucius, whatever. They are, he said, selfish, thinking only about themselves; they are individualistic in ways that no generation of Chinese has ever been.

Zhou said that rock music is subtly protesting youths' ambivalence and their sense of insecurity. Rock lyrics say that the State should no longer insist on leading or ruling, that it should throw off the "iron chains" and give the people back their "flesh and blood."

I can understand this now, somewhat. The young have to be confused, since the government now is forgoing ideology and starting up a free-market economy, which is most certainly a democratic, non-communist system. How can the government continue to talk out of both sides of its mouth? How long will it be before the bright youth rise up again in protest, rebellion? Mr. Zhang says that the government, of course, can always bring in the tanks. But doesn't <u>that</u> get old, too?

March 13

Jan

Our day was taken up with visitors. Ms. Wu, a former student of mine, brought her friend, Zhou, over. He is an intellectual who speaks English, French, German and Chinese, and knows a lot about literature. He wanted to meet Dave. Dave asked him how he had time to read so much since he is the general manager of a company. He said that <u>because</u> he is a manager, he can find the time to read. It is his "passion," he said.

March 13

Dave

Maintaining. Learned more about my heart test. I have no muscle damage, according to David P. The "defect," if it is one, occurred just after maximum exercise. And the EKG didn't change one iota, and everything was back to normal on the second scan an hour or so later. Hence, it's only a temporary glitch, if it is a glitch, and I really think it's a movement artifact, as they call them. The machine detects very minute details. I remember changing my arm position during the scanning. Anyway, no blockage was found, and my heart was pronounced "very strong" by the head doctor. I need to just go with that. Obviously, there's nothing seriously wrong with my heart.

David P. said, as my other doctors said, keep moving, keep working out, playing racquetball, running, climbing mountains if I want to. The point is that exercise is probably the best thing I've done for my health thus far in my life. I don't intend to quit, especially since it makes me feel so good, and keeps my weight down fairly well.

I'll have some setbacks. Before, I relied on beer to calm me. No more. So, I'll be jittery in company, for instance. I need to just accustom myself to this. Take my time, eat slowly, talk with others, listen to others. Deliberately take control of myself and maintain control.

March 14

Dave

Felt a pain in my chest last night in bed, don't know if it was real or a dream—I do think it was real. Muscular? I've felt the same pain before; this time I magnified it 100 times probably. The slightest unease becomes chest pain for me. I know I'm going to have these miscellaneous pains. It can't be angina, can it? In the middle of the night? No exertion, really, and angina is associated with exertion. I have a strong heart; it has to be muscular. I lifted a bar bell last night. Maybe that was the pain in my chest.

Jan says I need to forget it. She's right. Otherwise, I won't be able to focus.

...The young man who translated my story for Mr. Zhang's journal seems down on the U.S., but when I asked him where he'd most like to go outside China, he said, without hesitation, the U.S. Our country has a lot of negatives for some of these intellectuals here—they've gotten all the bad news on violence, discrimination, etc.— but they know, deep down, that the U.S. is far superior to China in many important ways. Living conditions are a basic human requirement. These people know that there's no comparison between the two countries on that matter, overall. And they know the freedoms. If I were a Chinese writer, I could not say anything against the government. I would be punished if I did. That is another basic. What is more basic to art than freedom of expression, the sheer, simple, rock-bottom freedom to say whatever you want on canvas, in stone or on paper? Otherwise, why even <u>be</u> an artist? The privilege of art is undermined to the extent that the artist qualifies what he/she says about power structures, about anything, for that matter. Anything.

March 14

Jan

It was a rainy, gloomy day. But since we needed food, we went to the market on our bikes.

...Guo came over for a dinner of soup, rice, pickled vegetables and scones. He was a little nervous eating at first, but overcame it. He watched Dave put crackers in his soup, and did the same. He was a little awkward with a fork, but said he didn't want chopsticks. He asked innocently, as we were eating scones, if they were part of the dinner. He had two helpings of soup and said he liked it. He wanted to wash the dishes after dinner, but I said it wasn't necessary. After dinner, we showed him our Michael Jackson video. Like so many Chinese students, he loves Michael Jackson and wants us to get a copy of the tape for him if we can.

Guo said he feels very lonely these days. His wife is in Chengdu. He talked about the lack of freedom in China, how he has to go to political meetings each week, and say that he loves the Party above anything else. He says everyone must say these things, but nobody means them. He says he can't speak freely to most people, but feels he can talk freely to us. As we were talking, he said we could call him Xiao Ming (Little Ming), or Ming (his first name), which are forms of address you can use when you are good friends. He said it is thought to be impolite to call someone by his or her first name, unless you are good friends. By Chinese standards he would have to call us aunt or uncle, or Mr. and Mrs., but never by our first names. So it was difficult for him at first when we told him to call us by our first names. He stayed until 10:00 p.m., and then he had to get on his bike and ride in the rain for 40 minutes to get home. He planned to stop by the post office on his way to call his wife. He said she was on duty and would be feeling lonely.

...Dave was having chest pains, so he took some Tylenol. He has serious concerns about his heart.

March 15

Jan

Today Dave's pains were in his left cheek and jaw. He thinks the pains are moving from his chest, to his left shoulder, to his cheek. I worry about him, but I don't let him know that I'm concerned. I feel that he is healthy physically. We can't be unhealthy in China!

...One of my students writes in her diary that she is bored and lonely, especially on weekends, because her parents won't allow her to go to movies or dances. Young people feel strongly about obeying their parents' wishes and normally won't act against them, even when they are far away. Married adults also feel that they must follow their parents' advice. While students are living at home, their mothers choose what clothes they will wear and what food they will eat. They are almost totally dependent on their parents for everything. It's not surprising that many of them feel lost when they first leave home.

...A phone call came for us from the U.S. while we were out for dinner. Julia answered it at the front desk and told them to call back at 7:30. We waited, but the call never came. So Dave spent the rest of the night worrying about the call. I used to be the one of us who would worry. Now, Dave worries for both of us.

March 16

Dave

Yesterday, most of the day anyway, I had the best day I've had so far in China in my second half of the year. I spent the morning and much of the afternoon revising a story; I felt terrific. I ran 2 1/4 miles. After my nap, my face began to hurt some. In the evening I was a little nervous. Slept well last night. I'm definitely losing my nervousness, returning to normal, but still not completely normal. The jaw ache bothers me. If it weren't on the left side, it would be better. I keep trying to connect it with my heart, yet I know it can't be related. This is a steady ache, more or less; at least, when it's there, it lasts for a while.

...Sleep is glorious. Oh, do I love sleep. Nature's soft nurse. I wish I had thought up those words instead of that guy from Stratford.

...Overcast sky again. I hate it. Yesterday in the afternoon the sun came out, but it was still cold. What wouldn't I give for sun....

...The other night Jan's former student, a young man studying dermatology, told us that he and his associates are constantly having to pretend to like their work and the Party. This is especially true at meetings, at which everybody sits around praising the Party line, apparently. No criticism, no objections to anything. Everything is simply accepted as right. He spoke of the "freedoms" in America, said his father has said he should go there and live. He is restless, unhappy, lonely for his wife back in Chengdu. He asked me if I was lonely; I said I am, that I miss my children. He was sincere in his question. He is a lonely young man.

What kind of a life is it when you have to always be praising the people in charge of you? Where there's no room for objections at all? That is really slavery, bondage. And the Chinese spend most of their time at work: six out of seven week days, seven to nine hours a day. That, a life?

March 16

Jan

After Dave was up for about an hour this morning, he went back to bed. He had drunk a cup of caffeine coffee and thought it had an effect on him. He also thought the cole slaw he ate upset his stomach. I think the gloomy weather has something to do with his mood. If it had been a sunny day, he probably would have felt better. It has been gloomy for several days.

March 17

Dave

Broke through another barrier today, ran <u>three miles</u>! That's an important victory, since now I know that my heart is strong. The first two miles
were a little "windy" at times, but then at about 2 1/4 miles I was hardly
breathing. I know my heart was pumping very efficiently for that last mile. I
felt terrific.

And yet, I felt some twinges in my chest, mid-center, but I am
extremely sensitive to any sensation/twinges in my chest. These are
normal, I know now. And my left arm aches a little because of a mus-
culo/skeletal problem. It comes and goes, as does my jaw/face ache,
which I'm convinced is psychological. I can see the use of yoga now. A
person can certainly learn to control some involuntary bodily functions
by deliberate concentration.

...Yesterday I was miserable; I felt sorry for myself the whole day
almost, but went to bed optimistic after a little walk alone. Walks are
rejuvenating. I'm feeling much more normal today. Amazing how my mind can
"switch" from one mood to another. I'm in the right mode/mood today,
essentially. I have to expect setbacks, negatives. The point is that I do
wake up in the morning, and I am sleeping well. "The long habit of living
indisposeth us to dying," said Francis Bacon.

March 17

Jan

We invited Ms. Hong over for dinner tonight. Our cook made a typical
Chinese dinner which, although not impressive, was okay. Hong brought some
special kinds of grass for dinner—one that she had cooked at home and
another that she had the cook prepare for dinner. She said that this is the
peak season for these grasses. The taste probably has to grow on you.

Hong's father died last December. She said he suffered terribly
from the Cultural Revolution. He was "labeled," which meant that he was
criticized and punished. He had worked for a newspaper in Hong Kong at

one time, and the leaders felt that he must be a counter-revolutionary, a rightist. She said that the leaders were required to produce a quota of people to persecute, and that her father happened to be on the first list to fill the quota of his section. She was emotional as she talked about his suffering. She also said that, as a member of his family, she has had to be quiet. If she were to be questioned for any reason, she would be looked at as not having a clean background because of her father.

We talked about the young people of today, and Hong said she just doesn't know what is going on. She said that now they are all talking about "lovers." She doesn't think they know what that word actually means. Young people are also concerned about the "third" person in a relationship. She says there are more men having extra-marital affairs; thus, more divorces and more unhappiness.

There is now a new late-night call-in show on a radio station in Nanjing that many young people listen to. The hosts of the program offer advice about love and relationships between young men and women. Hong is worried about the increase in boy-girl relationships on campus. She says most of these relationships will have to end after graduation, because the students will be sent to different areas and won't necessarily be able to stay together.

...I was asked by the English section to have my composition students write an essay on "Is Money Everything?" The trend today, in China, is to think that money is everything. The Chinese people have felt deprived for so long that their main goal in life now is making money. The young people don't talk about happiness and basic traditional values much. They talk about making money.

March 18

Jan

My cold is better, but the cold weather is still here. Dave is getting a cold now. I hate it when he's sick because he doesn't deal with it very well. A cold, along with his "heart problems," will be difficult.

224

March 19

Jan

Dear Sarah and Chuck,

How is everything? It's always good getting your letters. Thanks for taking care of our house rental problems. Life for us here continues to be captivating, if not unusual at times.

On our walk today, we stopped to watch something that was unusual to us. A lady was selling tea eggs, which is not unusual; but she was also selling another kind of egg—a large white one. What caught our eyes was a mother peeling one of these eggs and preparing it for her young daughter, who was about two or three years old. As she opened the egg, we could see a small, perfectly formed duck embryo with feathers and all. The mother plucked some of the larger feathers out and handed the peeled egg to her daughter, as the egg lady poured some salt into the girl's hand. The young girl first bit off the head of the embryo and then continued to eat the rest of it. These eggs are boiled and completely cooked, but they don't look like something we would want to try. Eva, a teacher from the Philippines, told us later that they are called "ballute," and that they are quite tasty and also nutritious. She said you usually suck all of the juice out first and then eat the rest of it.

Tom, our friend and colleague, called today to arrange a time for me to color his wife's hair. She was at home, but Tom called. I tried to imagine Dave or Chuck making our phone calls for us to arrange for hair coloring, etc. What do you think?

Sarah, you will appreciate this: I had a problem for which I went to see Cathy, a physician's assistant (an American). Dave has had appointments with her husband concerning his heart and his anxiety, which he's been having a lot of recently.

They have two small boys, ages two and five, and they live in a three-room apartment. They've been given the use of a medical examination room and an office, which is next to their apartment.

Anyway, when I got there, Cathy was feeding the boys a lunch of rice and vegetables. The apartment was a disaster. I can imagine that with two small boys and her busy schedule of learning the Chinese language and seeing patients, she has little time to clean. Her husband is as busy as she is.

She decided to do a pelvic exam on me, and since the youngest boy cried and clung to her and wouldn't let her leave the apartment to go to the exam room with me, she decided to check me right there in their bedroom. Cathy put a large towel on the bed, which her youngest son promptly jumped on, and then she had me undress and lie on the bed. She gave me a tiny hand towel to cover up with and asked me to scoot to the bottom of the bed and put my knees up so she could do the exam. She had to sit on the floor to check me, since the bed was so low. Before she did this, she bribed her son into going into the other room and locked the door and told his older brother to entertain him. This wasn't anything like the checkups I've been used to getting back home. I was hoping the instrument she got out of her closet was sterile. I was satisfied, though, with her knowledge and her recommendations. I know that if I had gone to a Chinese doctor I would have felt much more uncomfortable, especially with the lack of communication skills. I'm sure there is traditional Chinese medicine available that I could have used, but I feel more comfortable with Western medicine right now. What an experience.

Had better close. Stay in touch.

Love,

Jan (egg watcher)

March 19

Jan

Dave woke up with pains in his chest, a stomachache and his jaw hurting. He feels great stress today, after having had such a good day yesterday. He even got out the doctors' reports on his heart and read them yesterday. He hadn't read them earlier because he was sure they were too horrible to face. I had tried to reassure him that they were good reports, but he wouldn't believe me. It's a day-to-day thing with him. My stomach also hurts, and I think it may have been the chicken we ate for lunch yesterday. But I can deal with the pain. Dave can't. He has trouble with any kind of discomfort. He has a terrible fear of having a heart attack here. And if he did, he says he is sure he would not survive with the kind of medical care available. I told him that if he died in China, I would not be able to take his body home. It's the law. I asked then, "Should I scatter your ashes on the campus grounds in front of the English Department?"

"Throw them off the Nanjing Drum Tower," he said.

...Qian came over to give us some items she got in Shanghai. She had talked to her leader this morning about being sent to a factory to teach. She was in tears. She originally was supposed to go for two months and get Y1000 per month, which she could have handled easily. But now she has been told she has to go for four months, get only Y500 per month, and not have a summer vacation. She's extremely upset. She can refuse to go or she can ask for extended sick leave, but this would mean she would get even less money to live on. She is already paid very little. She can resign from her job and take a chance of finding something else. She doesn't know what to do. She loves teaching at Nanjing University and is a good teacher. That's part of the reason she was chosen, because she will do a good job of teaching for which the factory will pay a lot of money to the university. She says they are just using her to make money for them. She has come up against the leaders and dares not challenge them. She says this is not the Cultural Revolution and that she should not be "sent to the countryside." She just recently won a top prize for her presentation at a translation conference.

...All three of us decided to try to forget our problems and ride our bikes to the city wall. We climbed up a steep flight of steps and walked along the wall. Dave and I thought it was the most beautiful area we'd seen so far in Nanjing. It was quiet and peaceful, and the renowned Purple Mountain was visible in all of its splendor. The area where we walked, however, was dangerous. There were steep drop-offs on each side of the trail and no railings. I couldn't imagine parents bringing their children (as they often do) and having them near those ledges. (This is one of my great fears.)

...We attended a Y50 per plate fund-raising dinner at Brian and Chen Loo's apartment. They are trying to collect money for the dramas they are directing.

Chen told us about her problems with casting and organizing the students for the dramas. It sounds as though she is being too dictatorial and demanding. She admits that she is not always a nice person to the students. She says they won't like you any better by being overly nice to them. She thinks many of us foreign teachers go out of our way to be nice and that we believe the students when they say they like us or give us compliments. She says they don't mean it.

March 20

Dave

I continue my roller-coaster life in China. Yesterday morning I felt lousy. Woke up with what I thought were pains in my heart, but now I know they weren't. They were probably from lifting the night before; the pain was more in my pectorals. Also, I get twinges when I sleep on my back. Always have. Last night I slept on my side and had no pains at all. Feel good now. I can live with my condition. I'm healthy, normal. My weight is down well, I'm drinking only one to three beers per week, which means I've cut down my drinking over 90 percent. Still have an ache on the left side of my face; psychological yet? Probably stress. Gradually, I'm getting better. Had a long bike ride yesterday with Qian and Jan—went to a pagoda and wall, did a lot of walking, climbing steps. It was a good outing.

March 20

Jan

Today is the first day of spring, but it's not spring-like. Dave's face pains have subsided, but now he has pains in his chest. There's no end to it.

March 21

Dave

Slept seven straight hours, the best so far. A victory. Woke up, though, and started thinking of my condition, and made it—as usual when

I think too much of it—worse than it is. It isn't bad, my condition—it's mostly good. The good thought I had yesterday that should be a milestone thought for me is: The stress I've been having—but which I'm gradually, by degrees conquering—is the price I have to pay for a better, healthier, longer life than I'd have without it.

March 21

Jan

Dave is bothered by left shoulder and chest pains today. He thinks it may be arthritis or something like that. I think it's anxiety. He needs another appointment with David, his shrink.

March 22

Dave

Now I believe what I have is bursitis. The discomfort is in my left shoulder and left side of my chest and even my neck. The weather here is very damp right now, and I've had this condition before in damp weather. It even hurts in my back at times.

I don't want to have to resort to the Xanax. I haven't had one since the first week I got here. It's already the sixth week of school, actually. I'm catching up on my classes, having extra classes in case we're gone to Kunming in April. Maybe a little travel would be good for me. Get out and around. Keep busy— that is my best strategy right now. Sometimes I actually feel good and can enjoy my stay here. But I need to realize that I'm okay.

...Woke up with fast pulse last night: around 70. Ate too much chocolate, maybe? Brownies, chocolate candy. Need to stay away from caffeine. As well as beer. Did have a beer and a half last night. A beer now and then is not going to kill me.

March 22

Jan

We had a restless night. Dave woke up at one point and said his heart rate was too fast. I found it to be about 68, which is a little high for him. He probably had a nightmare. Can his mind create all of these discomforts he is experiencing, or are they real? If they are real, what is causing them? He made an appointment to see David P. I feel stressed.

It's raining and cold. I hate this kind of weather. I hate having Dave sick.

March 23

Dave

Decent night all around. Right now, I feel that, even if I'm not a perfect specimen of health at 52 going on 53, I am healthy and, if I take care of myself I can live a long time and enjoy my life. And not have to cut back on anything to speak of, except booze and fatty foods. I need to live my life deliberately, the way Thoreau said it ought to be lived, day to day; to do the things I enjoy, to be with people I enjoy being with; to help others; to be calm, confident, cheerful, useful, compassionate and kind whenever possible. I should avoid conflict when it harms me or others; I should avoid anger, and not hold grudges. I should be forgiving and open to suggestions and criticism.

Take the moderate way from now on, I need to tell myself, since I'm no longer a 30-year-old. It's time to shift gears. Fifty-three is not young, but it's not old either.

My nerves still bother me, but I am learning to deal with them. I need to relax. Relax. Relax. Relax. That is what I learned as an athlete, maybe the most important thing I learned as an athlete, and it holds for everything, just about. Relax. From the top of the head all the way down to the toes. "Let your soul stand cool and compos'd, before a million universes," said Whitman. I agree. RELAX. That's 99 percent of it.

March 23

Jan

Dave went back to bed this morning after he was up for about an hour. He didn't sleep well last night. His state of mind is not good. When will he stop worrying about his heart? And is there reason for him to worry about it? Now, he has started taking Advil. He saw David P. and felt better when he got home. David P. is going to be gone for a week or two, so Dave will, no doubt, be anxious about that.

...It rained and was dreary again today—not good for Dave's disposition. Deb and I had planned to go out shopping all morning since we don't have morning classes on Tuesdays, but with this rain we didn't do it.

March 24

Dave

Better day yesterday. The weather is still depressingly overcast and rainy and dreary. It's rainy and overcast all over China. One of these days we'll get some sun. But it's not easy to move around now. Still I try to stay on my feet. When I feel some anxiety coming on, I go out for a brief walk, which helps. Mentally, I'm getting along much better.

Calm down, Evans. Remember: calm down. And don't let your emotions carry you away. Figure it out. Believe in the hardware of modern medicine which says that your heart is "pretty darned good." You have a strong heart, "absolutely." That is the bottom line under the bottom line.

And, don't dwell on negatives. Dwell, always, on positives, on the good news, of which there is aplenty.

March 24

Jan

Dave is having pains in his chest and back. He thinks that he may have pleurisy or something similar. Another day, another pain.

March 25

Jan

Dave had a restless night because of chest and back pains, so I didn't sleep well either. He tells me now that he thinks he has an ulcer. I told him I wouldn't be surprised, since he is probably worrying himself into one. I think people can literally make themselves sick by thinking they are sick. Dave certainly has been thinking he is sick.

...It rained again almost all day and night. Dave rode his bike to class and got soaked. And my feet were soaked when I got to class, after stepping in several puddles. You can't avoid them. The insides of university buildings are almost as wet as the outsides. There are no mats in any of the buildings to help soak up some of the water, so it just accumulates. Street workers are always trying to sweep the water into drains with huge bamboo brooms, but with so much rain, it's impossible to keep up with it. The outside of our apartment building is like a lake.

...Angela and her parents got here last night around 10:00 p.m. Her parents were to land in Shanghai, where Angela went to meet them, but because of the heavy rain, they landed in Hangzhou. They were not allowed to get out of the plane and had to sit there for six hours (after they had already been in the plane for about 20 hours) before going to Shanghai. Angela waited at the Shanghai airport for them all this time. When they finally got to Shanghai, they all had to make arrangements to catch a train to Nanjing. The only seats they could get were hard seats. They have not had a good first impression of China. Angela's mother finds the spitting here disgusting. She's in culture shock and is also experiencing jet lag. She said she wanted Angela to come home, that she thought she was living in squalor. Angela told her that Nanjing is one of the most beautiful cities of China.

March 26

Dave

Better, better. Now that I know that the discomfort I've felt is not in my heart, and having talked to David P. for the I-don't-know-how-many-maybe-seventh time on the same, not-boring-to-me subject of my heart—I believe I've just been stressed out and feeling gas. May have the beginnings of an ulcer. I want to stop thinking about it and get on with my work now. Like revising stories, like writing stories. I've got a lot of work to do yet on my collection. If I can get two or three good ones done, I'll have a manuscript.

...Rain, rain, rain. My God, relentless rain. Is this typical Nanjing spring weather? It's hard to run in this rain, especially without a track now, which is under water. Jan wants to go out today and get some rainboots. Maybe I should, too. If this rain continues, day and night, we'll need them to save our shoes. We haven't seen a sustained sun for weeks, most of March, actually.

March 26

Jan

Dave feels pretty good today. He jogged 2 1/2 miles; we walked for more than an hour; he had a class this afternoon; we went out to eat with Qian; and we watched a video, Emerald Forest. The weather is, however, still rainy and overcast.

March 27

Jan

Dave had another bad night and didn't get much sleep. He can't stop dwelling on his health. If we were in the States, I'm sure he wouldn't have these problems. His main worry is having something happen and ending up in a Chinese hospital.

It's very frightening to him, as it is to any of us foreigners, but the difference is that most of us just don't think about it. I'm impatient with him at times, especially because I don't think there's a thing wrong with him.

March 27

Jan

Dear Nan & Gary,

Your package has arrived. Since you've lived in China before, you can appreciate how happy we were to get it. This morning, as soon as the desk clerk gave us the notice that there was a package for us, we got on our bikes and rode 30 minutes in the dreary misty weather to the main post office across town to retrieve it. The mail clerk couldn't find the package, so she asked (motioned) for us to come to the back room to help find it. It took us a while to look through the many and various boxes, but we finally spotted ours—a package from you. We opened it in the post office, with an audience, and split it up into our backpacks to carry home. We loved getting the candy, coffee, game, playing cards, pens, puzzle book, cookies and Tums. You knew what to send. Thanks.

The English Department at Nanjing University is going to have a new focus. It will be more business oriented and less literature oriented, I'm afraid. The name will be changed to "The School of Foreign Studies." Students don't seem to want to study literature and poetry so much any more. They want to go into business so they can make money.

Wu, a department leader, brought a young girl over to our apartment who will be teaching in the English section next semester. Her field is International Relations, and he wants me to help her with her speaking, so she'll eventually be able to teach in English. I don't mind, since we are trying to build up some guanxi so that when we want to be away from classes for traveling, I won't have a problem. You know how these things work in China. People are always keeping track—building up guanxi. I do something for him, he keeps track; he does something for me, I keep track. Then when a favor is needed, we can count up the guanxi and, if warranted, comply.

We stopped by our friend's room (she's on the faculty here) in the dormitory to take her some of our home-made granola cereal which she likes. We had never been to her room before, and found it depressing to walk up the six flights of steps to get there. (There are no elevators). The stairway walls and floors were stained with spit and dirt. The floors were full of garbage and trash—dirty and wet. Our friend wasn't at home, so we left a note and the cereal with the women across the hall from her. Dave felt extremely depressed seeing where she lived and said he didn't want to go back again. I told him it was probably fixed up nicely inside. It's a shame that a teacher (or anyone else, for that matter), has to live in such conditions. I'm sure others have it worse.

Dave's mental health hasn't been great since we've come back to China from our semester break. He continually worries about his heart. I think his heart is fine, but I do worry about his mental state. It has been difficult at times to deal with. But we <u>will</u> make it through the semester.

Again, thanks. Stay in touch. We love to get your letters.

Love,

Jan (hanging in there)

March 28

Jan

It was a nice Sunday—quiet and lazy. I read an Ann Tyler book most of the day instead of correcting papers from my writing class. We went to the market and almost stepped on a dead rat lying on the street, smashed, with its mouth open and its teeth showing. I made vegetable soup with tofu for dinner, and we watched a good video called <u>Stealing Home</u>.

March 29

Jan

Another bad night for Dave. This morning his jaw hurt and he had chest pains after he walked up three flights of stairs to Deb and Tom's apartment. He needs a counselor to help him deal with his anxiety. I've been reading that these symptoms are fairly common when one is worried about his or her heart. I don't think Dave has anything to be worried about physically. His mental state is another thing.

...The sun is shining today. It's a nice break from the rain. It also makes Dave feel better, and anything that makes him feel better is good.

March 29

Dave

Limping along. Not a good night. Walked up three flights of stairs and just afterwards felt a tingling in my heart. What the hell is it? I thought I was in shape. Is it the sudden exertion after being quiet for a time? I had jogged for 24 minutes earlier in the day.

Not doing well. Not sleeping. And that is not good. Still haven't found an anchor here. But today the sun is out for the first time in weeks. That may help. It will help! by God.

David P. is gone too, and I won't be able to check in with him for a while. Maybe that's good, not to have to rely on him.

March 30

Jan

Dave was miserable today. He had a bad pain in his chest when he got out of bed this morning, and as the day went on it got worse. He wanted desperately to go to Hong Kong to see a doctor, and even checked on flights. David P. is gone on vacation, and Dave has depended on him for reassurance. I feel helpless, since I have no good solutions. I try to help him the best I can.

By afternoon, Dave had settled down, so we rode our bikes to the bank to cash some travelers checks. We got there at lunch time, so we found the employees eating. They were sitting at their desks with their tin bowls filled with rice, vegetables and meat. They all appeared to be having the same thing and were using spoons instead of chopsticks. Every so often someone would throw something from their bowl into the garbage can—apparently something inedible. Nobody paid any attention to us. We waited for a while, until the person who handles foreigners finished lunch and returned to help us.

...Dave went to the campus clinic this afternoon to get some sleeping pills to help him sleep.

...During a debate today on the topic of women working outside the home, a male student said that women were "born to do housework." Another said it is impossible to have a marriage in which a woman and a man are equal. Their ideas are firmly fixed.

The young women in the class did a good job of debating with them, but I'm sure they did not convince the males to change their opinions about a woman's place in society.

March 30

Dave

Today I made a great discovery. I woke up this morning and felt a pain, sort of, in my chest, middle. Worried, worried, worried. Then another shortly afterward. Jan kept saying forget it, and pointed out that, according to the book we have on the heart, you can have heart attack symptoms without having the real thing. I thought I was having the real thing. Then later on in the morning, I took two aspirin and felt better. Then later, after lunch, feeling quite good, I walked up the stairs, kept walking up the stairs and down, up and down, and didn't feel a thing. Whereas I had some "chest pain" walking up the library steps and three flights in our building before. Now here's my discovery. My heart, if it was bad, and if I were having angina or a heart attack, would've noticed the strain. It didn't. Last semester I climbed up the Sun Yat-Sen steps, 395 of them, and took two at a time in places. My heart could not have deteriorated that much in a few months' time. The heart is a strong, over-designed pump, and it takes years for it to wear out. My moods explain the "chest pains" I had before. My mind affects my heartbeat partly, controls it, in fact. When I'm in a down mood or nervous, I sometimes have three little "blips," or skipped beats, but they are not important. They are fleeting, not angina. And, of course, since I was born with my skin inside out, I feel them as 100 times more powerful than they really are.

So, that is a crucial discovery. It opens the door. It says I may be on this earth a while longer, or at least that my heart is not giving out or giving in or giving up. The discovery should help me get back to a normal life of enjoying my life here in China. There isn't much time left to enjoy it—about three months, two months before David and Karen get here, anyway. I want to live my life here and live a good life of enjoyment, work, and of experiencing China. With Jan, of course. She does enjoy it so much. I want to be with her, here, for the rest of the term, and then we'll do something else, together. And again, and again....

Right now, I feel very good. I know I'll have setbacks, but my discovery today was crucial for me.

What is more important than breath? Just simple, plain, everyday breathing? Today, sunlight, blue, blue sky, all over the world.

I feel gloriously good. Took the day off running, tomorrow will get back to it again. Into my routine.

I did get some sleeping pills, trying to avoid the Xanax; but I may not need to take them if I feel really good tonight. My losing sleep, of course, was directly related to my worrying about my heart.

March 31

Dave

I wrote a letter to the Sioux City doctor today, asking him for an overall assessment of my condition. I wish I'd asked him more questions when I was in his office in January, but I was too nervous and we had to get up to Brookings. In the letter I asked him if he thinks I should go on with my exercise, and how I compare with men my age, at this time, given the tests I had in Wisconsin. It'll take at least a month to hear from him, I suppose.

March 31

Jan

With a sleeping pill, Dave slept better than he has for some time. This morning he went to the campus clinic to get a massage, but came back hurting. He said it was painful.

...I found out that the mother of one of the desk clerks committed suicide in the U.S. last year just before she was due to come back to China. Her mother was in the States on an exchange program and apparently had many problems. She was not well liked and was constantly harassing the administration to accept her daughter into the university where she was teaching. Her daughter did not have high enough scores to qualify for the tuition waiver, and not even high enough scores to be admitted. It was tragic.

...Dave didn't feel well this afternoon and evening. He was extremely tired. He had jogged and lifted weights earlier in the day. As I looked at him this evening, during a video he was watching with his graduate students, I thought he looked thin and pale. I'm worried about him. Will he make it another three months?

APRIL

April 1

Jan

Chen Loo called me at 7:30 a.m. and said she had to go back to Britain in five days, and then asked if I would take over the drama direction and production for her. I told her, seriously, that I had never done anything like that and didn't feel that I could do it. (I thought it was audacious of her to ask such a big favor in such a matter-of-fact way.) She let me try to get out of it gracefully, and then said, "April Fool's." She had me.

...In my class this morning, the first thing I told the students was that we would have an exam during the first hour and debates the second hour. They all began to squirm and protest, saying that I hadn't told them about an exam. I said I was sure I had told them about it last week. I let them worry for a while and then said, "April Fool's." They burst into laughter. I don't think April Fool's Day is a Chinese tradition.

I tried to fool Dave in the way I've fooled him in the past ten or more years—telling him he had a hole in his pants. It has always worked, but not this time. We had talked about it being April Fool's Day already, so he was prepared this time. I was still disappointed that he didn't fall for it one more time. I'm sure it will work next year.

...Dave took another sleeping pill last night and slept fairly well. The pills don't sedate him as he thought they would. I don't know what they are, since he got them from the campus doctor. They probably are not as strong as western sleeping pills.

...I've started doing some exercises with Eva and some young Chinese girls. We use two bats with nubbed rubber balls on the ends. We do low-impact aerobics exercises and hit ourselves with the rubber balls on the acupuncture pressure points on our bodies. The Chinese girls look so graceful when they do this, but those of us learning are not graceful. We hope to improve. It's not as difficult to learn as Tai Chi.

...Dave looks sickly and has begun taking aspirin and Tums for his pains. What he is dealing with is a psychological problem—one for which

239

he needs counseling. And there aren't any counselors around here. The head of each work unit in China is responsible for his or her workers' mental and physical health. I don't think our leader could help Dave. From what I've read, the sort of pain Dave has can, and often does, occur when people have anxiety about their health. The next three months could be very long and difficult if he doesn't stop worrying about his heart.

April 2

Jan

We can now tell who is calling on the phone or knocking on our door. A Chinese person will always let the phone ring many times before hanging up—sometimes more than ten times; a foreigner will usually let it ring only three or four times and then hang up. A Chinese person will knock very lightly on the door, sometimes so lightly the sound is difficult to hear. Foreigners will almost always knock loudly. Several foreigners have signs on their doors for Chinese guests that say: "Please knock loudly."

April 3

Dave

Up and down, up and down. Got very tired the other day. <u>Very</u> tired. Had to be nerves. Today I feel a little better. I'm sleeping about six hours total each night, which is down from my regular eight or so. I do what I can do. I had some pains, but I think they're gastric, related to an ulcer. Exactly like the ulcer pains I had about 30 years ago. I'm not having caffeine or beer, so that will help. I'm eliminating my pains, slowly but surely. What I had after sex yesterday was a tingling in my chest, right side, fairly high. Having sex, they say, is the equivalent of walking up a couple of flights of stairs. Yesterday afternoon I walked up six flights of stairs and I felt nothing. I know that the tingling is nerves or gas, which is constantly rising in my chest. Had a slight panic attack yesterday; did some walking, which helped. Something grips my chest sometimes, and I just have to ride it out. Keeping busy helps.

I need a mood change. It's not that I need euphoria; I just need to feel fairly normal. Seems like there's always a payoff if I get too high/euphoric. I'm learning a great deal about myself these days—about my health, both mental and physical. Mental health is probably just as important, if not more.

...Today we're going on a little one-day trip to the new campus and a park. I don't want to go, but...I know Jan does. It'll be good for me to get out and talk to people. I need to be more sociable.

...I had a great class in British Council literature last week. I never feel great going into that class, but usually manage to do a good job of teaching.

April 3

Dave

Dear Jim,

Thanks for writing. I appreciate your sending the prose works by Meissner, too, though I'd seen the one about Kirby Pucket's legs. And the Wells visual on baseball actually brought tears to my eyes. I don't know what I miss more: baseball or America. I've been thinking about opening day, and hate the idea of not being there when it happens. I hope we can get up to another Twins game this season. It sounds like the Twins could be real contenders again. I didn't know that Winfield signed with them. Where will he play? Maybe a DH? First base is taken up, I assume, by another guy who grew up in the Twin Cities area—yes?

So you saw the red-winged blackbirds! That's always a good sign, I'd say. They remind me too of the sound of baseballs slapping into mitts, the crack of them off bats...

China is fine, but I'll be ready to come home. The crowds are starting to get on my nerves. And yet, we're still learning, in many ways still having a good time here. We'll have our son and his wife here near the end of May into June. That will be great, taking them around and all.

Well, I'll sign out for now. The weather turned warm here, almost 75 degrees or so the other day. Living here in July and August is almost unbearable, they say. Last September was bad enough. You just can't imagine how hot it gets.

So, keep in touch. Tell Dacey hello for me, too. The best to your family.

As Ever,

Dave

April 3

Jan

The Waiban took several of us foreign teachers and some Chinese teachers to the new campus that is under construction in a place called Puco. It will be very nice when it is finished (in about 10 years). As we were looking at the scale model for the new site, Brian asked: "Where is the coal heap?" We have huge, unsightly coal heaps out in front of our apartment next to the campus restaurant. Some of us foreigners found the remark humorous, but the Chinese didn't catch the sarcasm.

We also visited a petroleum factory and a place called "Pearl Spring," a scenic area. We threw coins into the water and clapped our hands to make the bubbles (pearls) come up from the bottom of the spring. If your coin stays afloat, it means good luck. My first coin sank immediately; but my second one stayed afloat, so I felt relieved. Pearl Spring is an area much like a camping site in the U.S. (without litter regulations). You can even rent a tent for camping. There was a hedge maze close to the Pearl Spring that we had fun finding our way through. Qian was animated as she led us through the maze. Dave sat in the van, depressed.

April 5

Dave

Decent day yesterday, good evening, and then I woke up with pains again—nerves, I think, since I don't want to go to Hangzhou. Jan does. I don't want to go to Kunming either. But yet, I know it's good to get out and just go.

...Sleeping is so valuable to me, and I'm not getting enough of it. I hate being tired all the time. Though the other night I did sleep almost seven hours, a real breakthrough for me since I've been here this semester. I simply turned the clock over so I couldn't read it, and went to bed, and slept, getting up only once for the bathroom. Sleep, gentle sleep. Oh, how much I need my sleep. I never have had problems with sleep.

...When I get back to the U.S. I may need to take a tranquilizer daily. Need something to calm my anxiety. I wake up breathing fast sometimes and anxious.

...I have only about eleven weeks to go in China. I'm near the top of the hill...

...Jan calms me as much as she can. I hate dragging on her, but she does understand me. I need to be stronger for her as well as for myself.

...Yesterday I revised another story and like it pretty well. I've revised two stories this semester so far. Not bad, given my nerves these days. I need to find out how to switch out of my Diablo and into my calm Dave personality. They are always at war. Diablo has the upper hand lately, but Dave is learning some new strategies. He'll eventually win the war, and Diablo will go down forever.

Much of it, Dave knows, is about trusting his heart, trusting the technology that says his heart is stronger, much stronger, than most 53-year-old hearts. Dave wants so much to believe it, and he's moving toward total belief, slowly, if even inch by inch, daily. He has some setbacks, but he's coming on, coming on. He's capable of taking control of the matter. He's learning how to deal with Diablo. He'll have him beaten soon, soon. It's just a matter of time.

...Soon it'll be May, the month that son David and his wife Karen come to China. By then, I'll be much improved because Dave will be in charge. Dave is smart, and he's tenacious and ambitious.

April 6

Jan

About twenty or more students came over for my office hours. I showed them the movie Grease, which I hadn't seen for 20 years. I actually enjoyed watching it with them, since it brought back memories

Students watching television in our apartment

of my high school days. They liked it a lot, but all agreed it wasn't anything similar to their high school days.

April 6

Dave

Fighting depression. Worried about leaving my home base here in Nanjing and traveling to Hangzhou for a few days. I must stop worrying about such things. I get very depressed. Took a Xanax last night and did sleep, but was tired this morning, too. I can't seem to click in my good character, Dave. Diablo is in charge, mostly. Control, control, where is it? I'm not so worried about my physical health anymore. May have to rely on Xanax to get me through this week, to Hangzhou and back. I hope not. We're going with Deb and Tom, as we did last semester to Shanghai and had a great time. Why can't I have a great time this semester? I will try. "Roll your apple cart right on," the saying goes. Keep on your feet and going.

...I think it's China that's got me down. The crowds and noise, the disorder of it. I'm such a routine person; I need to have my routines, and China doesn't allow that.

I'll survive China. I'm stronger than I thought, really. Nobody can ever know, fully, another person's suffering or another person's joy. Human beings live mostly inside their minds, and in secret.

I suppose I can help myself by just behaving as if everything is okay, even if it isn't. Maybe the "normal" behavior will trigger the normal feelings. I'll give it a try; I <u>have</u> given it a try. I'll keep at it.

...Today, sun. That helps. Outside our apartment some young girls, workers in the restaurant, are playing a game with a sand bag, one of them trying to hit another one in a line, an the one who is hit becomes the thrower. They're so young and seem to be enjoying themselves so much. Oh, to be enjoying myself like that! To be able to forget myself and just have a good time. To forget myself, to look outward, to live in harmony with my associates, the people around here, everywhere I go. To get some balance between the inner and the outer. That is what I need.

April 7

Dave

David Jr.'s birthday. Wish we were there to celebrate it. But he'll be with us next month, and we'll celebrate both our birthdays, maybe on the Great Wall of China.

...I felt, yesterday afternoon and evening, the very best I've felt here this semester. Yesterday morning I was feeling sorry for myself again, really down. Then, in bed for a nap, I had a talk with Jan, and she said I need to be up and around and doing things, involving myself, and that I'm not sick, so why act like I'm sick? That helped turn me around.

I feel good except for a little upset stomach, probably anticipating the trip to Hangzhou this morning. It should be a good trip; back on Sunday. It's one of the cities we wanted to see and now we're about to see it.

They key is to stay busy, to not let Diablo, who is clever, get his words in. Cut him off before he gets started. Last night in bed, I couldn't believe how good I felt. The best I've felt in years, I think. And it wasn't because of any drugs: the Xanax (three-quarters of a pill) I had taken the night before; the effects had worn off, and they weren't good effects anyway. The pill brings bad dreams. I'm going to try to avoid that pill, have already, pretty much. Still have 36 of the 40 left, and I got them two months ago.

April 7

Jan

David Jr.'s birthday today. When he was born, his head was covered with thick, unruly blond hair. I thought about how the Chinese people are fascinated with blond, blue-eyed babies, just as most Americans are fascinated with black-haired, black-eyed Chinese babies. It's the sharp contrast we are curious about.

...Even though Dave was not feeling great, the two of us, along with Tom and Deb, left at 7:00 a.m. to catch a mini-bus to the train station to go to Hangzhou. Since we couldn't find a mini-bus, we had to get on a city bus and stand up all the way because the bus was so crowded—stressful for Dave.

We stopped in a city called Wuxi and had to change trains. We had about three hours to wait for the next train, so we walked around the city and bought some pottery, a silk hat, some shoes and some clogs. Wuxi is an interesting city with few tourists; a crowd gathered every time we stopped to look at something.

Deb and I decided we wanted to find some food to eat on the train, so, shortly before the train was to leave, we went looking for a food shop. It took longer than we thought, and we literally had to run to make it back to the train station on time, with only two minutes to spare. Dave was about to have an anxiety attack when we didn't get back. Missing a train in China is serious business, because there are usually no other seats available.

From the train we saw, in the countryside, many burial sites with wooden sticks protruding from them. These burial sites are hills of dirt with stone markers on top. "Hell money" is impaled on the sticks and burned; it's the belief that it will burn away evil spirits.

April 8

Jan

Dave got up almost every hour during the night with frequent and burning urination, so we didn't get much sleep. He has been stressed about being away from his home base in Nanjing. The drama continues.

We went to the Shangri-la Hotel and had a breakfast buffet. Dave and I decided to move there since it was so nice and Dave didn't feel well. It cost $125 per night.

This evening I went with Tom and Deb to a night market while Dave went to the room to rest and worry. We had fun buying pottery and various gifts. A young couple saw us and came to talk to us. They said they were students, when they saw that we were teachers (we had our Nanjing University badges on), and wanted to be our guides. We said we didn't need guides, that we were just looking. They continued to follow us everywhere. At one point, when I said I liked the girl's necklace, she took it off and handed it to me. I told her I couldn't take it and, when she refused to take it back, I put it down on a table. She picked it up and said they just wanted to be our friends. They continued to follow us around for about an hour until we were ready to leave. At that point, the young man asked us if we could help him out with U.S. dollars or F.E.C. money. We finally found out their motive. We suspected there would be one—an ulterior one.

April 9

Jan

We slept late, relaxed, enjoyed the huge king-size bed, watched CNN (a real treat) and went for a walk. It was a pleasant morning. The plum blossoms were in bloom, as well as some roses. Dave was fairly normal.

We met Deb and Tom at noon and checked into the cheaper Overseas Chinese Hotel for our last two nights. We didn't want to pay $125 per night for two more nights at the Shangri-la, even though we liked it. Our new view of the lake was good, but we were right on a busy, noisy street, with horns continuously blaring and people frantically trying to get somewhere.

After eating lunch on the 18th floor of the Friendship Hotel, with its beautiful view of the city, we took a cab to a Zen Buddhist temple, an intriguing place with ornate rock carvings and huge golden Buddhist statues. We went to the famous ("famerse," as the Chinese say) Dragon Well. It was a dud, just a hole in the ground surrounded by stones. Nothing like what we had expected from the advertisements. Since this area is the site of the famous dragon well tea, there was a lot of tea for sale. The little tea stands were surrounded by tea fields. A nice touch. There were many hawkers around.

April 10

Jan

Dave had a miserable night. He is falling apart with worry, pain, stress. He is talking about going back to the U.S. early. He doesn't seem to be able to cope. We haven't told Deb and Tom about Dave's health worry and depression.

Dave went to the room to rest and Deb and I went shopping all afternoon. Tom rested and walked around town. I bought Dave a snake-skin sword and a musical Mao cigarette lighter for his birthday. It plays a tune called "Dong Fang Hone" ("East is Red"), popular during the Long March.

April 11

Jan

Today is Dave's birthday, a milestone for him. He now has made it past the age of 53—the age his father was when he died. I think this has been weighing on him: he's had it in his mind that he could not out-live his father.

April 11

Jan

Dear David, Kari, Shelly,

First of all, David, Happy Birthday late! We thought about you a lot on the 7th. How did you celebrate? Today is your dad's birthday and we have just returned from a trip to Hangzhou, a beautiful city with a wonderful lake and beautiful parks—one of the best places we've been to in China.

We went with Tom and Deb, teachers at Nanjing University. When we got on the train, it was a struggle to find our seats, since they were already occupied. We got the people to move out of our seats by showing them our tickets. These people had no seat tickets, so they had to stand in the aisles. There were no extra overhead spaces for our luggage, so we had to hold some of it and stuff what we could under our legs. One lady yelled at your dad as he tried to put a bag near, or on top of, hers. People were chain smoking, and the people sitting across from us began eating a foul-smelling instant fish and noodle dish. People hovered around us. One old lady was sitting in the aisle holding a young boy. Later, she stood up and braced herself against your dad's back. People without seats were thinking that since we were foreigners, we would possibly move to the "soft sleeper" or "soft seat" section (which we were intending to do) and that they could then get our seats. Tom was back in another car negotiating with money for better seats. Your dad turned his walkman on to try to distract himself and stay calm. I could tell that the situation was difficult for him ,and I worried about his state of mind in this crowded, noisy, dirty train. Deb and I were smashed together. I managed to drop my glasses on the floor between my legs; and with the luggage there and the limited space, I couldn't get to them. Deb was able to struggle and retrieve them, while the people across from us were trying to push our luggage away from their legs.

Finally, Tom came back with soft sleeper (more comfortable) tickets in hand and we began to try to move. As we tried to get up, people were crowding desperately right in under us to get our seats. The old lady holding the boy sat right on top of Deb and had her hand on Deb's thigh. Deb had to push her away to get up. At that point I stood up and was squeezed in the middle of the two seats and wasn't able to move. Finally, with help from Deb, I got out and we made our way down the crowded aisle to the soft sleeper section, feeling greatly relieved. On his way down the dining-car aisle, your dad knocked some styrofoam food containers, filled with food, off the table. People had their legs sticking out in the aisles, making it difficult to get by. And other people were standing and sitting in the aisles, making it almost impossible to move. I don't know if we could have remained sane, especially your dad, during a nine-hour ride in the hard-seat section.

We rode fairly comfortably with two other gentlemen in our room. Your dad got up on the top bunk with the luggage for a while and rested. The older man with us said he had been a former guard for Chiang Kai-shek. He was also a fortune teller/palm reader. The old man had written books on palm reading. The younger man said he never did anything without first consulting his friend. (Your dad definitely did not want his palm read; he was too paranoid about what he might find.) Both men were from Taiwan and were in mainland China to do some kind of business. Only the younger man spoke English. It would have been intriguing to hear what the older man had to say about Chiang Kai-shek and the seven or eight years he spent with him.

We got home to find that Qian, our friend, had cooked your dad a birthday dinner of friend noodles (symbolic of long life—a typical birthday dish), chicken with green pepper, shrimp and water chestnuts, soybean noodles, cucumbers, tomatoes and peanuts. She gave your dad a book of Chinese poetry and an Easter lily. The Waiban had a cake for him in the office, but they didn't bring it over. It is their custom to bring cakes for all the foreigners' birthdays. We assume that if the birthday person is not around, the Waiban keeps the cake and eats it.

Anyway, the trip to Hangzhou was mostly fun, except for the train experience. And even that, after the fact, was captivating. Stay in touch. Love,

Mom (ticket holder)

April 12

Dave

In Hangzhou the last four days. Had a fairly good time, but I was uptight leaving my home base, and Hangzhou is extremely noisy and busy. I didn't sleep well, couldn't take in the sights that Jan wanted to take in.

That was not good. I have to get better and stop worrying about my health. David P. said that if my doctors had felt any concern about my condition, they would not have favored my returning to China.

...It's time to think about other things than my heart, dammit. Like my writing, like my teaching, like going to Kunming, which, hell, we might as well do for a week at the end of the month.

...Saw a beautiful Zen Buddhist temple in Hangzhou, the largest temple I've ever seen. But I find the Buddha faces mostly unpleasant to look at. The moods they display are not necessarily pleasant; it seems to me they're the opposite, sometimes downright menacing.

Later, same day:

...I was depressed, so I decided to move around, to ride my bike down to the Central Hotel for a paper, to get into the black-headed, flowing traffic of bikes. On the way home I felt a little better—my moods these days are not so extreme: I find, today, I can even cope with a little half-hour of depression—I stop by a bike repairman in a lane nearby. I motion that I want my seat lowered. The man's hands are black from handling bike parts all day. He has slippers on. But I'm thinking, looking down at him as he sits working on a little apron by the side of a busy, narrow lane: he is not depressed. He is merely focused on doing his job, making a living. I look around me; people in cars, on bikes, in trucks, all of them, if I look at their faces, seem, if not happy, not unhappy; seem not concerned about their health the way I am at this moment concerned about my health. Now, looking down at the bike man, I begin to lose my interest in my health, and begin to focus with him, to be patient with him, as he takes off my bike seat, which is broken, turns it over and lays it on the ground, begins to take a piece of flat steel out of it, and then, because it's broken, begins to fashion another piece the same size, hammer it on a small piece of iron, crease it and bend it back and forth until a crack appears, and then gives way, and the piece divides in half; pokes a hole in it and starts to put it back into the seat's innards.

The bike seat, lying there on the cement—looks like the underside of a hog or steer face in a packing house. I saw thousands of them when I worked in a packing house. This upside-down skull's jowls are showing through. It depresses me momentarily. But I know it is <u>not</u> a skull but only a bike seat. And then, once more I begin to take an interest in the man's work. I watch him as he fails again and again to get the metal piece's nut in place, using a long, needle-like piece of steel—again and again he fails, but keeps at it. At one point I want to try to tell him to give up, to let me have my bike, to put the broken seat back on and let me go home with my sack of bananas and oranges. But I watch. I keep watching him, I merge my mind with his, my eyes with his, my hands with his, until we succeed, by God, until the nut is in place, screwed in, the seat positioned back on the bike, tightened, and just right, just right. I take out my money and give him five yuan and he starts to make change. I say "No, okay," and show him two thumbs up and say "good, good," and he smiles, puts two thumbs up, puts the one yuan back in his little metal box, and I ride off. I go home with a better seat and a little better mind. For the moment, but moments become hours, and hours become days, and...

If I wrote a poem about this it might so something like:

> The old bike repairman with awkward fingers
> takes off my bike seat and lays it
> on the cement upside down.
> Why does the seat look nothing like a seat
> but like an animal's head in a packing house?
> Meatless jaw, tendons of steel, the exposed
> underside of a braincase.
> Where are the eyes that stare,
> the teeth, done crunching,
> the brain, done thinking about food.

April 12

Jan

Back to classes, back to students. The commercials I had my students prepare didn't take as long to present as I had thought they would, so I had time to spare, time to fill with something "meaningful." We played some word games, but I was tired and felt like I was coming down with another cold.

...Dave went to visit David P. and felt better after talking to him, as he always does. Poor David P. is not trained to do counseling, but he's doing it.

...While a few students were here this afternoon, they talked about the plays they were working on for Chen. They said she is very strict, and they feel somewhat intimidated by her. She tells them they must have good manners and act like "proper young ladies and gentlemen." I told them that Chen will make them work hard, as well as teach them something. She has had experience directing plays before in England, and I think knows what she is doing. It's good for them to get to know all kinds of foreigners.

April 13

Jan

Dave was not able to sleep last night, so he was particularly stressed today. I constantly worry about whether we should stay here or go back to the States, since he is having so much stress. It's difficult seeing him this way.

...My students and I watched <u>The Accidental Tourist</u> during my office hours tonight. It lasted until 9:30, and they felt guilty about staying past my scheduled office hours. I offered them tea or coffee, as I usually do, but none of them would accept the offer. They did eat some cookies that I handed to them directly. Chinese students typically will not accept an offer of food or drink. You must insist. Sometimes I insist, and sometimes I don't. It becomes tiring to do so. In the classroom, if I direct a question to the students in general, nobody will offer an answer. If I call on someone individually, he or she will respond; or if I appoint someone to be first to present a speech or a report, he or she will do so without hesitation.

April 13

Dave

I've lost my center point. Today, jogging, I lost my breath momentarily. A cardiologist in Wisconsin told me that it's only a sensation you get when your heart is palpitating—not a serious problem. That's probably what it was, but it bothered me. Then I ran when I was stressed out anyway, which is not good either. Then I had a tingling in my shoulder, which I still have, and have had in my upper chest sometimes after exertion, like sex—when I'm under stress. David P. says it's all stress-related, that if it were serious it would happen every time, and it doesn't; only when I'm stressed. When I feel good I can run and run and climb and climb steps and there's no feeling at all. It's a matter of mood.

Today I decided I might as well go ahead and use the Xanax I brought with me. I've only used six tablets in about two and a half months. "If you need them," Jan says, "take them." I suppose she's right. I can't function this way, always off balance, always half depressed or altogether depressed.

David P. says when I get back to the States I should probably seek some mental health advice, and he's right. I had already thought of it. I don't know how much of my agitation is because of my "heart incident" or because of just living in this crazy, loud country called China. It's both, a combination. I'm ready for some peace and solitude. I need to be in a quiet place, or at least close to one I can get to when I need to.

My work has fallen off. I need to write, but all I've done is some revising. I've been de-railed. And yet, I think I can get back. I know in my mind I don't have anything seriously wrong with me physically.

I hate the thought of having to feel good artificially, but if that's what it takes, I'll have to do it. When I get back to the States maybe I can get some better, daily medication to settle my nerves.

I want so much to feel good when David and Karen come here.

April 14

Jan

In my writing class today we discussed an essay by Martin Luther King, Jr. on non-violence. Most of the male students disagree with this philosophy of non-violence; most of the female students agree with it. It was an interesting discussion in the context of Communist China.

...Dave went jogging again today and is doing better. He was able to sleep last night.

April 14

Dave

Better today. I slept last night, slept well. It's necessary to get myself tired during the day: jogging, walking, working, always moving. Depression comes, but depression, like everything else, dies. The depression I've suffered lately seems not as intense and not as long-lasting as it did before. And the good feelings I have are not euphoria. They are just more like normal feelings. Hell, I don't want to feel great, I just want to feel normal. When I feel great, then the opposite feelings seem to barge in on me soon after to let me know that the dragon is still loose and in charge. Maybe I should, instead of fighting the dragon, instead of fearing it all the time, wink at it, praise it, welcome it. After all, it does show me that life is a matter of contrast. Without lows and highs, without the gnawing feeling of insecurity once in a while, life would have no real value. The value of life is that it is short, it does have an end to it. Life's essence and joy is in its brevity. William Blake knew this:

> He who binds himself to a joy
> does the winged life destroy;
> but he who kisses the joy as it flies
> lives in eternity's sunrise.

...Sunrise. Yes, the sun is out this morning. And I want to enjoy it. And I also started a short story yesterday.

April 15

Jan

Dave's students came by to watch The Accidental Tourist this evening, and I made popcorn for them. Chinese people like sugar on popcorn. In fact, all of the popcorn we've bought on the street in China has sugar on it. Ugh.

...A former student of mine from last semester brought me some snow tea. It's a white tea from the southwest part of China. He tells me

256

it's good for your health. We'll give it a try. According to Chinese people, all teas are known for some kind of medicinal value. Maybe it will help Dave.

April 15

Dave

The very night after my most extended period of feeling good (an evening and a full day after), I couldn't sleep. I had done plenty of physical stuff that day—jogging, walking, etc. But I couldn't sleep. The next day I was very tired; bad day overall. Last night I slept fairly well, and even "slept in" this morning after Jan got up—something I haven't been able to do since I got back this semester. My mind works on me when I'm unaware. And beats up on me when I least expect a beating. I must be vigilant always. I must find ways of tricking my mind into thinking I'm okay. I do think I'm okay, I am okay, dammit. I believe that I was better able to handle China last semester because I drank three or four beers every night. This relaxed me; I slept better. China had gotten to me even last semester, I know now, in retrospect. And I dealt with it partly by drinking plenty of beer.

I'm now on the downhill side of my stay in China. This should relax me somewhat; it does, just thinking about it. I need the calm and peace and quietness and population sparsity of South Dakota and Iowa, of a good lake, say, the frog pond near Moville. Never again will I live for an extended time in a crowded foreign city. It's not for me; I'm too sensitive.

I took a Xanax yesterday and all it did was increase my fatigue. And then I had another weird dream this morning, that Jan and I had brought back to China with us a "baby," which was a little face on a watch dangling on a chain. If you put a gold coin close to its face, the hands would spin around in excitement—the "baby" loved it. We were showing at around to friends and other jock friends of mine from school; it looked like a locker-room situation. To hell with Xanax, so far. If I have to resort to it I will, but it doesn't make me feel any better, so far.

April 16

Jan

When we were at the market today buying beans, a peasant lady tried to overcharge us. We knew it was too high, and Dave told her "tai guila" (too expensive). A crowd gathered as we were arguing. Finally, Dave gave her all the money she asked for (pushed it into her hands) and then we walked away refusing to take the beans. We had only gone a short distance, when she came up behind us and gave us the money back. She had to "save face."

April 17

Jan

We woke up to find a sack with two wonderful chocolate brownies hanging on our doorknob. Kate had made them for us.

...Eva and I caught the mini-bus to go to the bird and flower market to buy a plant. I was to be home by 1:00 p.m. for an appointment with a young girl, but the bus we took went a different way from what we thought it would go, and from what they told us (what we <u>thought</u> they told us) it would go. That made me late. Dave told the girl to come back later, but she didn't show up. Communication is difficult.

...Dave had yet another restless night and day. He is having stomach pains, possibly an ulcer, he says. We talked about whether we should go back to the States because of his continual stress, but we agreed that it would be too complicated to arrange. We'll stay and try to cope.

...This evening, Deb was showing us some of the Mao memorabilia she and Tom have collected over the years. Just then, someone knocked on the door. Deb quickly gathered the items into her bag to hide them. I can't imagine there being a concern about a collection of this kind. Maybe I'm naive. Maybe I need to be more cautious when I'm buying a Mao lapel pin or a Mao book on the street....

April 18

Dave

Yesterday was not at all good, and I had to resort to Xanax. I didn't run either, didn't sleep much the night before. Seems like it's every other night for a good/decent sleep. I have to break that habit somehow. I think I'll break it with exercise. Now, I know that the pain under my rib cage is an acidic stomach and not something serious; I can relax better when I run. Today I intend to run and air it out. Confidence is a major problem, I see now. Confidence for me has always been mostly a matter of physical exercise, and when I can't keep up that level of exercise, I hurt mentally and emotionally. I <u>must</u> get back up to my running level, get my heart beat up to 60-70 percent of the maximum as I run. No sense in fearing; it has to be done.

...Today the sun is out, it's already 70 degrees at 8:00 a.m. I feel better. Today will be a good day, or else.

Midnight:

Can't sleep. It's my every-other-bad-day, it seems. I dozed on a chair, reading, and about 9:30 Jan said, "go to bed if you're tired." I was. But not when I got into bed. What is it, this inability to sleep? The one thing I've always been able to do—sleep. Sleep any where, any time. Such a wonderful talent it is. To just pass out and sleep for an hour or two in the daytime, and then, always, at night, past, say 9:30, to go to bed and not wake up until 7:00 a.m., unless to pee. Always, this talent intact. And now, not any more. That is very depressing in itself. I am anxious about going to Kunming, of course; I don't want to spend a week there and do the rounds with all the people we know. The lectures, the sight-seeing. I am just not up to it at this point. Jan is. She's so game to go, to see, to socialize. It's hard keeping up, but I am not normal these days. I'm still not on top of my problem. I really have no significant problem, and yet I'm in a constant, general panic. Such a frail person, such a panicky person. I asked Jan: did you know I had this side of me? She said something like she did now. She <u>did</u> know.

I'm typing these words tired, yet wide awake, unable to sleep. I would like to simply sit here and type until I fall asleep at the computer. But I can't even do that. I'm too tired to work on anything, to write, and I'm too tired to sleep. I'm caught—trapped—between sleep and waking, between work and non-work. It is a bad feeling, all the way around, not to be able to sleep and to dream pleasant, normal dreams. Even my dreams are off-center, out of sync. A face of a baby as a watch dangling on a chain, for instance. Not even Franz Kafka could have dreamed that one.

I'm hurting as I write. Gas has risen in my chest on both sides, and my breathing is affected. I don't want to take Xanax again, two days in a row. I wrote my doctor today and asked for 25 more pills; I hope he'll send them to me. If I have to resort to them on a more or less daily basis, then the 25 will just about do me until I leave this crazy prison of a country. I'm anxious also about having David and Karen here. I want to feel good, and to show them around. I must learn to straighten up—to think positively, somehow.

I'll be seeing David P. in the morning. And I want to keep jogging, which I did today for about 27 minutes and felt decent when I got home—for a couple of hours at least, and yet, uneasy, too. As if the wolf was just waiting, out there behind a tree, waiting for me to weaken so he could once again come down his well-worn trail to my house and have to be let in, again, again. I want to blow his head off with a shotgun, but I don't have any gun to do it with. I wish I could do that, and then go on with my life.

I'm tired. Tired. Too tired to sleep, or is it too <u>un</u>tired to sleep? Both at the same time.

Okay. I'm going back to bed. I'll take up a book again, lie there until my eyes go shut, and try that technique for sleeping.

April 18

Jan

It was a beautiful, sunny, warm day; Dave and I walked to the bookstore and shopped at various street stands. Dave jogged and seemed to feel good after that. We watched a video.

April 19

Dave

This morning I went to see David P., described my depression, and he gave me a supply of Zoloft, which is similar to Prozac but has fewer side effects, he says. Headaches and nausea in much less than two percent of those who use it. He says it restores two chemicals in the brain, one of them serotonin.

I'll need to take it (half a pill) for about six to eight weeks and that should get the chemicals back up to normal. No booze at all during that time, which won't be easy. But I'll trade good feelings for booze any day. This depression is intolerable, and it has to stop. He said go ahead and go to Kunming. I intend to, and I intend to get well. Otherwise, I might as well go home, even if there isn't a house to go back to, or an income, at this point.

I feel better right now because of all this. I know that my depression is only temporary, that I will eventually be normal again. Many people have to have treatment for this problem; I'm not the first. I'll eventually get control of my emotions, my life, the way I had control before. I'll make it. I'm looking forward so much to having David and Karen here.

April 19

Jan

Dave seems to sleep fairly well only every other night. I think China is closing in on him. We talked to a foreigner in Hangzhour who said that China has a way of doing that. Dave feels trapped, depressed. He had an appointment with David P. this morning and got a new kind of pill for depression—Zoloft. David P. said it should help him. I hope so, because we both need some relief.

...Along with Mike and Lida, we had dinner at Cao's apartment this evening. She lives in a crowded, three-room flat with her 85-year-old mother, her college-age daughter and her husband. Cao's husband recently spent two months in the hospital, was released and then had to go back in a few days. He is suffering from asthma, she says, caused from allergies. She looks like she has lost weight, probably from worrying about him and from the extra work of preparing his meals and taking care of his needs while he is in the hospital. She reminds us of a good friend we had in Kunming back in 1988-89.

April 20

Dave

It's difficult. I took my first anti-depressant pill this morning. I need to hang on to see how it affects me. Very tired this morning, weak. I need to cut back on liquid because I get up about five or six times a night, which keeps me awake. If I can hold on today without Xanax, that will help. And if I can do some jogging, though the weather is getting so hot now that I should probably do my jogging in the mornings. Saw David P. jogging this morning; good idea to do it in cool weather.

...I don't want to go to Kunming. Dilemma. Jan wants to, I know, very badly. So she'll be disappointed. But I'm not up to it physically or mentally right now, though the pills may help by then.....Stay in there, Dave. Fight it. Fight it. Lay up and survive. Keep your center point.

April 21

Jan

One of my students wrote a paper about school dances. She called boys who go to dances "male love hunters," not a bad metaphor for young males. Another wrote a paper about how one has to buy gifts to get special favors and build up quanxi. It is expected and practiced widely. Her sister failed a senior high school entrance exam, and her father had to buy expensive gifts to gain her entrance. People are "used" quite readily for personal gain.

...The cook still has not had her glasses repaired. She has them taped together in the middle with white tape. I'd like to offer to pay to have them fixed, but know I can't do it. It would be improper.

...We had what was called a "press conference" in the Waiban conference room this afternoon. All of us foreigners were requested to attend. We were given various statistics about the university and its future plans. Then there was opportunity for questions and complaints.

Some in our group asked about future faculty housing. The apartments we are now living in are scheduled to be remodeled, and at that time faculty will be moved to the nearby university hotel. The hotel rooms are small and there are no cooking facilities, which would be unacceptable to most foreigners. The complaints then began about how unattractive the surroundings are and how much noise there is around the faculty apartment building. As Suzanna, a German teacher, was about to ask a question, the lights and camera were directed at her. She held up her hands and told them not to film here. She said, "This is not a zoo." I thought some of the complaints were unnecessary. After all, we chose to come to China— not to live in luxury, but to experience life in a foreign country, to live like the local people do, to learn to survive. This is part of the attraction for many of us. That is not to say that we don't want a certain standard of comfort. When I think of how the rest of the Chinese people live here, I know that we are living in luxury. But many foreigners would not come here if they knew what they had to put up with concerning noise and living conditions. I'm sure many of the Chinese think we are pampered.

April 22

Jan

Dave felt so terrible this morning that he had to dismiss one of his classes early. He has lost weight and generally does not look well. I think he would be better off in the U.S., but our leaving would mean that our students would be without American instructors for the remainder of the semester, and it would probably be next to impossible to get our tickets changed to go back early. We also have one more check from the Fulbright program due in May, and a friend and our son and his wife are coming to visit us in May. Someone is living in our house in the U.S. until the end of June. Just too much to consider and deal with. We'll have to stay and try to cope. It's not easy for me because I worry about Dave, but I know he is the one who is suffering the most. My emotions range from fear to anger to frustration with him. And I feel selfish because I don't want to go home.

...We talked about superstitions in class today. The Chinese superstitions mentioned are different than we know, but make about as much sense:

Do not stand your chopsticks straight up in a bowl of rice—it's bad luck and you won't live long.

If your left eye twitches, you will have good luck; if your right eye twitches, you will have bad luck.

The head of a cooked duck or fish should always face the oldest person at a table during a meal.

Burning hell money (a kind of bogus paper money) at a burial site will send this money to the heavens to be used by one's deceased relatives.

Never sweep your floor on the first day of the annual Spring Festival—it will bring you bad luck.

A crow is a sign of bad luck, just as the black cat is in the U.S.

Don't ever give someone a clock as a gift—it means they will die soon.

Don't give an umbrella for a gift.

Never cut a pear in half to eat it.

The students were animated as they remembered these superstitions, and they laughed when I told them about the superstitions that I knew.

...I finished the individual conferences with my writing students. One subject that came up often was their interest in finding a boyfriend or girlfriends. Their concerns are much like the concerns of junior high school students in the U.S. Since they are not allowed to have a friend of the opposite sex during high school, this kind of a relationship is all new and mysterious to them when they get to college. I thought about how Dave and I began "going steady" when I was 14 and he was 15, and married when we were 17 and 18.

April 23

Jan

As we walked across campus, I noticed how beautiful the roses, poppies and plum blossoms were. The campus looks festive, with huge balloons in the sky and banners posted all around for Sports Days. Sports Days are similar to track meets in the U.S. Students, as well as faculty, compete in various sporting events. Classes are canceled for two days. The atmosphere is cheerful.

...This wasn't a good day for Dave. In fact, it was the most difficult day he's had so far. These past two months have been hell for him. He's not able to concentrate on anything. We didn't join the other foreigners for the Friday night dinner at the Sprite. Mike had invited us to his apartment to watch Apocalypse Now, but we didn't go. Probably not an up-lifting kind of film right now. It makes me feel somewhat isolated when we don't take part in these activities.

We played UNO and Scrabble for a while this evening. Dave played, but I knew he was having trouble concentrating. It wasn't much fun.

April 24

Jan

Letter not sent

Dear......

HELP! Dave is falling apart. He's anxious, depressed, unable to sleep, dependent—a total mess. He went to see his "physician's assistant/psychiatrist" the first thing this morning after spending a miserable night. He was up at least every two hours. He is in serious trouble and needs some kind of help. Maybe the pills he got will begin working in a day or two. He was told they could take from a week to 10 days to be effective. Dave is talking seriously about going to Hong Kong for medical care. I try to help him the best way I know how, but I'm not always successful. He wants me near him at all times. Now, I know what the word dyadic means. He's full of despair and says he feels trapped. He can't sleep, which is something he has always been able to do at will. He continuously has some kind of pain. Maybe we should go home, but I think Dave's problem is one that he has to deal with and overcome while we're here. If he doesn't stay and deal with it, he'll feel worse when he gets home, knowing he gave up and did not finish his assignment. I wish I had the answer and could be more helpful. I'm frustrated and angry with him at times, and I also feel sorry for him. I'm trying. My optimism is waning, but I try not to convey that to Dave.

Yours,

Jan

April 25

Dave

Slightly better this morning, but not far from depression. Slept badly last night, worried again about my heart. Constant battle in my mind between "it's good" and "it's not so good." I need to simply say yes to the "good." Emphasize it, and close all else out. I have a good heart, by all the tests, and the fact that I was given no restrictions, that alone should allow me to affirm the good. Say _yes_ to life, Dave.

Sixth day on the depression pill. I feel slightly better; maybe it's taking hold, though it may be giving me some depression in the process. But it causes headaches and nausea. I need to stay up later to sleep better. Waking up tired is no good for me. I need to do some jogging today, get back in the rhythm.

April 25

Jan

The night was again long and arduous, but Dave seemed somewhat better for a while this morning. He is exhausted all the time from not sleeping. He has always needed at least eight hours of sleep a night. Being in China this second semester has changed Dave. He just can't cope with the noise and the crowds. Last semester, he could deal with them.

Even though all of this, we have maintained a good physical relationship. That is the one thing that keeps us going. David P. told Dave to concentrate on the things he likes to do, and certainly that is one of the things he likes to do. I call it his "sex therapy," and kid him about it. We need some levity. If we didn't have that, we would have to go home.

April 26

Dave

As I'm writing these words it's 3:00 a.m. and I've only slept about an hour since I went to bed at 10:00 p.m. Again, I'm preoccupied with my health. I can't reconcile with the so-called "defect" in my heart muscle. Sometimes I think my mind is a battlefield where two armies are trying to destroy each other, and there's no hope of a truce.

...Today I was uptight because I had to give a lecture with a Fulbright contingent from the U.S. I did it and did it fairly well, I think. I had run earlier in the day, and it was hot. My pulse got up to 80 when I got home and stayed there so I couldn't nap. I am always aware of my heartbeat; I can hear it and feel it, it seems. I would give all my possessions for the ability to sleep. The lowliest, poorest peasant in China is far superior to me in one way: he can sleep. I've seen them sleeping on the sidewalks, on cardboard; I've seen a beggar sleeping on ashes at the train station, in the hazy, cold darkness. These I envy more than I can describe.

...Sleep. What is more important than the basics: sex, food, sleep. The day is rounded out with sleep; the morning is renewed by it. Our daily lives are given meaning by the sleep that comes between night and morning. We're supposed to wake renewed, refreshed, ready to begin. Beginnings come out of sleep.

But now I have no beginnings. Is it China that's doing this to me? Is it my health worry? A combination of the two, plus other things? I don't know, but I've always been able to go to sleep, anywhere, anytime. Eight hours of sleep has always been my quota. A given, an assumption.

Now I lie in bed and stare at the dark, wide awake, at 3:00 a.m. Or 5:00 a.m. How do I solve this problem? I worry about David and Karen coming here and my not being able to sleep.

"Sleep that knits up the ravelled sleeve of care." This has always been one of my favorite lines from Shakespeare. Now I know what it means, having been robbed of sleep, I hope only temporarily. Nature's soft nurse. Balm of hurt minds. But not this hurt mind.

Sleep. When will it come? I try to read in the middle of the night, but

I don't enjoy what I read. That is not the time to read; it's the time to be sleeping, snoring, dreaming.

I feel like a recluse. All of China is sleeping, and here I am typing on a fucking computer in the middle of the night.

It does not make sense, what I have thought myself into lately. It does not make any sense at all.

When will the pills begin to take effect? Maybe they will help restore my confidence. I lack motivation. I'm going on automatic pilot. I want to go home, for sure. I believe that I have a better chance of solving my problems there, among people who speak my language, a place with medical facilities that can help me. I need to sleep.

I think I could probably sit here until dawn and just type, and not go to sleep. But I need to get back in bed and try. Trying to sleep is probably not a good idea either, because I try too hard.

Sleep, gentle sleep. Where are you? What must I do to allow you to come to Me?

Later same day:

David P. gave me some Halcion, sleeping pills, that I'll begin taking tonight. During the day I can teach my classes—I only have six weeks of classes left, actually, after this week.

It's hard to concentrate, to work on my writing, to do my classes, even. But I can go for some time on automatic pilot. I know the stuff I'm teaching, and I'm good in the classroom; that helps.

April 26

Jan

A minor victory! Dave slept from 10:00 p.m. to 3:00 a.m., which is something he has not been able to do lately. But from 3:00 a.m. to 7:00 a.m. was another story. The Fulbright people from Beijing were scheduled to come today, so Dave was worried about that. Early morning seems to be the worst time for him. He is suffering intensely. Another several days for these pills, and then maybe they will begin working.

April 27

Jan

Dave didn't sleep last night. He was anxious and deeply depressed. He was exhausted. We went together to see David P. this morning and got the first of our two Japanese encephalitis injections. We then talked to him for a while about Dave's condition. He tried to reassure Dave, as he has tried many times, that his heart is strong and that he should not worry about it. Depression is an overwhelming mood disorder, and is, David P. says, fairly common. Fortunately, there is now medication for it.

Dave has never had this kind of depression before. He had problems dealing with his father's death, but he was able to cope with it. This depression is the result of his worrying about his heart, and being back in China. Dave didn't want to come back for the second semester. He wants to go home; but if we did go home, he would feel defeated and guilty. We'll get through this, with the help of David P. and medication.

April 18

Dave

The rain this morning doesn't help me. But last night I slept because I took Halcion. Good to sleep, and yet maybe I'm too awake this morning. Maybe the sleep disturbances that accompany depression occur to sort of keep the victim knocked out, drowsy—maybe there's some mercy in that, I don't know. But I feel different. Agitated, nervous. A whole day ahead of me, and I'll be indoors most of it. I need to walk outside.

...My dreams are abnormal. Accusative, paranoid. In one dream, or sudden image that came to me as I dozed, David P. looked like a panther: sharp jaw, inset eyes. I like this man; he is helping me. Yet this image comes to me. It's scary. I don't need it, and yet there it is. I may as well acknowledge it, face it. There's a lot that I need to face these days, a lot that I would, under more normal circumstances, turn away from and forget, suppress.

Is there a slight, a very slight letup in the depression this morning, or is it my imagination? I know it will be gradual, getting better. It's a matter of having the two chemicals build up in my brain. I am anxious for it to come, which is not good either. I need to stay busy writing, reading, preparing for classes.

I could escape China and go home early, but that would be a mistake. I'd feel like a failure because I didn't stick it out. Here I am; I must make the best of it.

Later, same day:

One big difference between Jan and me: she always has something to do; I don't. I get bored easily. Before, I could sleep an hour or two after lunch, then eight hours at night. Now, I can't sleep much at all. So I have this extra time to fill up, and I don't feel like working. I suppose that's the depression again. There was a pace to my life before; now, I go from hour to hour.

It's raining out; I can't go for a walk, get the paper. Those little things I did even yesterday I can't do today.

The old Fear is still there whenever I'm in bed. One side of my mind wants to believe I'm okay, the other side says, "not so." and the <u>not so</u> is winning these days. This will turn around. The medicine will start working and I'll start getting better. Just this morning when I was in the bathroom, suddenly I got a glimpse of better feelings. I just felt better; it was momentary, but it was there. I felt it. And then it passed and the anxiety was back.

Jan says I should maybe take up cooking. But that doesn't interest me. I like to draw, and I do some drawing. Nothing interests me to a high degree. Again, this, David P. says, is what depression does. It saps one's motivation.

I wish I could get into a short story; I need to get at those. I have done some revising this semester, at least, and wrote two stories last semester. Writing short stories does interest me, and I enjoy reading them. But right now I don't have much desire for either.

I will have to endure this. I know that millions of people endure exactly what I'm going through. And many don't have the money for medicine. When I get better and begin to live a more normal life again, I will have a different view of depression, and of illness in general. Never again will I take my good health for granted. Never again.

270

Dave's drawing of his heart

Same night, around midnight:

Can't sleep. Suddenly, an image of a surgeon comes to me as I doze. Green gown, short, like the cardiologist in Sioux City, the nightmare man who told me my thallium test was "less than perfect." And yet, in his report, which I took to China, he said that my thallium test was "also pretty good." What did he mean by those two phrases? I didn't stay for an answer. I was too scared to ask, and had to get to Brookings on a snowy highway. I should have asked him more. I've written to him, but he hasn't responded. It's been over a month.

"Less than perfect." What does the cardiologist's phrase mean? Does it mean, as I think it does, that there are degrees of wellness when it comes to cardiac cases? But what if he'd said "almost perfect"? I'd take it that meant good, almost perfect....? Maybe medical students should be required to take a course in poetry, where they are sensitized to the nuances of words—not just denotations but connotations.

I need to put all this behind me. But I can't sleep. The doctor's words are too clear, too memorable. I can't get them out of my mind.

I'm not tired, I suppose, because I took a sleeping pill and slept last night all night. And paid for it this morning with bad feelings.

For over 35 years I have slept with Jan, slept <u>with</u> Jan in the sense of loving her and sleeping <u>at the same time</u>, every night, next to her, often

For over 35 years I have slept with Jan, slept <u>with</u> Jan in the sense of loving her and sleeping <u>at the same time</u>, every night, next to her, often with my arm around her.

Now, she is sleeping and I am up typing these words into my journal. It doesn't make any sense at all...how I've been intimidated by a report on my heart that really is a basically good report. It's the "less than perfect" that hurts me, and it's exactly this that I must learn to live with.

Sleep, gentle sleep. Where are you? I need you more than ever. I am tired and yet I am not tired. How can that be? I am evidently afraid to sleep. It's as if, by sleeping, I'd be vulnerable to some threat I can't quite identify. Isn't that why people have trouble sleeping...because their nervous system has decided that they're under siege? Just four hours would be enough. I could get through the day with three to four hours, if those hours were solid sleep. I'm in good shape; I suppose that's why I don't need as much sleep to function as others might need. Tomorrow I have two classes. I want to be fresh for them, to teach well.

April 28

Jan

Dave took a sleeping pill last night and slept well, but he woke up feeling groggy and depressed. Even though he wasn't feeling great, he talked to my writing class for the first hour. The students were completely attentive and really enjoyed him.

But at home, after the class, he began feeling terrible again. His moments of depression outweigh his moments of feeling good. I know this is one of the symptoms of depression.

...Our senior students are beginning to turn in the first drafts of their senior theses. Dave read through the first batch. One student had obviously copied much of her material and did not use quotes. The Chinese have a different attitude toward using others' words. They think that if something is written well, there is no reason to change it or to try to improve upon it.

...Dave did well at dinner with Mike, Lida and Angela. The cook made seven different dishes, three of which were extremely spicy. We sat and drank beer and talked for some time. Dave is not drinking because of the medication, and I think that bothers him.

April 29

Jan

Dave didn't sleep at all during the night. He was up every half hour or more. He is miserable and desperate. I don't know how much longer we can continue at this pace. If he takes a sleeping pill, he can sleep some; but then he feels miserable in the morning. If he doesn't take a sleeping pill, he can't sleep and feels even worse. His early mornings are filled with utter despair and pain. It's wearing both of us down. My emotions range from compassion, to empathy, to anger, to despair. He is dependent on me, and vulnerable. I feel as if I'm being suffocated with this dependency. I presume the pills will help and he will get better—at least well enough to get through the next two months. Once we get home, I think he will be fine.

...Most of the foreigners left this morning for a three-day trip sponsored by the Foreign Affairs Office. We hadn't signed up because it didn't sound like something we wanted to do and we thought when it was planned that we might be in Kunming. As it turns out, we did not go to Kunming, but we're glad we didn't go. It would have been too stressful for Dave right now. He can't relax and doesn't enjoy participating in activities.

...Zhang came over to talk about the up-coming Language Poetry conference at Nanjing University in May and about a book on Midwestern poetry he is planning to translate. He had lots of questions. Dave was dozing off on a chair, but Zhang didn't seem to be bothered or offended. He and I talked, with Dave joining in occasionally.

David P. does not have enough sleeping pills to last the next two months, and suggested the Dave cut them in half. I told Dave that maybe he would sleep <u>half</u> the night with half a pill.

April 30

Dave

Last day of April. Terrible depression this morning. No relief from it. David P. said I could start doubling my dosage of Zoloft to one whole pill. I can't sleep except with Halcion, and David P. doesn't have enough left to sustain me. We hope the medicine will begin to act and make me feel better. What else can we do? What else can I do? My motivation is very low; I don't feel like jogging or reading. Self-confidence has drained out of my brain over the last month or so. The pills are supposed to restore it, somehow. How did people handle depression in the past? Of course, some didn't. I think my depression has been coming on for some time, maybe for a year or so. I remember sitting in my office at the university at home and thinking about my lack of motivation. Of course, I loved playing racquetball with my friends and I was writing some fiction, hanging out with friends, etc. But I'd noticed some draining of my motivation for teaching.

Where does it come from? What is its purpose? I've been taught that all physical and physiological things have a function, otherwise they wouldn't occur. What in <u>hell</u> is the purpose of depression? How can it be helpful to a person who has it? What does it mean?

...Read some poems by a "language poet" last night and liked the free form poems. The language poems I don't get, but I'm beginning to see something there, maybe. An attempt to find new forms, structures, meanings, whether organic or inorganic.

...Sometimes I just cry. But at this point I can't cry anymore. All my tears have dried up.

April 30

Jan

Dave slept most of the night, but woke up around 4:00 a.m. with a headache and depression that lasted all morning. His moods seem to be cyclical—worse in the mornings and better in the evenings. He is also having some urinary tract pain, probably brought on by stress. Does he have other physical problems that need treatment? David P. told Dave he could increase the dose of Zoloft to one pill per day. This may speed up the relief. But I wonder if these pills actually <u>increase</u> the depression? Pills can have strange side effects. I feel torn and confused, but I don't want to create doubts for Dave.

David P. asked us both to come in so we could all talk about Dave's condition together. He's doing the best he can under the circumstances. He had questions about whether Dave is hearing voices or seeing things that aren't actually there. If that were the case, he said he would consider Dave's problem more serious. Dave says he's not having these symptoms, although he does see what appears to be frightening eyes in our overhead light at times, usually in the morning. I can see them myself, and I'm fairly normal? It's just the way the sun shines through the window on this light. David P. said we made a commitment to these pills and should give them 10 days or so. If at that time they don't seem to be effective, we'll have to consider something else.

...I opened Dave's letter from the cardiologist in Sioux City (something I would not have done earlier and that I fell guilty about doing). I wasn't worried so much about what the doctor had to say, but about how Dave would interpret what he said. Dr. C. said, among other things, "the 'thinning' in once section of the heart can suggest the presence of mild coronary artery disease.... He went on to say that Dave's heart tests were, however, "quite good," and that he could exercise and do anything he wanted to do, with no restrictions. The letter was positive, but Dave probably would take the few statements that suggested it <u>could</u> possibly be this or that, and become obsessed with them. I've decided to hide the letter. I'll show it to him when we get back to Brookings.

...We had a FAX from Barb telling us of her arrival plans. We sent a return FAX to tell her we would meet her in Shanghai and asked her to bring some sleeping pills for Dave, since David P. doesn't have any more.

MAY

Qian and Jan at market

May 1

Jan

Today is a holiday in China—Labor Day—so there are no classes. It's Saturday, and Dave and I don't have classes anyway, even though almost everyone else does. Labor Day is celebrated here much as it is in the U.S.—to honor the working men and women. Schools and colleges, as well as many places of business, are closed. Banquets and parades are held, but we didn't take part in anything special.

...Dave didn't sleep well since he only took half a sleeping pill, but he did sleep some, actually about half of the night. I shouldn't have told him he would sleep half a night with half a pill. He woke up early this morning feeling great for a while, but his depression returned, although it was not as severe as it has been. It has rained the past two days and is dreary and chilly, which doesn't help his disposition any.

...Qian came over and brought me some flowers for the holiday. We made chocolate chip cookies and muffins, and she made some corn soup for us for dinner.

May 2

Dave

Bad night. The depression is virile right now. I keep thinking it may be lessening—I've been on the pills for 12 days now, this is my 13th—and yet I don't feel any different. Had a "high" two mornings ago, but that, I now suspect, was the Halcion. What a feeling—it was like I was totally normal, and that my problems were over. I could get up, walk out of the bedroom into the normal world. But it didn't happen.

Jan seems to be tiring of me and my negativism. I can't blame her. David P. says that depression _is_ negativism. Depression is negativism, directed inward at the self and outward at the world. I feel paralyzed by negativism right now. And yet, Jan says that, even before this problem, I tended to emphasize the dark side, the down side of things. In my present state, every little problem is a big problem to me: for instance, having to bike to class in the rain, which I used to enjoy. I know Jan is right. I am uptight, and I must learn ways to just let go and not get so damned excited at the least little problem that comes up. Jan, being so easy going herself, can do that. It's her natural way. I can't imagine her ever being depressed. She always finds something to do, never is bored. I get bored easily. But I've always had the ability to go to sleep or do <u>something</u> to keep me going. Now that ability is gone, at least temporarily. David P. says that when the pills restore my levels of chemicals, the sleep problem will disappear. I hope and trust he's right. The last place on earth I want to be is where I am right now—China. On the other hand, if I solve my problem here, and I don't panic but stay in and take it, endure it, and teach my classes and all, that will be a large victory.

My writing is on hold. I go over my short story manuscript and try to revise, but my mind is not in it. My classes are still working, though I don't feel comfortable teaching them right now. I want so much to get better so I can go into a classroom and relax, the way I did last semester. And have a good time with my students, besides discussing literature.

...Invited to Eva's for dinner tonight. I don't want to go, but will. Being around people agitates me because I assume they're all having such a good time. The contrast is intimidating. It diminishes me. This morning I felt slightly better than yesterday morning—in fact, quite a bit better. But then yesterday I had just come off that Halcion high. And David P., I knew, was out of town, so I couldn't get hold of him if I wanted to. But today I'm a few percentage points better. Maybe the drug is beginning to do what it's supposed to do. What's the difference between taking a drug for your liver and one for your brain? They're both organs, both run by chemicals.

Emotion is a matter of chemicals. That is in a way a depressing thing to say, but if it's true, it's true.

...When I can't nap, the day is a hundred times longer. When I can't work ....

May 2

Jan

Again, Dave woke up about 1:30 a.m. and had trouble getting back to sleep. He finally slept some and then was restless from 4:00 a.m. on. It frustrates me because he tosses and turns and tells me about how horrible it is for him, how miserable he feels. I just want to sleep. Even though I try to empathize and be supportive and rub his back for what seems like hours, I feel like he's being self-indulgent. And then I feel guilty about feeling that way. He's going through hell. He has a fear of dying in China. His mornings have not improved any. Sometimes, during the day, he has moments of feeling fairly decent. But these moments don't last long.

...We went to Eva's for dinner tonight, along with several other people. Dave made it through the evening, but felt lonely and unhappy. He at least is making an attempt to be involved with other people.

...Eva talked about the recent Waiban trip, the one Dave and I decided against. She said they mostly visited factories and didn't have any time for looking around or shopping. They went to a city that is known as one of the richest cities in China, where most people have fancy automobiles and large "villas." Everyone was assigned to stay with a peasant family overnight. Eva said the "villas" were more like poorly maintained condos, without water. The group of foreigners were taken to a dance, and most of them were led around by young children who had memorized things to say to them in English. The youngsters sounded good, but if they were asked a question in English, they couldn't understand, and, of course, couldn't answer.

Those who went believe it was all propaganda—a photo op for the Chinese. Eva said the people with whom they stayed were not typical peasants, as the group had been led to believe they would be. They all had printed name cards to present to their guests.

Eva said she wrote to tell her husband, in Michigan, that she has finally "slept" with someone here. At the peasants' home she and a woman she didn't even know had to share a bed.

May 3

Dave

Bad night, bad morning. Very depressed. Last night was especially hard. I was sitting with Jan and five or six of our colleagues for dinner, and feeling isolated, not a part of the group. I'd listen to somebody talking about a person or situation that I would usually be interested in, but I had no interest, and my lack of interest made me extremely uncomfortable. I simply was too into myself to feel I belonged there.

...This is the second week of the medicine. No break. Yesterday afternoon I felt better, almost normal in fact. It's overnight that gets to me. The Halcion is good only for half the night. I wake up at 4:00 a.m. and can't get back to sleep. Toss and turn, wake up Jan, which I can't keep on doing.

I feel very lonely right now. I go for a walk and just wander around thinking about myself. That doesn't make any sense at all. I must get out of myself. I must stop worrying about my health. Today I'll jog; that will help.

I've got to be building up some medicine in my brain by now. The third week should do the trick. That is the usual time—between seven and 21 days, David P. says. I'm going to talk to him this morning.

Later, same day:

Saw David P. He told me I was getting better, that I appear to have more confidence. I don't know if he's right, but I do know that I feel awful most of the time, and totally preoccupied with my physical and mental health—

whether from the pills I'm taking or from just the general galaxy of symptoms that surround a depressed state of mind. David also suggested I might need to probe deeper conflicts when I get back to the U.S.

He's probably right. I need to lay some things on the table and deal with them. For instance, my relationships with colleagues back in the U.S. I tend to hold grudges against persons I have quarrels with. I must learn to deal with difficult situations and difficult persons more assertively, instead of hiding from confrontation, and bottling up my anger. I noticed a change in my life starting at about 50—in and out of the racquetball court. I wasn't able to make shots which were easy several years before; and also a slight lack of focus. I suppose most men my age—especially those who have been very physical all their lives—feel some sort of adjustment has to be made when they find they can't do what they did as younger men.

And yet, last semester here I was fine. I saw the doctor once: when I went to get a recipe for granola. I slept well, dreamed well, was basically content, and Jan and I had a good time together, in and out of bed. We went places, and pretty much enjoyed the travel. I was uptight sometimes, but then I've always been uptight sometimes. I did well, felt good. My drinking has been a problem. I hope I don't have to give it up completely but can have one or two beers now and then. I miss beer a lot.

Other ghosts need to be dragged out of the closet of my life. I'm willing to see a therapist and drag them out, if that will help me.

It's this daily depressed state I'm in that is so disconcerting, so, yes, depressing. I'm depressed about being depressed. Depressed about being depressed about being depressed. And so on. And anxious. This has to let up when I get my serotonin restored again. I'll be working on my third week with that pill beginning tomorrow.

I told Jan I don't want to recede from her. That I will be back—normal again. I constantly have to fight thinking negative thoughts, and belittling myself. I have to remind myself that I have done a few good things with my writing, with relationships, family, and so on. I need to practice tolerance of others and of myself. I need to relent, let up, try to understand others and not judge them. We are all mortal, subject to the same laws of the universe. All of us suffer; all of us have some joy; all of us die eventually. No one and everyone is unique.

Today I tried to rest, to sleep. Jan said, "Think of something pleasant and happy." I thought of my story about the two guys floating in the yard pool on air mattresses. That is a useful image to me. It helps me relax somewhat, though I didn't sleep.

Sleep is almost as important as breath. In a way, sleep _is_ breath— unconscious breathing. We all need to be knocked out by sleep every night. At this moment in my life, I have to do it with pills, unfortunately. But it will come back. I know it will. It will come back. I'm determined to work on it. To work on relaxing. I must get back my normal life.

I love Jan more than ever, need her more than ever.

May 3

Jan

I wonder whether Dave will _ever_ sleep all night again and if he will _ever_ feel normal again. The early mornings are hell to get through. He called David P. to make an appointment to see him this morning and spent 45 minutes with him. He always seems to make Dave feel better, at least temporarily.

This semester is turning out to be just a period of time to get through. Each day now brings anxiety and apprehension; last semester each day brought anticipation and excitement. I hope we get that enjoyment back before we leave in June.

...One thing I do enjoy is my students. The Freshmen English majors have been easier to teach, since their command of English is superior to the non-English majors, but I liked the Ph.D. students I had last semester a little better. They were more mature—some were almost 40 years old—and more dedicated as students. Working for the English section leaders has been much easier and more comfortable than working for the graduate school director. He embodied for me all that is negative, as far as a leader is concerned.

May 4

Dave

I feel slightly better this morning, though I wasn't feeling very good just before I got up. I took a whole Halcion pill last night, and so slept slightly better. No dreams. The pill just knocks you out. It's not a quality sleep, certainly. Instead of waking up refreshed after a good night's sleep, you wake up feeling that you haven't slept. But I was able to relax and lie there this morning and not be too uptight. Everything is a matter of being able to relax—to settle down. I must realize, as I do right now as I write these words, that I really don't have anything wrong with my heart or with my head. I need to open up more, be more conciliatory, agreeable, less belligerent and stubborn and resisting. This, at home, and here. I need to relax. That is the main thing. Even if I do have a slight defect, I've been told I can live with it without problems—no restrictions. Just go on jogging, go on living, as usual. I figure if I cut out the booze, which I have done pretty much, and practice a reasonable diet, I should be fine. And keep my weight down to about 185 to 188 or so.

The lack of sleep hurts, but it'll come back. It's on the way right now, with these slightly better feelings this morning. Today I'll do some jogging.

I need to get to the point where I'm not thinking about all these things in this journal—the point at which I can look outside of myself and start recording what I see, hear, feel, taste of China. Even if I'm not happy here, I can still enjoy some things.

Later, same day:

Got a FAX from David Jr. saying he and Karen will be on stand-by to come to China. This makes me extremely anxious. I hope I can feel good by the time they get here, or maintain when they get here if the medicine hasn't started to take effect. Today I feel rotten. It's as if I'm seeing the world through eyes that aren't mine, listening with ears that aren't mine, feeling with hands that aren't mine. Forgot my bike at the post office, thought I'd left it at the Waiban and that it was stolen when I went back for it. But then remembered it was at the post office. Jan says it's not new for me to forget like this, and probably she's right.

...David P. says I have to get out of China. Yes, I said, but I've got a month and a half of classes to teach. I can't run away. I'd like to go, but I can't.

I can't seem to stay busy, can't seem to get interested in anything. All I have is the basics: eating and eliminating—no sleeping except with Xanax or Halcion. I've got 30 Xanax left for about 50 days. I hope my doctor will send 25 more; I wrote to him about two weeks ago and asked him to send the pills. Or, maybe the sleep problem will lessen if the medicine kicks in; maybe I won't need any sleeping pill, or maybe only half dosage.

I feel isolated, lonely. I'm trapped inside my own mind, unable to take an active part in the world. It seems like I don't belong in it. I am completely locked into my own selfness—without joy, without hope except for the medicine I'm taking. My psyche is vulnerable to all sorts of negative bombardments. I'm so tired. I've been robbed of sleep. My past is attacking my mind—all the negatives, the failures and transgressions. I use my energy to muster some positive thoughts to counter these negative ones. I'm sapped of emotional and mental strength.

I can't concentrate on anything. At first, I could read in bed and enjoy, somewhat, the reading. Now it's more and more difficult to find something I like to read when I'm not asleep at 3:00 a.m. I'm withdrawing from society, from friends, students, even Jan.

Later, same day at 4:00 p.m.:

The worst I've felt so far....I don't know if I can make it here or not ... maybe it's the anxiety more than the depression, I don't know. Hard to tell, but I'm hurting. I lie down for an hour, but, of course, can't sleep but only rest in spurts.

Same day, 7:00 p.m.:

Went out for groceries and ate. Felt rotten, feel rotten still. All I can do is wait for 9:00 p.m. to take my Xanax. This condition is getting to me—is it anxiety or depression? Probably both. I feel absolutely totally rotten tonight. Tomorrow I have a class, talking about several Hemingway stories. Today I did little work—In fact, almost none. The depression is stealing all my ambition and motivation to accomplish anything. Usually at night I feel better—not tonight.

Do I want sympathy from Jan? Sure. I *do* want sympathy. I want anything that can in any way help my condition. Jan is so patient with her students. She's talking to two of them as I write. She takes her time, explains things in detail, slowly. The students like her because she's so accommodating and decent to them.

May 4

Jan

Dave took a whole sleeping pill last night and still didn't sleep well, although he seemed a little better this morning. I keep waiting for the morning when we wake up and he is fine. He can't concentrate on his writing. He takes a lot of walks during the day (on campus where there's not as much noise from cars) and enjoys watching videos. Otherwise, he is deeply depressed and unhappy. He has taken the pills for 15 days now. David P. said they could take from seven to 21 days to begin working, possibly longer. That's the part I didn't like to hear—"possibly longer."

...The U.S. dollar rate is over nine to one right now, so I will "change money" today. Dave won't change money, but I will. We've been told that government money changers are planted around town to catch people, but I'm not too worried about the place I go. The rate at the bank is only about 5.5 to one. I went into the inner room of a little noodle restaurant (the restaurant is actually a front, I think) and changed money. The man wanted to give me Y9.0 for $1, but I asked for 9.1. He agreed. Dave waited for me down the street and when I didn't come out after a few minutes, he worriedly came in to see what was going on. The man had to get more money from a different area, so it took a little longer. I took my Y2700 and stuffed it in my bag and walked away as if nothing had happened inside. We often get cheated on the street; this made me feel somewhat vindicated.

...A former student of mine brought a couple of pieces of calligraphy for me. A friend of his from Nanjing Normal University is studying calligraphy and did them. I've hung them on our walls. One says, "Where there's a will there's a way" (appropriate for us now), and the other says something like, "Bosom friends from afar bring distant lands near." I appreciated getting these. He was a good writing student last semester, and I've helped him a little with a report he is doing on advertising.

May 5

Jan

Dave had a miserable night. We were both awake most of the night. He decided this morning that he needed to leave immediately to go to Hong Kong to get some help. He said he couldn't take the misery any longer. He was going to cancel his 8:00 a.m. class. He then called David P. and talked to him for some time. Afterward, he took a pill and went to teach his class at 8:00 a.m. I also taught my 8:00 a.m. class, worrying about Dave and being stressed and upset about his state of mind. I was emotionally drained.

We went together to see David P. at noon and spent a long time discussing the situation. He decided he would take Dave off the Zoloft he had given him for depression, the very pill we had been counting on to cure him! He said it could possibly be adding to his anxiety and depression. It happens in some cases. Great news, I thought. It will take about five days to get it out of Dave's system. At that time, with the help of Xanax, we are all hoping he will be able to manage well enough to stay until June 23. When Dave has moments of feeling better, he says he doesn't want to go home early. It would be too difficult, with someone living in our house, with getting things tied up here, and with the feeling of guilt for leaving.

May 5

Dave

David P. took me off the Zoloft, says I'm not getting better, and am probably worse, which is true. I called him this morning and said I couldn't take it anymore, that I wanted to go to a Hong Kong hospital. But he said it wouldn't be worth it, that where I needed to go was home, if I needed to leave China. And he told me not to be rash about it, but give it a few days' thought. He said I could be treated for anxiety with Xanax.

My mind/emotions want to go to the U.S., and so I'm uptight about having to stay. To go would make Jan terribly unhappy. She does not at all agree with that idea. I'm going to have to do the best I can here. David Jr. is coming next week; that should pick me up.

May 6

Dave

Called my family doctor in the U.S. last night at 1:00 a.m., China time. He has read my heart report, and he said it was a good report, that doctors don't worry about such a minor thing as he saw on my thallium test. The reports then, were quite good, I can go on doing exercise as long as I feel good. Basically, he said I had a strong heart, that I had nothing to worry about.

No reason to worry about things that still come up—negative thoughts such as grudges, failures to confront others and speak my mind, a job that sometimes can be tedious because of apathetic, incompetent students. I can't allow them to intimidate me. I need to be less and less anxious about these things. Everybody has problems, big and little. I need to emphasize my victories, accomplishments, the positive side, always. It's hard to do this, of course, but I must do it.

Later, same day:

Very rough day, first day of withdrawal from the Zoloft, assuming that the Zoloft caused my depression to deepen.

I should start to rally now, since I did get a very good report from my hometown doctor on the phone last night. He said essentially that my heart is in good shape; even the thallium test showed that, and the treadmill had an even better outcome. He said I had a very good workup, and that all indications are that my heart is strong and durable. And that I had done "the right things" for my heart to be this healthy at my age. Being in good shape for 20 years couldn't have hurt anything, I would think.

Now I have to start healing mentally. Depression is like being caged within your mind and having no idea who has the key to the lock on the cage. It saps your energy, both mental and physical. I don't want to be in

China right now, but there's nothing I can *do* about it, except bear it the best I can.

Xanax is on the way from the States. I can take up to three per day, which I will continue to do. About five hours into a Xanax I feel groggy, as I do as I type these words. I don't want to try to go to sleep because I know it'll hurt me for sleep tonight. I have been sleeping slightly better lately, sometimes even dreaming, though the dreams on Xanax tend to be bizarre. Last night I dreamed about going to an ice arena or rink under- ground and nobody was in the stadium, no players, no spectators.

...If I could some day soon complete an actual sleep cycle, that would be a miracle. Just the smallest, most minute percentage point better. .00000000000001 would be something. A triumph. Depression is almost like being awake and in a coma at the same time.

It's harder and harder to maintain classes, though this morning the class got better as it went on. It's an ordeal, especially because it's a two-hour class instead of the usual one-hour length back home.

Tonight we'll watch a video. Maybe that will keep me quiet. I need Jan more than ever. I hate it when she leaves to go out shopping, as she did this morning. But I made it without her; tried to sleep. But when she's around I feel better. I'm very dependent on her. Between Jan and Xanax, I am surviving China. When I called my doctor, he mentioned that it's probably the loud, strange environment that is causing my stress, and it surely is. I don't like to walk out in crowds anymore, dodging people. Last semester I liked it. Sometimes I even enjoyed the feeling of being immobilized by numbers of people clogging the street—it felt good to just relax and let go and be carried along by the crowd.

Five more weeks of classes and we're out of here, up in the air and over the ocean blue. I look forward to that day the way a man who's been walking through a desert for days yearns for a cool glass of water. What wouldn't he do for water? What wouldn't I do for a normal, healthy mind right now? Or even one night's normal sleep, which I haven't had for almost three months.

I haven't run for about five days, and I'm nervous about that, too. I don't want my legs to turn flabby. David P. said I have a "good pair of wheels," and I do—born with good legs, and I've used them to run and play racquetball for a long time. They are strong; I want them to stay that way. I need to use them.

Of course, I can maintain somewhat by lots of walking and biking, but it's not like jogging two or three miles four or five times a week.

May 6

Jan

We had more sleep last night than we have had for some time. Dave hadn't taken his Zoloft. We got up at 1:00 a.m. and Dave called his doctor in Brookings to ask him to send him some more Xanax pills and to talk to him about his heart report. He reassured Dave that he had a good report and that he was a healthy person. That made Dave feel better. But this morning when he woke up, he felt depressed again.

...I read some poetry to my class today, and then they all took turns reading Mother Goose nursery rhymes. I was surprised to see how much they enjoyed this.

...Eva and I took a bus to go shopping at the other end of town, near the Fuzimiao temple. We planned to eat at the Kentucky Fried Chicken restaurant but because the electricity was off, it was temporarily closed. We were disappointed, since we had planned for days to eat there. So we found a Chinese hotel coffee shop and had lunch there. We suddenly realized we had run out of time, since Eva had to get back by 2:30 to show a film, so we took a cab instead of a city bus.

When we got back, Dave was in an extremely depressed state. I rubbed his back for about an hour and talked to him to get him past this crisis. I felt guilty for having been gone and for enjoying myself.

...Eva told me today that one of our colleagues has worms. He passed a large one and has been sick with stomach problems and a fever. Mike is also sick with a fever and stomach problems, and Deb is sick. What's going on?

A colleague heard yesterday that his Fulbright grant was not renewed. His name had been entered for renewal, but then was mysteriously withdrawn by this university. No reasons were given. This is China. Foreigners are expendable. I know he wanted to stay for another year and is deeply disappointed.

...Dave had the best evening he has had this second semester. He was juggling apples and actually having a good time. We watched a video, and later he read some poetry to me. He seemed normal and happy, more like himself.

May 7

Dave

Last night, I felt about the best I've felt this semester. Went to bed feeling strong, confident, on top of things. Woke up two or so hours later and there it was: total, relentless depression. Maybe the worst I've felt for some time. Then, I must've slept after Jan rubbed me some and woke up feeling a little better. But now, I'm very tired and very unhappy. And anxious about David Jr. and Karen and Barb coming next week.

I want to go home but know I can't—no place to live, for one thing. So I'm confined to China. How could I have felt so good last night and so lousy after I woke up several hours later? All this is wearing on me. I haven't done any jogging, my legs are getting soft. I'm in bad condition, and I haven't been in bad condition for a long time—many years. Still, I'm not totally out of shape because I do walk some, but I don't run. I must begin to do some slow jogging soon. Question: what's the world like without Xanax?

I am able to sleep an hour or so in the day time, and that's new. But the leap from great feelings to despair last night bothers me.

I live for nights. Those few moments when I usually feel decent. I like to think that there's some withdrawal from Zoloft taking place. I'm still suffering the half-life fading of the drug inside my brain. I do actually feel better about my heart, having talked to my doctor, who told me my report was good, that they don't worry about very "tiny defects" so-called, if in fact it is a defect and not a machine error. He said that I have a strong, healthy heart, and I believe he knows what he's talking about. He's an internist; he knows about these things; he said he's seen hundreds of these pictures, and that mine is a good one. I can live a normal, healthy life the way I am.

Later, same day:

I did a few things today. I told Mike about my depression. He listened well. He himself is a worrier; thinks he has throat cancer, is always checking his neck. He's vulnerable in ways that I am too. He's very bright, a friend who can listen and even help me by talking things out. That was good. I listened to him, too, and he also is sick of China.

I made love with Jan. I ran a mile and a quarter or so, very slow. But that was good, good. My moods change with the clouds, the China light. And, I haven't taken a Xanax more than once today. I'll take one for bed.

And, on my way home on my bike from the track, I saw a puffed-up bag that kids buy candy in and discard. When you throw it away it puffs up, and when you step on it (lots of them on the track) it pops. I saw it as I rode my bike, and turned my wheel and ran over it. It didn't pop...was already popped—but the fact that I did it is a happy fact. It shows I can find interesting things outside myself.

Last night, before bed when I felt so good, I read Jan the ending paragraph of William Faulkner's story "Barn Burning" and a page and a half of Raymond Carver's wonderful story "Nobody Said Anything." About a boy who tries to be a go-between in a fight between his father and mother. He goes out and catches a huge fish and brings half of it home (split it with another boy who helped him get it), and tries to please his parents with it. They are still arguing. Both of them reject his fish, and the story ends with the boy staring at the huge half of a fish.

May 7

Jan

Dave was up at midnight but went back to sleep until about 3:30 a.m. From then until about 5:30 a.m. he was in deep despair. He said he couldn't stand it anymore, that he desperately needed help. This made me feel overwhelmed with stress and confusion. I wondered what we should do—if we should talk to somebody else besides David P.? Should we try to go home? What will happen to Dave if we continue to stay here? I think part of his feeling is due to the withdrawal from the Zoloft. It is still in his system and David P. said it would take about five days to pass through. So I don't know if the depression is worse now because he isn't taking the pills, or if it is because he is adjusting to not taking them, or if it is from the Xanax he's taking to treat his anxiety and help him sleep. He needs some relief, and so do I. The trip to Shanghai to pick up Barbara, David Jr. and Karen is weighing on him. He doesn't know if he can deal with the crowds and noise in Shanghai.

...Qian came over and offered to go to Shanghai by herself to get Barbara if we can't go. We may let her, since Dave is worrying about going there, although I have really been looking forward to going. I feel trapped and restricted. I don't feel like I can be away from Dave for any length of time. He needs me there to help him get through crises, and I want to be near him to help in whatever way I can. But I feel a certain amount of ambivalence, since I want to go to Shanghai and other places, and I know I can't.

Dave took only one Xanax early this morning and then didn't take any more all day. He had a relatively good day. He jogged; we had a good nap; we went to eat at the Central Hotel; and we watched a video in the evening. David Jr. called to tell us when he would be arriving. Dave became quite anxious over the uncertainty of David's plans. David didn't know the actual date he will get a seat on a plane, and he will be arriving in Beijing instead of Shanghai. It will be extremely difficult for him to get a plane ticket to Nanjing from Beijing. He doesn't know how difficult. Karen will come on the 18th. There's no guarantee that we can even get tickets to go pick her up, if we don't get them three days in advance. And we can't do it in advance, because her seat is not guaranteed. I have to believe it will all work out somehow.

...Chen came by for a while. She said Premier Li Peng is in the hospital, but that it has not been announced in China on T.V. or radio news or in the newspapers. She heard it on the BBC. She said when a leader in China is in the hospital, it usually means something is going on. She says the unemployment is very high, inflation is soaring, and there is a general unrest in China. You see lots of fights on the streets. Chen Loo, who is Chinese Malaysian, says she can't understand the Chinese and has lots of criticism of them.

...A Chinese teacher, who had translated a story of Dave's and who had translated some Chinese poetry into English, stopped by this after-noon to visit. He ended up staying entirely too long. Dave excused himself and went to bed. When he got up some time later, the man was still here. Dave made some remark about us having to go somewhere, and the man finally left. I had given various clues or suggestions to him to let him know it was time for him to leave, but to no avail. I think he just had nothing else to do today and wanted to talk.

May 8

Dave

No better this morning. Can't sleep except in spurts. My sleep cycle is shot. Anxious about David Jr. flying into Beijing next week. How will I feel when he gets here? How will I manage to help him around? I feel just simply rotten. Jan thinks I had a better day yesterday; I don't know if it's true. I don't have any motivation right now. The rest of the world goes by merrily, and Dave Evans is feeling out of it. I'm off the merry-go-round. Everybody looks happy, content, unconscious. I'm too, too conscious.

I don't know whether to take a Xanax or not. Only have about 25 left; waiting for another bottle of them coming maybe within two weeks. Didn't take anything yesterday beyond 1:00 p.m., not even overnight. How can I maintain classes? Nothing interests me. I'm still functional sexually, but sex doesn't give me any sustained joy, I'm sorry to say. And I love Jan very much as I always have and always will.

Later, Saturday:

Jan says I've developed a habit of messing with my fingernails in company. True. And it's sometimes hard to look people in the eye and sustain eye contact. What is also difficult is to see so many normal, happy foreigners enjoying life in China. Life was like that the first semester. Now it's hard for me to enjoy China, since I'm so down on myself. Jan was quiet and a little distant today and cried some when we got home after going to the post office on a mini-bus. I was quiet, too, my usual self these days because it's so hard to enjoy anything. But Jan's quietness and distance is disturbing to me, and I think it perked me up a little after we got home. Tomorrow is Mother's Day; I have to get her some flowers and a card in the morning. I know I won't feel much like going out, but I have to do it. It's a sad situation we're both in here. I have to get home to see a

psychologist or psychiatrist with some regularity to get myself straightened out. I know I will eventually learn to cope.

...David Jr. comes next week. I want to feel better.

...This war in my mind has to end. I haven't been in the "other" good
phase for a few days now. Took a Xanax tonight at 8:00.

May 8

Jan

Dave went to bed without a pill, at my suggestion. He didn't sleep
very well, but I think woke up slightly less depressed than he has been. In
the early morning hours, he usually says he needs to get to a hospital,
needs to see a psychiatrist, that he is extremely unhappy, has no
motivation and cannot concentrate. Sometimes I find myself becoming
irritated with him. I know he can't help it. Maybe I'm not basically a very
nice person, but I get extremely tired after hearing him complain about his
misery and his imagined heart problem, and after rubbing his back for what
seems like hours at a time. I know he needs this, but I am tired and want
some sleep. I feel like I did in the mornings when the kids were infants,
when I had to get up every few hours during the night with them. I want
Dave to get better and for us to be able to enjoy this last month and a
half in China. Maybe he'll improve with David Jr. and Karen and Barb here.
Maybe he'll get worse, I don't know. He's very anxious to see David and
Karen, but worried about himself in this situation. He doesn't want his son
to see him depressed and unhappy.

... I went to the drama practice at the University today, and as I
was coming out of the building, I saw Dave coming up the sidewalk, waving
his hand wildly at me. He looked troubled. He said he couldn't see very well,
that everything was blurry. He was scared. I was worried and thought to
myself that he could be going blind or that he may have a brain tumor. He
has been complaining lately of having strange feelings in his head (I'm
starting to think like he thinks). I went back with him to the apartment,
and after a while his eye problem cleared up. It seemed to be another
stress-related incident. I feel sorry for him, but I don't know what we can
do. I even thought that he should see a Chinese doctor (David P. had told

us not to do that; he said it would be too difficult and that they don't have the right kinds of medicine for depression). We sat around for a while and then decided to catch a mini-bus to the post office to pick up a package. I thought this would help take our minds off Dave's problems. The package was de-caf coffee and tea from Bev. I was feeling the stress of having little sleep last night and of having Dave in such a bad state. I don't feel like I can do anything without Dave. I can't leave him alone, since he is so dependent on me. And there's so much I want to see and do and buy before we go home. If we weren't having all of our company, maybe we would try harder to go home early. It's not good living like this.

...A small thermos exploded in Dave's hands after he bumped it this afternoon. I think he was actually using it for an ashtray for his pipe. It was a huge explosion and scared the hell out of Dave. Tonight, while he was up on a chair hanging something on the wall, he slipped, and stepped down into a plastic wastebasket and broke it. It also created an incredibly loud noise and scared both of us. I tried to make light of these incidents and told Dave he was a danger to himself, as well as to me.

May 9

Dave

Better day. I took a Xanax at 8:00 p.m. last night and slept better, didn't have to lie awake much, "woke up" about 5:00 a.m. Depressed this morning, took a Xanax whose effects wore off about 2:00 p.m. Made love, and it was better, better, closer, much closer now, to the familiar love-making we've been used to for so many years. Went jogging—1 1/2 miles. It felt good. Slow, but good. After the jog, felt quite good. Played a little "tennis" (no net) with a couple of my students. The sun's coming out this afternoon helped a lot. The light in China is different from the light in the U.S., I swear. Hard to get used to.

...I went out to eat with Jan and Eva and over to Eva's for cake later. Felt good, feel good now. The diminishing of the Zoloft in my system is making me less depressed. I'm glad I don't have to take the stuff to feel better. My main problem now is stress, not depression.

...I need to keep on my feet on the track—keep doing my laps and giving my heart a workout to keep it strong and healthy. I've done it for 20 years; why stop now? Jogging and working out has become a part of my life. It has given me great peace and joy and comradeship with others. I need to keep it going, and nobody said I couldn't or shouldn't.

...Work has fallen off. Not just a little either. I must get back to it as soon as possible. Reading for classes is one thing—I haven't slacked off much on that. It's my writing. I need to be revising stories for my collection.

...I got flowers for Jan for Mother's Day, and reminded her of how good a mother she is.

...I'm going to try to avoid having to see David P. for a while. That is one of my goals now. To wean myself off his advice. I like him, and he has helped me a lot and I told him so; but I must go on my own as much as possible from now on.

May 9

Jan

Dave took a Xanax before bed and had a fairly good night. He didn't wake me up with complaints about being depressed. This morning he took a Xanax and was better than he has been any morning for the last month. He went out in the rain and bought me a beautiful bouquet of flowers for Mother's Day. Things are looking up.

...We had a nap; Dave jogged; we went to the department store; and later we went with Eva to the Danube restaurant to eat dinner. After dinner, we went to Eva's for cake, fresh pineapple and coffee. Dave has been great today. He actually feels fairly decent. I think the effects of that horrible pill are wearing off. I'm happy David P. made the decision to take Dave off the pills (not happy that he gave them to him in the first place).

May 9

Jan

Dear Nan & Gary,

It's been a while since we've heard from you. How are things going? What's new?

What are your summer plans? We look forward to seeing you when we get back on the 26th of June. The 27th is Gary's birthday, isn't it? Maybe we could bring him a "lard frosting cake" from China. What do you think? I'm sure you remember them from Kunming.

We've heard from the Swedlunds in Kunming, but have not made it there. We probably won't now. This semester has been a long one for Dave. China is wearing on him, and we're ready to come home.

It's wearing on another teacher here, too. She's a young woman from the States, and she's having difficulty with one of her junior classes. The entire class walked out on her the other day after she criticized a student in front of everyone. She is about 24 years old, just out of college, and this is her first teaching job. I don't know what all has taken place in the classroom, and don't want to know, but I believe the students' walking out was a way they could legally protest without negative consequences from the authorities, as far as the administration is concerned. The teacher is "just a foreign teacher" and the students' behavior could probably be understandable. Anyway, it has been difficult for her since that incident. This little foreign community produces some soap-opera material, let me tell you.

Another colleague told a group of us about living in the Philippines—about having worms and lice as a child. When they had worms they all had to line up and take castor oil and then fast for a whole day to get rid of the worms. When she had lice, her aunt's pet monkey sometimes would pick the critters out of her head. She said it felt great—like a massage. It was too bizarre. As she was talking about lice, we all began to scratch our heads. At least I don't think there's been a lice problem here. We have other kinds of bugs, but not lice.

Only a little over a month to go, and there's so much to do and so much to see. Will we get it all accomplished? Probably not. But we'll try. See you soon.

Love,

Jan (scratching)

May 10

Dave

Best night of sleeping so far this semester, probably, though I have to qualify it as a Xanax night. If that's what it takes to sleep, then that's what it'll have to be until I get more relaxed, focused. Xanax feeling this morning: thick-headed, not rested, though I know I slept a good six to seven hours. First night for months I didn't wake up and have to read for several hours.

I'm not as depressed this morning, but I don't have a lot of motivation. I will do some work today on my classes at least. Not nearly as desperate this morning. I'll make it.

Later, same day:

No motivation, no desire to read or write. I jogged, but it required a gigantic effort. Feel terrible. All I wait for is 8:00 p.m. when I can take my Xanax and begin to feel better.

...One of my biggest fears is not being able to adjust when I get back to the States. I know that I will eventually get back to "normal," but I don't know how long it will take. I used to be able to pace myself. Now, something is pacing me instead. Something terrible in my mind. Sometimes I actually feel something crawling under my scalp behind my left ear. Is it the Zoloft fading? I think I've felt it before, before China. A momentary strange feeling of something moving around in my brain.

I'm withdrawing. I don't feel like going out. I expressed this fear to Jan. She doesn't understand because she is so healthy and tough-minded. Maybe she'll never understand.

I think too much. Before China, I had the same problem, but I could do things to shut off the valve of my thoughts so the stream didn't get too heavy: play racquetball, drink beer, work on a poem or a story. Now, it's not so easy,

Later, same day:

NINE LINES BEGINNING WITH "AND"

AND then I wake up for the first time
AND also the last time
AND rub my eyes
AND look around
AND I'm in Hell
AND the Main sign (there are millions
AND all of them begin with
AND) says:
AND NO SLEEPING FOREVER

Maybe now I can begin to write some poems that tell the truth based on my experience. This is not a pleasant poem, but it's a truthful poem. Maybe I should call my next book of poems Xanax Poems?

May 10

Jan

I was upset with my classes today; they were too noisy when their classmates were in front giving talks. I had to keep stopping the presentations to ask them to wait until everyone was quiet. The students would quiet down, and then start up again. These students are sometimes like elementary-age children.

May 11

Dave

Depressed, anxious again. Woke up worrying about David Jr. getting here, about Barbara, about them finding out about my state of mind lately. But as Jan says, they're coming here to see China, not just me. That makes sense.

David P. says I should take as few Xanax as possible. I'm down to 17 and a half, so I'll have to conserve. If David Jr. brings some, I can use more if need be. And then I'll get my supply from my doctor.

I guess if I can just maintain, do my classes...that's all I can expect until I fly out of here and get home to better care. Main feelings are still persisting, but with time and good advice and counseling I know I can whip it and get back to normal.

But oh, it's hard, hard, hard to do right now. Mainly, I need to do some writing and reading. Even reading for classes is an ordeal. At first I could do it fairly easily; not now.

May 11

Jan

Dave woke up at 1:30 a.m. worrying about running out of pills before they come in the mail from Dr. J., worried he won't be able to make it without them. We asked David Jr. to bring some, but we don't know if he'll be able to since they are a prescription drug. Dave finally went back to sleep but woke again around 4:00 or 5:00 a.m. complaining and worrying. I was so tired, and told him it was not right for me to have to be awakened by him complaining. My patience is wearing thin. I know I need to help him, but I wasn't in a very good mood. Early mornings are difficult. Dave thinks he is seriously ill and thinks he needs to see a psychiatrist. He has always been the kind of person who exaggerates. His imagination runs wild when he focuses on his health. We only have 34 more days to spend in China. Can we make it?

...We went for a walk this afternoon, but it wasn't fun like it used to be. We went with a group of foreigners to eat dinner at the Sprite this evening, but Dave didn't enjoy it. Later this evening Dave said he felt good about his heart, that he thought he didn't have a problem—a good sign, I thought. All of these contradictions are mind boggling. Sometimes he tells me he's going to be fine and a little later he says he's not going to make it.

May 12

Dave

Slightly better, maybe, today. Taught Hemingway's two stories, "The Killers" and "The Short Happy Life of Francis Macomber." Didn't take a Xanax this morning before class. The class went well, although my students were their usual quiet selves. Last night I was awake a lot, thinking about my heart.

The trouble with depression is that you have too much time to think. Suicide has occurred to me, but as I told David P., I wouldn't have the guts. When I mentioned suicidal thoughts, he asked me how I'd do it.

"Climb a building and jump off."

He said that as long as I didn't have any specific plans, I'd be okay. Otherwise, he'd send me home. The bottom line is: I need a way out of this depression. That's why suicide comes up. I dread jogging at the track because the tallest building on campus is next to it, and I've had thoughts of jumping off of it from the very first day I got back in February. Most times when I go over there to run I forget those thoughts. But the thoughts are, in themselves, intimidating.

This morning, on the way back from the post office in the mini-bus (I hate to go there because the traffic is so loud and congested) I felt a little more relaxed, as if I were actually getting back to normal.

Took a short "nap" and actually slept for maybe 30-40 minutes, but was startled awake and then felt terrible, waking up. That is a no-good feeling. But—I did manage to sleep a little, and I was tired.

May 12

Jan

Dave expressed concern about not being able to teach his classes when he gets back home in July. He always has something to worry about or has some kind of pain. He is suffering greatly. I try to imagine being that depressed, but I really can't.

...We had another package to pick up at the post office, so we caught a mini-bus. The traffic and noise are unbearable in that part of town—horns blaring, bumper-to-bumper cars, trucks, taxis, carts, bicycles and an over-abundance of people all rushing to get somewhere. It's a desperate feeling, one I experience here often, with so many people. I sometimes feel like I'll be completely consumed in a crowd of people and never be heard from again. Images of stampedes also come to mind, when people just can't get away from what's coming toward them.

May 13

Jan

It rained and was dark and dreary all day.

Dave and I each showed films in the apartment for our classes today. I went on the mini-bus alone to the post office to get another package, since Dave was not up to struggling through the traffic and noise. I was the topic of conversation on the bus, as people were looking at me and making me feel like an alien. I could understand a few of their words. Today was one of those days when it bothered me to be the center of attention. I wanted to be anonymous. I was the only foreigner on the bus.

...The afternoon was bad. Dave and I both felt depressed about Dave's depression. There is not much joy or humor for us right now, and these things have always been a apart of our daily lives.

...Qian came by to tell us she would go to Shanghai on Saturday morning instead of on Friday, to pick up Barbara. This means she won't be able to visit her grandmother and aunt and uncle, whom she was looking forward to seeing. She can't go on Friday because she has to give a talk for one of the leaders. She had given one for him the other day, and only two people attended. She doesn't want to go back and talk to the same two people—it's not worth her time and effort. But she has to go. It's a 40-minute bike ride for her each way.

...I bought and prepared some strawberries, even though we've heard it's not safe to eat them. I soaked them in potassium permanganate and in salt water. We can buy two kinds of U.S. ice cream—"Bud's" from San Francisco or "Meadow Gold"—to put on top of the strawberries. Even though there is fairly good Chinese ice cream for sale, we usually opt for the U.S. brands. Dave says he still won't eat the strawberries. He's heard too many horror stories about food-borne diseases, some about strawberries.

May 14

Dave

Yesterday, rain. Wasn't able to jog. Next time maybe I can jump rope or walk stairs here for 15 minutes. That'll be something. Slept better last night, didn't wake up worrying about my heart. That's a victory. Even slept after the Xanax wore off, from 4:30 a.m. to about 6:30. Maybe I'm getting a handle on this.

It's amazing how my anxiety-into-depression has allowed all sorts of other things to come in: guilt, hang-ups, phobias, worries, etc. I suppose that is the nature of the disease. I need to take the good thoughts that break through and emphasize them. It's not a matter of either/or. It's a matter of degree. I must stop pitting opposite against opposite, black against white. For instance, I shouldn't believe that a person or an event is altogether bad. The Chinese understand this. Their Yin/Yang symbol blends the white into the black and vice versa. Dichotomizing is a destructive practice.

...David Jr. should be here in a day or two from Hong Kong. I want to relax and have a good time with him, and then with Karen and with Barb, too.

...This morning I'm ill at ease, but I feel slightly better. Today I'll probably do some jogging, and walking with Jan. I should be less dependent on Jan, less worried about what others think of me, less uptight about the future.

May 14

Jan

We had a relatively good day today. We went for a 2 1/2 hour walk like we did last semester. I bought a nice leather backpack.

...Barb will be here Sunday night with the help of Qian. David Jr. called from Hong Kong to tell us he arrived there. He has a contact person in Hong Kong, so I hope he stayed with him. He could arrive tomorrow, if he is able to book a flight. I hope all of this company will help bring Dave out of his depression.

...My hair needed trimming, so, in desperation, I asked Dave to trim the back. I can't believe I let him do it, but he didn't do too badly. Under normal circumstances, I wouldn't let him get near my hair with a scissors.

...I had blood in my stool today, so now I'm thinking I probably have a horrible disease. Maybe it's stress; maybe it's nothing; maybe it's China. I seem to feel okay. If I had Dave's disposition, I would think I was near death.

May 15

Dave

Woke up with bad depression. I am sleeping better, thanks to Xanax, and I'm not having to read in the middle of the night. But the depression bothers me considerably.

Jan said this morning, "I miss having you around." I haven't been around for most of the semester. I have to get straightened out. Drugs, therapy, a combination...whatever.

I hate having to tell son David about all this, but I must, because he'll know my change immediately. I like to think his being here will help me.

..…I must learn to be less hostile toward people I argue with or don't always like. Hostility is dangerous, destructive. If I could learn from Jan about this...she doesn't have any hostile feelings that last. She blows off steam, but then she's back to normal in a few minutes. That is health. The one thing I want to avoid is cynicism. I have never been cynical, though I've had cynical moments. My poems don't express a cynical point of view or philosophy. I have an upbeat, optimistic attitude, basically. That must be retained and maintained.

May 15

Jan

Dave woke up early feeling depressed, so he took a Xanax. That made him tired. He's either tired or depressed, or both.

...I have insect bites on me—one on my eye that makes me look like I have a black eye, one on my arm, and another on my finger. They are swollen and red and probably infected. I don't know what bit me, but it may have been spiders. I woke up during the night with my eye almost swollen shut. And Dave's feet and hands are itching. With the warm weather, we get the insects.

...Around 3:00 p.m. we heard a knock at the door. There were two of Dave's students, along with David Jr.! David had flown into Nanjing at noon and had taken a taxi to the campus. He was let off in the wrong place. After he had asked directions from several Chinese people without success, he finally just sat down to rest and wait to see if any foreigners would come by so he could ask them for directions. He didn't see many. As he was wandering around campus, these two students of Dave's saw him and recognized him from a picture we had shown them. They brought him to our apartment, insisting on carrying his heavy back packs. It was great to see him. It was very emotional for Dave, especially since he's been so depressed.

...David Jr. had his first experience of "real" Chinese food at a banquet we attended this evening. He liked the eel. After introducing him to many of the Chinese and foreign faculty, we came home and talked until after 10:30 p.m. David is experiencing jet lag. He spent last night in Hong Kong in a cheap, dirty hotel. His contact in Hong Kong turned out to be no help to him at all.

Having David around, I think, may help Dave.

May 16

Jan

We took David to the market to buy some food and show him around. As we were walking along, a string of firecrackers exploded behind us, scaring us. It was a celebration for the opening of a new store. Coming from America, one automatically thinks of gunfire when hearing these firecrackers go off. David was fascinated with the market.

...Barb and Qian arrived from Shanghai around 5:30 p.m., just in time for chili and grilled cheese sandwiches. We were grateful to Qian for helping us. She even bought some Western food for us in Shanghai. The Asian Games were being held in Shanghai, so Qian had problems finding them a decent place to stay. She and Barbara ended up in a cheap, dirty place. Barb was tired, so she slept well in spite of the poor conditions.

May 17

Dave

Worse. I take only one Xanax these days, at night to sleep, but woke up this morning very depressed. Does the Xanax contribute to that depression? And maybe my Cardizem blood pressure pill is making me tired, especially after a 2 1/2 mile jog? It does say on the pharmacy sheet that came with the pills that you shouldn't tire yourself out. I should've asked these questions when I got the pill in the first place.

I'm having considerable stress right now. Barb is here, David Jr. is here, Karen is due in on Thursday. The only good time for me is just after running and after dinner, and then best when I've taken a Xanax and go to bed and hour and a half later. But then I wake up feeling terrible.

May 17

Jan

Dave woke up depressed, after feeling fairly good last night. Barb came over early this morning. She was talking to Dave, and when I walked into the room, I could see that she was in tears. Great, two depressed people on my hands. She and Dave can commiserate with each other. They both have problems. She said she cried herself to sleep last night, and wondered why she came to China. She said, at the last minute, she didn't want to come but couldn't change her plans. Her room isn't great, but it isn't terrible—it has two twin beds, a T.V., two chairs and a dresser. Granted the toilet leaks, the carpet is filthy, the lighting is dim and there are no screens on the windows, but not a bad place.

... This evening we treated Barbara and David to dinner at the Sprite Outlet. Barbara innocently asked if there was a bathroom in the Sprite. That is not a usual thing to have in a small restaurant in China. So Dave took her across the street to an outdoor W.C. (a squatter), which made her literally sick to her stomach. Welcome to China, we told her.

... Later, Mr. Tso, a Fulbright professor from Shanghai, came by. He hadn't shown up for dinner last night as we thought he would. He's originally from Taiwan and does not like China. He's anxious to go back to the States. He brought us a huge teapot with a broken handle, something he picked up at an outdoor market. It has a poem by Li Bai, a famous ancient Chinese poet, inscribed on it. We were touched by his thoughtfulness.

May 18

Jan

Deb, Barbara and I went to the bank, did some shopping and went to Smoky Joe's to change money. We had a good time laughing, shopping, being crazy. This is such a contrast to what has been going on with Dave this semester, I feel a sense of relief.

Tonight we (foreign faculty) got dressed up, mostly to please Chen Loo, and walked en masse to campus to attend opening night for the dramas. The basement of the English Department building was transformed into a theater. The plays were all by British playwrights; one play was an absurdist drama about a dog that had been hit by a car. The entire play was an argument about whether the dog was dead or not. The students used perfect British English. Many Chinese have learned British English, but say they prefer American English.

Unfortunately, Barbara had taken an allergy pill before we left for the play and became very tired. She kept nodding off during the performance, and her chair was so weak and wobbly she was afraid it would break and she would end up on the floor. Dave took her home just before the last play, which was the best of the three, but he didn't mind leaving early.

...Barbara and Dave have had some good conversations about depression and how to deal with it. She has been depressed and understands how it feels. She also said she has cured herself of serious health problems by thinking them out of her body. Dave had a good afternoon and evening—the best in months. He was laughing and even sang "Laredo," for us.

May 19

Dave

Fact:

The Chinese word for <u>crisis</u> has two characters: the first means dangerous; the second means opportunity.

May 19

Jan

Rain...Dave woke up less depressed than he has been for some time. He and David went out for lunch, while Barbara and I went to Deb's apartment where I colored her hair.

...Dave, David and I talked to Eva's class this afternoon. It's a class for English teacher training. She wanted an American family to speak to them on cultural topics. It was fun and Dave and David each recited some poems. The students liked it.

The cook's dinner was especially good this evening. David and Barbara were impressed with it. She still hasn't had her glasses fixed.

May 20

Jan

Rain...David Jr. talked with my conversation students. They liked speaking to a young American.

...Qian, David, Barbara and I decided to go to the Sprite for lunch. It was raining so hard the paths on campus and the side streets were flooded. I had boots on, but the others didn't. Raw sewage, above-the-ankle deep, was running through the streets. Qian decided to go back home when we were half-way there. She had had enough. David went back home to get the bicycle to avoid walking any more in the dirty water in his good tennis shoes, which were already soaked. Barbara and I went on, worried some about illnesses such as typhoid and worms. We had our lunch in the Sprite and then walked around town to shop for rubber boots and floor mats. Barbara and I are having a lot of fun together. She makes me laugh. Her ways of dealing with the frustration of being in a third-world country are humorous to me. She's enthusiastic, curious and has an artist's sensibility.

Dave jogged this afternoon when the rain subsided and then became very tired this evening and went to bed at 8:00 p.m.

Today is Lida's birthday, and Mike had asked us earlier to come to their apartment for cake. But today, he didn't mention anything about it. We bought Lida a glass paper weight and Barbara blew up about 12 balloons and we left them in her apartment. They had the party without us. Why?

Barbara tried to call United Airlines for two hours today to get her return ticket straightened out. She never was able to get a call through and became totally frustrated. She decided that she would FAX her husband and have him take care of it from the States. As I had warned her, making travel arrangements is a task always filled with anxiety and stress in China.

May 21

Jan

Barbara, David and I walked to the market to buy food. Barbara got some good pictures of the live chickens, eels and fish.

David and I caught a cab to the airport to see if Karen would be on the plane from Hong Kong. (Karen and David weren't able to get tickets together because there was a scarcity of seats.) While there, we called Dave at the apartment and found out Karen had sent a FAX saying she wouldn't be in until Monday. She had sprained her ankle stepping off a curb. She found somebody to share a room with in Hong Kong. I think David's worried about her.

We all had dinner at Tom and Deb's apartment. Deb made a vegetable soup and curried chicken. I made spaghetti, and Barbara made garlic bread and fixed some snacks with the food she brought from the U.S. We also had strawberry shortcake with real whipping cream that Deb had purchased in Shanghai. It was a feast. We had fun talking, and Barbara and I got to laughing so hard at Deb we couldn't stop. She was talking about her misunderstandings with Chinese people and various awkward situations she has found herself in. Dave didn't join in much.

...David is finding his way around and doing lots of shopping. As many of us are, he is frustrated by the difficulty in communicating.

May 22

Dave

Walked with David Jr. today for two hours. While walking, a motto occurred to me:

Lie down and die or stand up and keep walking.
It helps to have my son here.

May 22

Jan

Dave took David Jr. to the bookstore and to a part of town David hadn't seen. Barb and I planned to leave at 11:00 a.m. to go to the Fuzimiao Confucian temple area, an area full of outdoor shops comparable to a U.S. shopping mall, but Eva came down and brought me a rose and stayed to talk. We ended up leaving at noon. David had come back from the bookstore, and he wanted to go with us. We enjoyed looking around and drew huge crowds of people. David had a tank top and shorts on. He's so muscular and blond that people can't help watching. Barbara gets nervous and sweats just as I do when I'm trying to buy something with so many people watching, pointing at me and laughing.

...We ate left-over spaghetti for dinner and made popcorn later while we were sitting around talking about Dave's depression. David Jr. decided to go to the English Corner, a place where people gather on Saturday nights just to speak in English. David said he felt like a prophet. Hundreds of people gathered around him, ten or so deep, asking questions. He was the only foreigner there. He didn't get home until after 11:00 p.m. I was worried the gate would be locked when he came home. It was an interesting experience for him. The people there want him to come back.

May 23

Dave

Tough morning at first. The day starts out bad and then gets gradually better. Then, after supper, I come around somewhat; in fact, a lot, sometimes. And I haven't had a really bad fatigue spell in the last couple of days. Need to keep on my feet and moving.

I think China is about 75 percent of my problem. When I get home, out of this violence and noise and crowding, I should feel a lot better. Quiet is what I need, and my own environment, which I have some control over.

Jan is so steady. I envy her, wish I could be that way. I wish it a hundred times a day. I need to be able to get that way, or on the way to that way, at least.

To relax—that is what I need to be able to do. Just lie down and go to sleep at night or in the afternoon, which I've been able to do for almost 53 years, until this fibrillation episode in January.

...I think I'll try to forgo "naps." I'm so used to napping, it'll be hard to wean myself, but I should try.

...Took a walk with David Jr. tonight. That's what I wanted to do so much when I learned he and Karen were coming here. Feel awful that I'm mostly not into it this semester. I hope he understands. I'm sure he does; he's like his mother, mostly. He's pretty steady.

Dylan Thomas: "I have been told to reason by the heart,/ but heart like head leads helplessly."

May 23

Jan

Dave is still depressed much of the time, but has periods of near normalcy. His worries have not decreased, but the intensity is sometimes less. He tried to go to bed without a Xanax last night, but had to get up at 2:30 a.m. to take one when he couldn't sleep.

...Barbara and I walked to the arts and crafts building and David Jr. went for a walk. Dave and David went to the Sprite to eat lunch but found that it was too crowded and that the food and service were not good.

As they were attempting to eat, a cat got sick and vomited near their table. Then a young girl squatted near them to pee. Dave wanted to come home.

As Barbara and I were walking, we saw a crowd of people gathered, so we stopped to have a look. There was a young, terribly deformed boy who was attracting the attention. He looked like the "Elephant Man" with a badly misshapen head (a huge bulbous growth on top), eyes wide apart, ears toward the back of his head, and a hole in the back of his head. It was horrible to see. People were staring, and we even saw one man getting up on a stone fence to get a good photo of this person. The boy's father or guardian was collecting money for him. The boy was moving around, writing on his own hand with a pen. I can't get the image of this boy out of my mind.

Barbara said she wonders why she was told that Nanjing was a beautiful city. I told her we have not gone to the beautiful areas yet. Nanjing has many beautiful and historical sites, such as the Yangtze bridge, the 1000-year-old city wall, the Ming Tombs with gigantic concrete animals, temples, an observatory. But the rest of the city can be bleak and dirty to a foreigner. I guess we are used to it and don't see it so much. Actually, Dave sees it and is depressed by it and by all of the noise, but I'm okay.

The girl at the reception desk told Barbara that she would have to move out of her room, that they needed it for people attending a meeting here. So Barbara began to panic until Dave and I went to the desk to straighten it out. At least we think we straightened it out.

Barbara is hungry all the time, so I told her it was the beginning of her tapeworm. She worries about the food and water here, and we, of course, told her about the huge worm that Kevin passed.

...We had asked to have a bed moved into our apartment for Karen, so the fuwuyan (maids) came to the door carrying a cot. I shook my head no and said "chuang," which means bed; so they went to get a bed. Karen could not sleep on a cot for several weeks, especially that cot.

May 24

Dave

Bad dream last night, can't remember the content, but it was one of those either/or dreams where I was stuck between the either and the or, and there was no solution, no compromise.

...One day less than a month away and we fly out of China forever. I can't wait. I don't feel good today, but the depression is not as intense as it has been. Women do not understand men; Jan does not understand me. Men—yes, I know— do not understand women either. Jan assumes I'm feeling better than I am feeling. I know all this is a drag on her, this depression. But...I'm surviving and maintaining. I don't know how, I feel so lousy.

May 24

Jan

A nice, sunny, warm day, but the first thing I hear when I wake up is a complaint from Dave. He either feels terrible mentally or has some physical pains. It makes me feel resentful, but I know I need to help him as much as I can. I want him to stop taking Xanax and take an over-the-counter sleeping pill that Barbara brought along, but he won't do it.

...Barbara spoke to one of my conversation classes again this morning. The students were fascinated by her and her artwork. She showed them some of her collages, which consist of "found" materials placed in various angles on a canvas. This type of art is completely alien to them.

Barb's still waiting to hear from somebody about her return ticket to the U.S. She says she thinks everyone at home has forgotten about her. I told her that is usually what happens. As of today, she says, she has decided to have a different attitude about China. She is going to be positive and try to enjoy each moment she is here.

...David tried about 40 times to call the travel agency to find out what time Karen's plane will arrive today (and we don't have a push button phone or a re-dial feature). He was never able to get through, so he and Dave went to the Jinling Hotel travel agency and found out. David Jr. has a cold and a sore throat. This happens to almost everyone who comes to China. New germs, body rhythm disturbances and different food.

Karen arrived at 8:30 p.m. (1 1/2 hours late). She had a horrible time in Hong Kong trying to live on limited funds, and had sprained her ankle.

She thinks Nanjing looks great compared to where she's been.

Qian stopped by to meet Karen. As I was telling everyone about Qian's beautiful singing voice, she began to sing "Killing Me Softly With His Song." This brought Barbara to tears. An emotional moment.

May 25

Jan

Karen's first night in our apartment, and she woke to find three huge cockroaches in the room. I also found a big one in the bathroom. My roach houses have apparently expired. I got out some spray and "fumigated" the apartment. These creatures could have been brought in with the bed. At home, I would have been embarrassed about cockroaches in my house. But here, it doesn't bother me.

...We went to dinner with two American language poets who are traveling through China doing lectures and readings. We went to a little alley restaurant that had a patio with lots of trees and shrubbery strung with Christmas lights. We were happy to be able to eat outside in this pleasant setting, but the wind suddenly came up and we all became extremely uncomfortable with the sand, dirt and gravel getting in our eyes. We had to go back inside to eat.

...Dave has seemed fairly normal today. He's still having trouble sleeping and insists on taking a Xanax to relax him. They are not sleeping pills, and the rest of us have tried to convince him to take the over-the-counter sleeping pills that Barbara brought along. During the daytime, he tries to nap but can't. Then he gets frustrated. He's now worried that the lack of sleep is harming his heart and body.

May 25

Jan

David Jr. and Karen are having a good time walking around the city taking videos and snapshots and shopping. They get along well.

...Dave was depressed and tired this morning. He's so preoccupied with himself that he doesn't give me the attention I'm used to getting from him—just little things like hugging me or touching me whenever he goes by me, making humorous comments, laughing with me or at me. I know it's because of his depression, but I don't like it. He and Barbara went to lunch at the Sprite; I didn't want to go. I had fried rice and vegetables with Eva; Karen and David went to the Black Cat restaurant.

...David and Karen went to the city zoo and took pictures of the German Shepherd and the Persian cat which were safely behind bars. They were amused.

...We all went out to eat and took Qian along. The menu was in Chinese only. The restaurant was unusually noisy and the service poor. Dave and David left a little early, since the noise was getting to them. The rest of us stayed as Qian argued loudly with the waiter about the check. Qian is so good at bargaining that she got the bill reduced by Y30. Chinese people believe that a successful party has lots of noise, a big mess and plenty of leftovers. I think the people next to us at the restaurant had a "successful" dinner party. At one point, when they couldn't get a wine bottle open, they hit it loudly against the doorjamb to loosen the cap. They also turned the volume of a large T.V near our table up high to add to the atmosphere.

...I invited Chen Loo and Brian to our apartment for cookies and coffee as a farewell to Chen Loo, who is going home to England tomorrow. She spent much of the afternoon and evening complaining about the drama production and certain frustrations that she had experienced while directing. If they want to present plays, she believes they should do new ones under a new director and not repeat the plays she has been doing. This foreign experts building will be somewhat less colorful after she leaves. And Brian will turn into a different person without her around, the kind of person he was before she came.

May 27

Jan

Rain...Dave had almost no sleep all night and complained about not sleeping, so I didn't get much sleep either. Sleep is such a valuable thing, something that we have always taken for granted. I assume this will pass when we get back to the States.

...The two language poets spoke to Dave's class and other students this morning. I don't like language poetry much nor do I agree with the ideas and philosophy that go along with it. The interesting part of the talk by Sherry and Lazer for me was to watch the students' reactions to it. They had not been exposed to language poetry before, and they appeared to be confused. It is so unlike traditional Chinese poetry. I prefer traditional poetry, I've decided. One of Sherry's poems was a recital of the 50 most used words in the English language, and that was it. Barbara, however, loved their poetry, since it is similar to what she is trying to do in her art. Her art is modernistic and deals with similar themes.

...Dave felt miserable this afternoon because he couldn't sleep. I joined him for a nap and made him feel much better. He went to bed this evening without taking a Xanax. He took a sleeping pill instead. Another victory.

...For dinner we had hor d'ourves of soda crackers with peanut butter and cheese (from the U.S.), tuna and noodles and blueberry muffins. We played the game "Taboo" and laughed a lot.

May 28

Dave

Felt bad last night, but took a Unisom instead of a Xanax, and slept better. Maybe I can break the Xanax habit and I'll be better.

...Karen says her athlete sister was told she had a heart murmur but went on with her life as though she hadn't heard that news. I suppose that's the best way, especially, as in my case, when they say "no restrictions." That means "carry on." It becomes a problem when you start fearing your condition. I should simply carry on as though nothing has changed. That is my attitude right now, anyway.

I really don't think I "have" anything but depression right now. No delusions, no huge paranoias, though I've always been slightly paranoid.

I feel better this morning. Felt lousy last night.

May 28

Jan

Rain again. Dave actually slept last night and felt decent this morning.

...We left for the Nanjing Museum with our umbrellas and rain coats. We got to the museum just before noon and were told to come back at 2:00 p.m. (after nap). So we walked around and found a place to have lunch. The first place we went to wanted to charge us a flat fee of Y300. We said "tai guila" (too expensive), and went to another small place and ate for Y49. It wasn't aesthetically pleasing, but the food was decent. The museum had many interesting relics from various dynasties in history. We weren't allowed to take snapshots, but David videotaped much of it. Dave was tired throughout most of the day. Again, I worried about him having something else wrong with him. He can't seem to get with it. He looked worn out.

...The cook fixed our dinner tonight and Zhang joined us. He has many plans for introducing Barbara to artists in the area. He seems to feel responsible for making sure we are meeting the kinds of people we want to meet. He's very helpful. Dave was not very sociable.

...A student came over with a video he had promised to bring us: "Shocking Asia." We thought we might want to get a copy of it from the description he had given us earlier, but it's not something we will try to copy on campus, or anywhere. It's full of violence, sadism, masochism, brutality, kinky sex. I was surprised that he brought it to us, or that he even had it.

As this student and Qian were here, Dave, David and Karen watched a Star Trek video. The student and Qian didn't like it and talked loudly during the movie, so Dave got up to turn up the volume on the TV. It was an awkward situation, one in which I was not comfortable. I was surprised by Dave's behavior and embarrassed. My student had actually come over to talk. He and Qian left after Star Trek was over.

May 29

Dave

Feel terrible, no real change, though I don't feel so much depressed as just sick and tired. Headache. Took a Unisom last night, it didn't work very well at all. Very tired. Will I have one good day before I leave China? Will all this make me a cynical man? I hope not. I believe China is about 40 percent of my problem. Or 50, or 60. I don't know when I'm awake or dreaming these days.

I should go with David and Karen to the Sun Yat-Sen memorial today, just to go somewhere, do something. And yet I want to stay here. I want to see if I can actually work on some writing. I have to stop feeling sorry for myself, stop asking for pity: from others and myself. It is a hard life. Nothing from now on is going to be handed to me on a silver platter.

...Talked with the two language poets from the U.S. They say there's no theme to language poetry, very little narrative and description. But isn't the lack of theme a theme? They don't talk about poetry as art. What is it, if not art? Karen is right: It's all very pedestrian and boring. No lift to the language. One of them is no poet; the other is a good free verse poet, but he's going over the deep end.

The world is screwed up, fragmented, the language poets say, so we need poets who speak to that more appropriately. Also, they want to break down the relationship between artist/poet and reader. Reader and poet, they say, should be on an equal level. Authority breaks down. What about apprenticeship, then? Trying to "come up" to the master writer, the authentic practitioner? That, too, is gone? How do you evaluate language poetry, in which author and reader are equal? Does the poet still get royalties? Put his/her name on the published book?

To me it's a silly game, this language poetry. A blind alley. Nothing will come of it unless it's good poetry, good poem-making. I think it's a joke.

May 29

Jan

   Beautiful, sunny day. Qian was supposed to take all of us to Purple Mountain today, but we decided to go tomorrow instead. Dave was too tired; David Jr. had a severe sinus headache; Barbara had to try to get some business cards printed; and I had lots of papers to correct. Also, Barbara and I had to go to the travel agency to pay for our tickets to Beijing. A hectic day. Dave was crabby. David and Karen finally decided to take a bus to the Yangtze River bridge, with directions from Qian.

   ...As Barbara and I were walking across an alley-way, after paying for our tickets, a man driving an expensive, shiny, black car pulled right out in front of us and almost hit us. Barbara let go of a string of epithets, the most foul swear words possible, that made us both laugh so hard we almost peed our pants. The driver's window was open, and even though he didn't know what she was saying literally, I think he had an idea of the content.

   ...Dave tried to nap, as usual, and had trouble falling asleep, as usual. He called me in to talk to him and told me he thought he might not live through the year. He feels like his entire life is changing; nothing is quite right. I was frightened to hear him talk this way and thought I should call David P. or someone to tell them about it. Instead, I talked to Dave for quite a while and changed his mood, at least temporarily. I'm worried about him.

   ...David, Karen, Barbara and I went to Qian's apartment this evening. She had a variety of food set out for us: peanuts, dried salted peas, pepau fruit, bean paste dumplings and some rum or tea to drink. The others didn't stay long, but I stayed to looked at her photo albums and her stamp collection and had a few shots of rum. She was pleased that we were there. Her room consists of three sets of bunk beds, a desk, a bookcase, a black and white portable T.V., a table and a big stereo-tape player. She's on the sixth floor of a dormitory, with a view across the yard into the freshmen boys' dorm. We looked in their windows and saw some of them playing table tennis, some playing cards and some studying. Qian is not sharing her room with anyone at present, except for a lady and her young daughter who come in daily for a nap. The other two roommates have moved out. Someone may be assigned to share this room with her later. It is set up to have three persons.

...Barbara met someone from Holland on the street today and planned a meeting at 9:00 p.m.

May 30

Dave

Do I feel better today? A little, it seems, though I am tired. Less tired than yesterday. Maybe I'm digging myself out, toward the sun, which is shining today. The way I felt when I woke up this morning—I did sleep fairly well, though it was with a Unison—I can't afford to be depressed, because that means not getting my work done. I have a lot of work to do: I have a collection of stories to get finished and published. That is primary, and I have a living to make, and I can't make it by sitting around feeling sorry for myself. Nothing worse than self-pity, than <u>asking</u> for pity from others. Pity is not what I need. I need to get my work done. Period.

...Today Qian took David, Karen and Barbara to the Sun Yat-Sen Memorial and other places. They'll have fun. I remember last semester feeling so good out there, taking two steps at a time up the 395-step memorial. Feeling awake and alive and young. I want that feeling back, and I mean it. And I will get it back. It will take work, but I will get there. Much of it has to do with attitude, no doubt. There's always been a good correlation between working and integrity with me. And being recognized. Plenty of work to be done. And I have ideas in my head for new and good stories and poems.

Onward!

May 30

Jan

Qian took Barbara, David and Karen to Purple Mountain to see the sights, David videotaped much of what they saw. They were impressed with the mountain and its purple cast. Barbara almost lost her glasses in a W.C. She was squatting with her glasses in her T-shirt pocket, when they fell out. She was able to hit them with her hand and knock them away just as they were about to fall into the hole (which was full-to-over-flowing).

Dave and I spent the day at home alone. As I was beginning to prepare food for Eva's potluck dinner party, I ran out of bottle gas. We were supposed to have a new tank by 2:30 p.m., but it didn't come until almost 5:00 p.m.; so we were late getting the dishes prepared. We got to the party after 5:30. Dave, Karen and David were asked to read some of their poetry after dinner. Everyone seemed to enjoy it. Dave was a little depressed at the party, but came alive when he read his poems, and said he enjoyed the party. Barbara seemed uneasy during the evening and left a little early. I think she had made arrangements to meet someone and was anxious to go.

May 31

Dave

Tired, tired, tired. Pain, or dull ache in my chest all night, my jaw hurting too. Tossed and turned all night. I know what "tossed and turned" means now. I've lived it. All the cliches are true. All I've been doing these last few months in China is surviving. I've hated it here. I know that China excites me in bad ways.

Actually, last night I felt decent; went for a beer with David and Karen. A beer, a glass of beer. No more 4, 5, 6 beers as in the "old days." One or two will do it. I wish I could afford the luxury of drowsing out on four or five cans at night; I think I'd sleep better. David P. says I've got a lot of adrenalin surging inside my chest. My awakeness is a curse. And then I _try_ too hard to sleep, and sleep won't happen. I should try _not_ to sleep. Just read until I can't hold my eyes open anymore.

May 31

Jan

Eva left a note under our door this morning commenting on the poetry. She had appreciated and enjoyed it. Eva is one of the people here I have liked most. She's interesting, enthusiastic and sincere.

...We are hearing about typhoid outbreaks in Nanjing. Students are being inoculated. Dave and I had inoculations before we came to Nanjing, but David and Karen haven't had any. I'm worried about them, but they don't seem to be bothered about it at all.

...Dave says he doesn't feel so depressed today, but is so incredibly tired. He seems most tired in the mornings and late afternoons. He sleeps off and on during the night, with the Unisom sleeping pills. At least he is not taking Xanax anymore.

...David and Karen went with Mike to have some beer, and ended up in his apartment until 1:30 a.m. Dave went to bed early, and I stayed up until 11:30, having some time to myself.

...Barbara had an exciting day with some artists and magazine editors. They want to publish some of her artwork and seem to like what she is doing. It's similar to what some of them are doing. She has another meeting tomorrow.

...I accidentally (on purpose) broke a leaky thermos bottle today. That thing had been left in front of our door one time too many. (The maids bring us boiled water twice a day.) I put it in our garbage basket and told the <u>fuwuyan</u>, "bu hao" (bad).

JUNE

June 1

Dave

Twenty more days and we're out of here, although not out of China (Shanghai). Agitated today; uneasy. But I can see living and liking living, eventually. I need a place I can relax to do my work. I really think a major trauma for me was quitting drinking, or at least turning into a "moderate drinker." I can no longer cut loose on the beer. I've lost my innocence on that matter, too. The way I see it: something serious has happened to Dave Evans. And Dave Evans needs to change his life to deal with it. Will he? Of course. Otherwise, there is no quality in the life. Being a grownup means to grow up; to relax and be calm. I don't have to get so excited about things anymore. Down the long road: look—there is nothing at the end except death—for everyone, not just Dave Evans. A man has been made a little more aware of his mortality. It isn't the first time for this to happen. It won't be the last either. I need to grow up. To change. Or else.

June 1

Jan

It rained most of the night and day. Eva was in our apartment most of the morning, and I had a class in the apartment this afternoon. Dave jogged but then felt tired and somewhat depressed.

...I'm worn out and feel fat and ugly. I'm anxious to get home to do something different with my hair and get back into aerobics. I lost weight when we were in China in 1988-1989, and even last semester. But this semester has been too stressful. We've eaten more Western food and haven't walked as much as we used to. I eat more when I'm under stress.

June 2

Dave

Bad night; my feet, both of them, twitched/jumped at about 30- to 40-second intervals, making sleep very difficult. As usual, I slept when it was about time to get up—5:00 a.m. on. So I'm tired, as usual. Called David P. He said China was my main problem, that when I get back to Brookings I'll be able to deal with my supposed problem. Jan mad last night; thinks I'm blaming her for my condition, my feelings; that I don't get close to her anymore. Maybe I do in part blame her—for not taking my condition seriously enough. She says she just doesn't want to dwell on it. I keep thinking the worst; that I'll have some permanent neural damage by the time I leave this hell called China. My title? At least for the second half of my journal? "This Hell Called China"? or "Double Happiness, Double Hell"?

...I feel so bad that I haven't felt worth a damn for David Jr.'s visit. That really hurts me. Deeply. I'm hurt for all sorts of reasons. Not a day has gone by this semester without feeling stress. Not one.

Like Alice, I've fallen down a hole into another world. I need to climb out into the normal one again. Today is beautiful. Sun, cool. Walking would be great, but I don't feel like it right now. David and Karen went for a walk.

June 2

Jan

I don't think I slept any during the entire night. Dave was having spasms in his feet every 30 seconds all night long (I timed them), which kept me awake. He dozed off and on, but I couldn't. What would cause these kinds of spasms—it could be a neurological problem. I want him to see a doctor in Beijing when we're there, but he says he won't.

...I made a pot of chili and had Barbara and Eva for dinner. Eva said that our colleague from the U.S., who is a political science/history professor, talked to her cross-cultural communication class. During the talk, some of the students wanted to leave, because they didn't like what they were hearing. One even passed a note to Eva asking to be excused. An example of what they didn't like is that he said Lincoln should have let the South secede from the Union. This didn't agree with their Chinese sense of history. (Is this why he wasn't asked to come back next year?). He is intelligent and well read—a Renaissance man—and outspoken.

...David bought a harmonica from a street vendor today, and Karen got a pair of softball/tennis shoes for Y13—less than $2.00 U.S. They're having fun walking around and shopping.

On our walk this afternoon, we found a man sitting on the street with a huge piece of tanned leather selling made-to-order belts. Dave wanted to watch the procedure, so he ordered one. We watched as the man cut a shape from the leather and proceeded to turn it into a belt. Dave paid Y10 for it, a little more that one U.S. dollar for a leather belt—not bad. It's not fancy, but Dave likes it. We were captivated with the man's skill and continued to watch him until a crowd gathered to watch us.

June 3

Jan

Off to Beijing on the airplane at 10:30 a.m. We had some difficulty at the airport, but nothing more than what is usual in China for foreigners. Barbara was completely frustrated and I couldn't help laughing at her. She kept asking "Nar? Nar?" (where, where). It sounded hilariously funny to me, especially with the look of desperation she had on her face.

David Jr. was pale-faced throughout most of the flight to Beijing. He's afraid to fly on China Airlines because of their past safety record. We mentioned that CAAC means, "China Airplanes Always Crash," which didn't help him. Lunch on the plane included meat and a bun for a sandwich. As I looked around at the Chinese people on the plane, I didn't see any of them making sandwiches. They ate the meat and the bun separately. Sandwiches are not what Chinese people are accustomed to eating. This lunch was obviously for tourists.

...Dave was much better today, more like himself. He's no longer taking any medication to sleep.

June 7

Jan

Dear Shelly, Kari and all,

This will probably be my last letter to you from China. We look forward to getting home and spending time with you. It has been a long semester. We'll call to make the final arrangements for our return trip.

We just returned from a trip to Beijing with David, Karen and Barbara, our friend from Iowa.

A Mr. Xing, friend of a friend of Barbara's in Iowa, picked us up at the airport when we arrived in Beijing. After a scramble over whether we would take a bus or a taxi, we opted for a taxi. At the hotel, Barbara became uncomfortable because she was going to share a room with your dad and me. Your dad said he didn't want a third bed brought into the room because he thought it would be too crowded. He just wanted the two of us to sleep in one twin bed. Barbara thought this meant that he was uncomfortable and needed his "space." She said she wanted to get her own room and began to cry. She was near hysteria. I tried to reassure her that this arrangement was fine with us. It's what we had planned. The cost of a single room for her would be too expensive, so we agreed that we could manage just fine. Mr. Xing was caught in the middle of this discussion and had a bewildered look on his face. He was confused and uncomfortable with us Americans. I felt sorry for him.

After we settled in, Barbara told me she had been invited to spend the night with a friend whom she had met in Nanjing, who was in Beijing for a few days, so she was happy.

David, Karen, your dad and I ate in a small restaurant around the corner from our hotel, one David and Karen had found on their walk earlier. The man seemed friendly. As it turned out, he conveniently couldn't find the English menu, and we didn't ask the prices as we ordered from the Chinese menu (pointing out our choices). From the looks of the place, it appeared that it wouldn't be very expensive, but we ended up paying way too much money. We can get a similar meal in Nanjing at the same kind of restaurant for 1/4 the cost. We felt exploited. I wanted to buy some

David. Jr. and Karen at Tienanmen Square

glasses in the restaurant that said "pijiu" (beer) on them. The man told me that <u>for me</u> they would be free, but I knew better. When the check came, there was Y30 added on for them. The man said his boss wouldn't let him give them away. I think <u>he</u> was actually the boss.

On the fourth anniversary of the Tianamen incident, we all walked on Tianamen Square and felt close to what happened there. At one point, Barbara began to cry. Mr. Xing was concerned and said, "You mustn't think about it. It is all in the past—we must only look forward."

Seeing Mao's body for the second time was, again, an eerie experience for me. He is encased in a domed glass or Plexiglas coffin, on a raised platform and is separated from the crowd by chain-linked floor guards similar to those in front of airport ticket counters. People are instructed to walk by quickly and quietly while armed guards watch intently. People are not allowed to carry purses, backpacks, cameras or anything else into the area. There are stalls all around the outside for checking these items.

We asked Mr. Xing and his wife to be our guests for dinner at a roast duck restaurant. It looked, from the outside, to be a decent place. The food turned out to be horrible and completely over-priced. We paid over Y300 and had only two dishes! The duck was almost all fat. It was a disappointment, since Peking roast duck is usually excellent and we had been looking forward to having it. Thus, we felt taken advantage of again. We didn't say much because of Mr. Xing and his wife.

We came back to the hotel and had drinks at the bar. The drinks, too, were over-priced. Barbara went to the room.

David, Karen and Barbara went to see the Great Wall with Mr. Xing and his uncle, a taxi driver. He charged them Y425 for the day, a substantial sum. Your dad and I didn't go along, since we had been there three times already. Instead, we went to a Friendship store and then to McDonalds to eat. I'm surprised at how busy this McDonalds is, that there are so many Chinese who can afford to eat there. The cost for a family would be equivalent to one-third or one-half of an average family's monthly salary. The restaurant is a two-story restaurant with at least 20 check-out stations. It has seating for hundreds.

The ride to and from the Wall (one hour each way), in the small taxi, was extremely uncomfortable, David Jr. said, because of Karen's chronic neck problem and David's long legs. The driver constantly jerked the car from side to side, causing Karen considerable neck pain. At one point during the trip, Barbara asked David and Karen whether they had read The Ugly American. They were taken aback.

A hotel clerk called our room to tell us our "fly tickets" were at the desk to be picked up. The travel agency had delivered our airplane tickets to the hotel.

David, Karen, your dad and I ate at a great restaurant for dinner our last night in Beijing, and didn't get over-charged. The food was excellent— probably the best we've had in China, and the people couldn't speak a word of English. Ordering our meal was a challenge, but I was able to use my minimal Chinese vocabulary for words like chicken, pork, noodles, rice, etc., and we just pointed at some of the entrees. It was a successful meal.

We left at 10:00 a.m. to get to the airport for our 12:25 p.m. flight to Nanjing. Mr. Xing's uncle came to take us to the airport. We agreed ahead of time to pay him Y120, but the fare only showed Y105 on his meter. And we thought we were getting a special deal from him. Another lesson.

The flight to Nanjing was rough, with lots of turbulence. David was especially concerned. For lunch on the plane we were served just bread, nothing else.

We were glad to be "home." We've decided that we like Nanjing better than Beijing. We don't feel like we're being taken advantage of as much here. I'm sure large tourist areas in the U.S. take advantage of tourists, too. I don't think Beijing will be chosen to host the Olympics in the year 2000, even though they are making a major campaign for it. There are huge signs all over promoting the Olympics, and each taxi seems to have a sign on its bumper. China's unfair money system—with RMB for natives, and FEC for foreigners—is too confusing and complicated, and tends to make foreign people use the black market, and natives try to take advantage of foreigners. The unfair pricing system for locals and foreigners would make those foreigners attending the Olympics unhappy. And the trip to the airport takes an hour on an extremely congested highway. China has a lot of work to do to get the city ready for an event as huge as the Olympics.

By the way, while in Beijing, Karen found a $100 bill! She and David were just walking along near a tourist hotel, and there it was on the ground, stuck in a fence. They changed it immediately with one of the many money changers hanging around the hotel; they got Y1000, a lot of money in China.

Again, we can't wait to see you all.

Love you all,

Mom (coming home)

June 7

Jan

Dear Sarah and Chuck,

Thanks for the letter and the clippings. Enjoyed Andrea's and Ryan's letters. Sorry to hear your parents aren't doing so well.

We will be arriving in Sioux City on June 24 and will come to Brookings on the 26th, since Kari and Jef and the kids will arrive on that day. So we need to have our house by then. Could you tell the renters that for us? Maybe they will have their new house by then or have some place else to stay. It's going to be a hassle for us to get home and have Kari and family there, and then have to move everything back into the house. It will be almost as bad as a complete move. I don't look forward to that part, but we do look forward to coming home. We feel, at this point, like we have "done" China. It's time to come home.

Thanks for taking care of the window in Dave's office. The storm must have been a bad one.

We just got back from Beijing, where we took David, Karen and Barbara, our friend from Iowa, to see the Wall, Tianamen and other sights. We didn't have enough days to do everything we would have liked to do, but it was a nice break, and they got to see the major attractions. Barbara will leave on June 24th when we leave. We plan to go to Shanghai on June 20 to spend a few days before we leave for the U.S. Dave and I plan to get a luxurious hotel for our last days in China—a good exit.

David and Karen leave on June 16. We've enjoyed having them, even though our living conditions are not conducive to having guests. They've had a great time getting around the city on bike and on foot. They are so adaptable and easy to have around. They love China.

I'm far behind with my classes—grading and preparing—so I need to get busy. And we're starting to pack things for home, and are busy with last-minute get-togethers.

See you soon! Would you please be sure to talk to the renters. Thanks.
Love,

Jan (almost home)

June 8

Jan

The exchange rate for one U.S. dollar is Y10 RMB, the best since we've been here.

...David, Karen and Dave couldn't sleep last night. David had nightmares about plane crashes, which must be disturbing since he's flying to the U.S. in about a week. He keeps thinking about CAAC and worries. Karen's back hurt. And Dave just couldn't sleep. I think he sleeps more than he thinks he does, but he was extremely tired today.

...I found a live snail in our bathroom medicine cabinet this morning. How long has it been living with us?

...David Jr. went to the campus barber today. He tried to tell him "just a little off," but when he came home, he had "just a little hair" remaining. The barber apparently understood his gestures to mean "leave just a little hair." He said that after the haircut, the barber poured a half of a cup of shampoo on his head and massaged it so hard it hurt.

...Today, David and Karen saw a man, who appeared to be a doctor, cleaning people's ears on the street. They said he used a long wire-like device and seemed to push it quite far in. They wondered about punctured eardrums. I tried to imagine having my ears cleaned on the street with thousands of people walking by. Actually, the only time a crowd would gather for this sort of activity in China would be if a foreigner were having it done.

June 9

Jan

Dave talked to my class today and we played some Simon and Garfunkel songs and all sang along. It was a fun class. Songs like "Homeward Bound," are meaningful.

...David and Karen saw a fight between two women today. They were yelling, pulling hair, hitting and kicking each other with passion.

...When David Jr. went to get his bike from a parking stall today downtown, he found it had been chained up by the parking attendant. He never did know why and got the bike lady to unchain it by pointing at his bike firmly. He probably scared her since he is so big, and so foreign.

June 10

Jan

Mr. Li, one of Dave's students, invited us to be his guests for dinner at a business restaurant. We borrowed two bikes for David Jr. and Karen and rode 20 minutes or so to get to the restaurant during the traffic hour. We had many kinds of traditional dishes and more than enough to drink. As soon as our glasses were about half empty, a waitress was there filling them up again.

...I had my last official class today. Now, only finals are left next week.

June 11

Jan

The English department had an official banquet for David Jr. and Karen today at noon in the campus restaurant. We had the usual cold dishes first, then a variety of hot dishes including squid, baby quail, pork fat, duck webs. David and Karen enjoyed the food. It is tradition for the department to host a banquet for guests of their faculty.

...Zhou's wife, with Xi Xi their four-year-old daughter riding on the back of her bike, and I left for the food market to buy food for the party this evening. I was impressed with Xi Xi's ability to hold on so well as she sat on the back of the bike with nothing to support her. It's very dangerous without a carrier, especially with all the bumps on the roads.

Zhou's wife is the master of masters when it comes to shopping for food. She bargained over every little item we bought, often heatedly, and I'm sure got the best prices available to anyone. She even pulled the skins off the garlic to make sure it was okay, and to make it weigh less. I wanted to tell her, as I was standing in the scorching sun sweating profusely, that it was okay if I paid a few jiao (less than a penny) more, but I didn't. She doesn't speak much English, so we had some difficulty communicating.

This evening, the preparation of jaozi (meat-stuffed dumplings) by Dave's students was quite a production. They made enough to feed the entire apartment complex, so there was plenty left over. They are all skilled at making jaozi. Zhou's wife took over the production. First, they made a huge ball of dough; then they tore it in tiny pieces and made perfect half-moon shapes and filled them with a meat and vegetable mixture. Then they pinched the ends together and placed them into a large pan of boiling water. They must boil three times before they are considered finished. Each time the water comes to a boil, a container of cold water is thrown into the boiling water and then re-boiled. A delicious sauce made from vinegar and soy sauce is served with them.

It was Zhou's birthday, so I bought a lard frosting birthday cake (the only kind available) in one of the department stores. The frosting is actually made with lard—very white and very lardy tasting. The cake was skillfully decorated. I hung a sign and some decorations on the wall for him and for his daughter, Xi Xi, whose birthday is tomorrow. Zhou was touched by it and said he would never forget this birthday. Dave gave his students some books and a few miscellaneous items we had brought with us to give away. They were thrilled with the books, since they have little access to books in English and almost no money to spend on them. David and Karen read some of their poems for the students, and the students asked for copies of the poems. It was a successful party. Xi Xi became animated during the evening and acted like any normal four-year-old—a little boisterous. After everyone left, Zhou came back and asked if he could have the birthday sign.

Earlier in the day, Qian went with me on the bus to get a set of dishes. She knew the perfect place. When we got off the bus, we discovered that the shop had been moved. So we walked around until we found it, not too far away. We spent over an hour purchasing the dishes. The clerks were not very enthusiastic about selling us dishes nor were they very helpful. They seemed to be ignoring us or they would tell us "meiyou" (don't have). This type of behavior is not uncommon in China at government-run stores. People are assigned to work in these stores and are not interested or excited about being there. No incentive for doing a good job.

We finally made a decision, at which time they said that all the good sets had been shipped abroad, that they only had seconds and thirds. So we had to open each box and look at each dish separately to see if it was chipped. They would replace a chipped one, but not one that only had a flaw on it. I was worn out after this ordeal and the dishes were heavy, so we caught a cab. Qian was more than willing to carry the heavy dishes and walk ten minutes to get a bus, and then walk ten minutes after we got off the bus to get to our apartment. I wasn't.

...I'm covered with bites that are red and swollen, and I couldn't sleep last night because of the intense itching. Qian says they are not mosquito bites and suggested that they may be fleas! I was horrified. She accompanied me to the campus clinic where I first paid an amount equivalent to less than ten cents, and then we went into a doctor's (she said skin doctor's) office. Four men were also waiting to see the doctor. We took a seat and waited as the others discussed their conditions with the doctor (no privacy). The doctor gave each of them a prescription and sent them on. Then it was my turn. Qian wrote my name in English for the doctor, and he promptly scratched it out and told her to write it in Chinese. He looked at a couple of my bites and wrote a prescription for two kinds of traditional medicine. We had to get one medicine on the first floor and the other on the third floor. The third-floor shop was already closed, so we went to the first floor. At the counter, which had an approximately 2" x 10" opening to talk into, Qian had angry words with the clerk and then went to another window. She came back, said a few more angry words, and the clerk threw the bottle of medicine at her. Apparently, they wanted me to pay, and our contract says we don't have to pay. Qian always looks out for us; we feel lucky to have her around. Other foreigners have commented that they are envious of all the attention we get from our contact person, since they get very little help from theirs.

June 12

Jan

Qian went with me to pick out a carpet, because we're packing our crate today for shipment to the U.S. and I wanted to get one to send home. She was able to get the price down Y100 because the rug has a tiny soiled spot on it. After the purchase, Qian tied the carpet roll, which was wrapped in plastic, onto the back of her bike and we rode home in the rain.

...Some officials came to check the contents of our one-meter-square crate and watched as we put our things into it. They asked us to open a few boxes to have a look to make sure we weren't taking anything home we shouldn't be taking, like valuable relics and artwork. After it was packed, the men pounded the crate shut with nails and put an official seal on it. (China loves official red seals. If something doesn't have a red seal on it, it's not valid, no matter what it is.) The crate will be picked up in a few days (we hope), and shipped to a port (we hope) in Chicago. It will take from six weeks to three months to get there (we hope).

...Zhang brought five men over to our apartment this evening—two poets, one playwright, a novelist and a critic. We served beer, cookies and peanuts, and tried to communicate. None of them spoke English except for Zhang, so he translated. It was frustrating not being able to communicate with them directly. The playwright, Chen, invited us to his home tomorrow evening. He is apparently very well known in China and is well taken care of by the government. He even has his own car. He has strong Party connections and is important throughout China for his role in the Long March. He wrote plays and poetry for the Red Army. During the March, he collected leaves and drew pictures and wrote poems on each of them. Recently a book was published with pictures of these leaves in it.

June 13

Jan

We went to the Black Cat restaurant for a Western breakfast, a place many of the foreign students frequent since it's near their dormitory. To see it from the outside, a person would probably have no interest in eating there or even in going inside. There is garbage strewn around the alley entryway, and a string of bleak-looking flats. But the inside is okay and the food is tasty. There is no bathroom inside the restaurant, which is typical for this kind of eating establishment. A sign on the restaurant wall says, "Follow the string of lights to the bathroom at the end of the alley." It also says, "Do Not Piss on the Neighbor's Walls!"

...We saw a sick-looking rat near our apartment today. I say sick, since they usually don't come around during the day. We haven't seen as many rats here as we did in Kunming. Streets are always being swept by women with tree-branch brooms.

...Mr. Chen's youngest daughter picked us up this evening and we walked 20 minutes to get to their home. He's the writer who was involved in the Long March. His home is a big, old, two-story home, walled off from the rest of the neighborhood. His wife and two daughters were gracious hosts. They served us two kinds of dumplings, one with sesame paste and one with bean paste, a burned-tasting brown sugar candy (a sticky glutinous rice ball with bean paste inside), fish-flavored chips and beer. Chen showed us some of his work and gave us one of his books—the one with pictures of the leaves he collected and on which he wrote poems and drew pictures. He opened a desk drawer and showed us the original leaves. They are beautiful. One daughter lives in America, is married to an American, and has a three-year-old son. She was visiting—the first time in 12 years. She and her son planned to stay until July. Her three-year-old son does not understand Chinese, so he and his grandparents are having trouble communicating. The daughter is expecting another baby in three months—a boy, she said. She hates the weather in Nanjing and thinks the people aren't friendly. She's anxious to leave. She has become Americanized.

...Dave has been more like himself. He's more fun to be around and is a little more relaxed.

June 14

Jan

This morning Dave got up, went jogging in the sweltering heat and humidity, came back, sat at his desk and had a cup of regular (caffeine) coffee. His heart began to palpitate and then slipped into an irregular rhythm. He was alarmed and called David P. He told Dave to first rest and then come in to see him in 1 1/2 hours. Since Dave did not feel well at all and didn't want to ride his bike or walk, we took a cab. David P. checked Dave and decided to take him to the People's Hospital to see a Chinese cardiologist. This alarmed me some, but I didn't convey this to Dave. The EKG showed that Dave did not have a heart attack, but they wanted to put him in the hospital until his heart went back into regular rhythm. Dave refused to be admitted, so they told him to take digoxin and sent him home.

When this happened to Dave, we were in the midst of making plans for a surprise party for Qian's birthday this evening, and I had two cakes to make and miscellaneous other things to do. It was stressful, since I was worried about Dave. So I postponed my two classes today. I had exams left to give.

Dave spent most of the day in bed, getting up briefly for the party. He broke out into a sweat several times and had some dizziness.

...To surprise Qian, David Jr., Karen and Barbara took her out for dinner and then brought her to our apartment where we were all waiting for her. She was surprised about the party and pleased with the suede backpack we gave her. She said it was the best present she had ever received. She has helped us so much and we wanted to get her something special. Barbara had bought one like it and I knew Qian had admired it. Karen made a huge birthday sign to hang on the wall and a sketch of a snake, since Qian's birthday sign is a snake. We decorated the apartment with balloons. It looked festive.

...Earlier today, Karen bought a bottle of drinking water in a back-alley store. After she had drunk almost half of it, she noticed that it tasted funny. She looked at it and, to her horror, found moss and/or scum growing up from the bottom of the bottle. I'm surprised she hasn't gotten sick here. She eats a lot of things on the street and once even drank water out of our faucet by mistake. I think she's probably healthier than the rest of us.

June 15

Jan

Dave felt miserable this morning, so I called David P. A little later his heart suddenly went back into rhythm. David P. came to the house, as did Dr. Huang, the cardiologist. We can't complain about this kind of medical care and concern.

...David Jr. and Karen left about 7:00 a.m. to go to the train station. I felt bad that we could not accompany them. We hated to see them leave. It's always hard to say goodbye, especially since Dave was not doing well. Qian gave them a tea set and some sandalwood fans. They were loaded down with luggage.

Dave was feeling a bit tired and he had pain in the center of his chest. We have always called it stress pains, but anymore I'm not sure.

June 16

Jan

David P. came to the house again to see Dave. Dr. Huang called to talk to him. We have been impressed with the concern and compassion they have shown to us.

June 16

Dave

Haven't felt like going anywhere lately. The trip to Beijing was okay. David and Karen got to see the Wall, Tiananmen.

...Now I have pain in my chest. I suppose it may just be stress, and my jaw pain continues somewhat, too. David P. says it isn't my heart.

I had another fibrillation incident, which does not leave me in a good mood. I'll have to solve that problem, somehow. Two episodes in six months. I think it was the caffeine in the coffee, but I had some beer (no more than a beer and a half) the night before. It may have been the combination again, or it may be that I am extremely vulnerable to caffeine. This was after I jogged a mile and a half and then had breakfast. The heartbeat went regular the next day, thanks I suppose to digoxin, which slows the heart down.

...Four more days in Nanjing, three in Shanghai, and we'll be flying out of this country, maybe forever. This has not been the best semester.

...Hard to say goodbye to David and Karen yesterday. Tough, tough to do that anymore. I'm getting more sentimental in my 50s.

...The Chinese doctor here, a most gracious man, read my reports, said that my "tiny defect" was nothing, that this kind of thing shows up on most thallium reports. That was reassuring. When he said I'd probably have to cut back to "moderate" exercise, that was not good news. But he admitted that he's conservative. Not good to fibrillate when I'm jogging, of course. But that has never happened. I'll have to have that problem solved. I will need to keep on exercising; maybe the intensity will have to lessen. I had already cut back before I came to China, but I was still in decent shape. That is what I want from exercise mostly, anyway. To feel good by being in decent shape. The intense competition of racquetball might be over. I know that will be hard to live with for awhile, but I can't be an athlete all my life. A person has to slow down with age; that is a fact of life. But I wish I could just be free from pain, whether it's real or stress-induced. I'll be home inside of ten days. I need to get free of China. That is my one main goal right now. I know I'll feel better back in my own surroundings, among friends, and people who speak my own language. And with good health care available.

I was feeling good just before I had my fibrillation. Went downtown with David Jr. the day before, had a good time with him. It seems that if I'm focused on something else, I don't feel any pain. What should that tell me?

June 17

Jan

My last class! There were some good speeches presented for the final exam. I received a big straw hat and a huge card with Greta Garbo on it from two students.

...I went shopping with Eva for last-minute items. In the bus on the way home an old man with a huge burlap bag was being severely criticized. We figured out that he hadn't paid his bus fare and didn't seem to have any money. After we listened to the bus attendant yell at him for a long time, and the old man begging for mercy, we took out some money and gave it to the old man. He was grateful and paid the attendant for his fare. The attendant then made the old man stand up over his huge bag, so he didn't take up any more than one space. Everyone stared at us; we could tell we were being talked about—a bit discomforting. Then the bus driver wouldn't let us off where we wanted to get off. We had to backtrack about two blocks.

June 18

Dave

Much, <u>MUCH</u> better today! My body is relaxed. I slept well, dreaming of baseball, the Sioux City Soos baseball team, in fact. Of a player, Billy Pavilick, or was it Eddie Bressoud—meeting him in a cafe. He was waiting on tables. I asked him to come over and talk, and he came over, very friendly, and sat down and talked. Talked about baseball, the Soos, the promise of life in that young, supple, vigorous body of his.

...This morning I feel good. Very little pain, only lingering pain from tightness (so it feels, anyway) in my chest. I think I'm as relaxed as I've been in months. I feel on top of my life right now. I have pretty much survived China.

June 18

Jan

It rained today, and I enjoyed riding my bike in the rain with my rain cape over my head. I felt the anonymity I've wanted to feel but haven't felt, since I've been in China. I look forward to being able to go shopping in the U.S. and not have anyone stare at me.

...Xia Ayi, our cook, came by and gave us a sack of tomatoes, two small flower buds and seven cloisonne bracelets. We managed to communicate, somewhat awkwardly.

...The Waiban sponsored a farewell banquet for us tonight at the campus restaurant. They gave us two beautiful eggshell vases and certificates with letters of recommendation about our teaching at Nanjing University. As I was sitting there eating Chinese specialties, I thought about how hungry I was for a hamburger and French fries.

After dinner we went to see Qian sing in a university talent show. I had lent her my new skirt, a blouse and a necklace. She looked great and she was pleased with how she looked. She came over after the performance and gave us some paintings, some big furry bunny slippers with floppy

Qian

ears for me, some ginseng roots, tea and a sandalwood fan. We told her we would see her off tomorrow morning. She is on her way to a small town to teach English to factory workers for a month.

...Eva gave me a necklace that she had gotten at a temple. Barb stopped over. She's tired of the hassles she's been having in China, especially those with the phone system. She can't ever get through, and when she does, there is so much static she can't hear. She had bought a carry-out chicken-with-peanut dinner with her from the Sprite to eat for lunch. Just as she was about to take her first bite, she found a big "fucking" hair in it, to use her expression. She just picked it out, threw it on our floor and began eating the food. I asked her if she had ever seen a hair under a microscope, which made her cringe.

June 19

Jan

We helped Qian carry her heavy bag for the 20-minute walk to a bus stop. I don't know how she would have made it alone. She had to catch the bus to the train station to leave at 8:24 a.m. She was pleased that we saw her off. Seeing someone off is important in China. It is considered an honor. We'll miss her. Our lives would have been much more complicated and less pleasant without her around.

...On our way home from the bus stop, we walked by an outdoor dance arena. Men and women (and some women and women) were dancing very properly at 8:00 a.m. (waltz, fox trot, etc.). We stopped to watch for a while. It reminded me of the dancing style in America about 40 years ago.

...We got home and then began the serious job of packing. Dave is stressed (as usual), but this time about having suitcases that are too heavy. They will be heavy and cumbersome, but there's no way around it. We mailed three boxes separately for Y700, and also a huge crate for around $300 U.S. And yet, we have too much to carry. Dave gave away most of his clothes to his students. I gave away a lot too, but have bought as many.

Four of Dave's students helped him carry the three boxes the four or five blocks to the large post office for mailing. It turned out to be a hassle, as I expected it would be, but they got them out. Dave then went to the bank to cash a traveler's check and he came home without his passport. Tomorrow is Sunday, but we think the bank will be open. He can't leave China without his passport. Just one more complication to add to his day. No wonder he is stressed.

Yin, my former student, and his wife came over with a scroll painted by his mother. It was our going-away gift from them. His wife also insisted that I take her handbag, which I had admired. I didn't expect her to give it to me and felt uncomfortable taking it. But she insisted. It was the first time I had met her. She seemed so young and shy. Shyness is a learned attribute for Chinese women.

Zhang stopped by, then Eva. We sat around eating popcorn, talking, feeling happy and content. I'll miss these kinds of evenings and these people.

June 19

Dave

My student Mr. Li, who dotes on me, gave me a painting and a poem he wrote (both pieces he had mounted, and he did all the calligraphy himself). The poem talks about my being a teacher/gardener who tended the young "sprouts" and some day, when I'm in America, I'll look back from a long distance and see the ripe peaches growing in various places in China. A fecund idea. I hadn't thought until he gave me the painting that, yes, maybe I did have an effect on my students. I liked them, gave them a lot of materials in class, taught with some passion, enjoyed talking about Twain and Hemingway and Crane and Carver and Faulkner with them. The conviction, I hope, came through. I taught with the handicap of depression at times, but I did it. I stayed in there. I will never forget the night I didn't sleep at all, and then got up at 7:00 and taught two two-hour classes back to back. That was not easy.

Feeling better and better.

June 20

Jan

Dr. Huang came over at 8:00 a.m. and brought me a beautiful necklace carved from bone. His shirt was buttoned wrong, with one side hanging way down below the other. He has a lot of nervous energy and says he also has stress. He understands what Dave is going through. He stayed for over an hour. As we talked, we wished we had met him several months ago. Dave would have had an easier time with his stress about his heart. As soon as he left, three of Dave's students came by. Some of my students came with gifts. It was a hectic morning. And we had packing left to do.

...Dave went to the bank, with a note written in Chinese, to retrieve his passport (kind of like a note from your mother when you're in kindergarten). No problems.

Many people stopped by to say goodbye and leave gifts. Zhou, Dave's favorite student, told Dave that he had changed his life. He was so grateful for having had him as a teacher. We talked about seeing each other again, either in China or in the U.S.

Mike, Lida, Tom and Deb took us to dinner for our last night in Nanjing. It was the only time I left the apartment all day—I was too busy packing and visiting with students and others who stopped by.

June 21

Dave

Last entry:

Feeling good. Sleeping, moving toward a relaxed state. Heading for Shanghai. In a few more days I'll be leaving China, the main source of my stress. That will make a difference. Yesterday I talked for an hour with Dr. Huang, who came to see me. He "promised" me that I have no significant heart problem, certainly no arterial damage to speak of—clinical ischemia, as he called it. He did say that I will need to learn to relax. He, too, is a nervous type, and as he spoke to me his knees kept knocking together—the faster he talked, the faster they knocked. He said he wants to keep in touch, send us Christmas cards. He is a great guy. He brought a beautiful necklace for Jan. I had given him a book of my poems.

What I need to do: cold turkey the caffeine, go easy on the beer (which Huang said probably does not affect the electrical system of the heart nearly as much as caffeine, if at all—though he thought the hard stuff is another matter) and get back to a running/workout regimen. That in itself (I'm about 15 percent off right now) will take care of much of my stress. I know how I feel after running or racquetball. I want that feeling back. No reason in the world why I can't do it. And no reason in the world why I can't learn to conquer, to a significant degree, my nervousness, my excitable heart.

June 21

Jan

Departure Day!

People began gathering around 7:00 a.m. Xia Ayi, the cook, took almost all of the stuff we had left in our apartment, and was excited about getting it. She cried when she told us goodbye.

The Waiban was supposed to have a van ordered for us, but only one small cab showed up. We couldn't even begin to get all of our eleven pieces of luggage in it. So they had to scramble around and get another car for us. We hugged everyone and said our good-byes. These people were a big part of our lives for almost a year. We'll miss many of them. It's always difficult to say goodbye.

Zhou, Zhang and Zhen went with us to the train station. Zhang will be in the U.S. next year as a Fulbright professor. We plan to see him then. Zhou went to buy us two cans of beer, two cans of soda and four meat sticks to eat on the train—a thoughtful gesture. We know he doesn't have much money.

As the train started to leave for Shanghai, I thought about how I felt leaving Nanjing. I felt anxious, apprehensive, sad, relieved, happy. I'm anxious to see our family and friends, anxious about adjusting to a slower-paced, quieter life in the U.S. without horns blaring, without the crowds of people everywhere, without the stares, without the need for bargaining for every-thing we buy. I'll like having space; I'll like being able to walk on our floors without shoes or slippers on; I'll enjoy a clean house. The conveniences will be easy to adjust to, but I'll miss not having to survive creatively with minimal resources. I'll miss walking around the streets of Nanjing seeing new and interesting things each day. I'll like going to the stores and being able to find what I want, being able to read and understand the language. I have essentially felt like an illiterate person here. But I know I will miss China.

This second semester has been hell at times because of Dave's problems. But I liked teaching, liked the schedule we had, the freedom to do what we wanted (mostly), and the togetherness we have had. It was great meeting new and engaging people, experiencing new kinds of activities, and most of all I have a particular fondness for the Chinese people. I admire them for their hard work and ability to make use of everything, and their seemingly positive attitudes. They are upbeat. Life for them is not easy, and most of them would do anything to come to America.

...When we got to Shanghai, after a four-hour train ride, a young man came up to us at the train, when he saw all of our luggage, and said he had a bus. We agreed to pay Y90, which we thought was a bit high, but we had lots of stuff. We were then taken to a station-wagon, not a bus. Two older women pulled our luggage in two carts, for which we paid Y5 each. We then paid the man who directed us to the station-wagon, and he left. It took some maneuvering to get all of our luggage in. The front seat had two large bags, making it impossible for the driver to see out of the passenger's side. I was almost buried with luggage. The driver kept talking to us, without much luck. "Wo ting bu dong," I said (I don't understand). When we got to the hotel we unloaded and he wrote up a bill for us for Y41. Dave said no, that we had already paid Y90. There was some arguing, with the bellhop being able to understand and speak some English. He translated our message to the cab driver while a crowd suddenly gathered. We held our ground and just went into the hotel and left the driver talking. The hotel bellhop brought our luggage in. It was another attempt by a taxi driver to rip us off. Paying Y90 was already too much; we wouldn't pay any more.

Our hotel room is okay, but not as luxurious as we had expected for $98 per night. It is a Chinese-run hotel and not a joint venture hotel, similar to a decent Holiday Inn in the U.S. We settled in to spend a few nights, and then found our way to the Kentucky Fried Chicken restaurant near our hotel for our first greasy, American-style food.

As we were walking along, we saw a woman walking on the street in her nightgown (a flowing, nylon, see-through gown). A strange sight to us, but apparently not to anyone else. We've also seen several men in pajamas walking around. Maybe this is a new fashion craze.

It began to rain.

344

June 22

Jan

Rain still. We slept well. It was the best night for Dave for a long time. He's better already. I think the fact that we're going home has had a good effect on him. We went to eat at the Shangri-la Portman Hotel for a Western buffet breakfast. It was very expensive, but wonderful.

When we showed our passports to someone at the hotel, we were told that they had expired; so we decided we'd better get them checked at the American Consulate. We couldn't handle being delayed at the airport. We caught a cab across town to the Consulate and found our way through a labyrinth of buildings, in the pouring rain, to get to the office. We were completely soaked. They told us we would be okay as long as we had our work cards which approved our stay in China until August, 1993.

Later, Dave left the hotel for a while and came back with a rose for me. It is the anniversary of the day we started going together 38 years ago! I was touched. I had actually forgotten. He has never forgotten. He's in a much better mood. We're on our way home!

June 23

Jan

I dreamed I was being attacked by a cat. It grabbed onto my hand and bit me and I couldn't shake it loose. I wonder if this dream was symbolic of trying to shake myself loose from China. It will take some time for me, I know, to readjust. It's a long process; at least it was when we returned to the U.S. from China in 1989.

...We met the Bausmans (Fulbright professor and his wife—Jack and Evelyn) and went to some arts and crafts studios in the French section of Shanghai. We bought some batik material and other small items. Then we went to the Bausman's apartment about 40 minutes away by cab. Their apartment is much nicer than what we had in Nanjing, with more space, hardwood floors—aesthetically more pleasing. However, the smell of rancid water from a river near their apartment was almost unbearable. It is worse than the packing house smells which we know about from living in the Midwest. We ate dinner in a restaurant outside of their apartment and had excellent Chinese food for our last dinner in China.

...Dave is taking Xanax to get by in Shanghai, which is noisy, congested, polluted. You can't walk on the streets without being bumped into every few steps. The traffic is insane. It's probably a good thing we weren't assigned to Shanghai. I tried to imagine how Dave would have been able to survive there, especially the second semester.

June 24

Jan

We met Barbara at the airport. She was still struggling. She had ordered some rice with vegetables and sauce, and had asked for some extra sauce. They would give her more if she wanted to pay more money, but she refused to pay more money. After the airplane had taken off, she came to talk to us and was in tears because she was leaving China. I remembered back at how she cried herself to sleep the first few nights in Nanjing because she thought China was so bad. Like most of us, she was affected by what she saw and experienced in China, and she fell in love with the people.

...As we were flying over the ocean on our way to America, we felt like we had literally survived China. Dave was happy that he didn't give up and go home when he was having so many problems. This was a victory for him. Would we do it again? For Dave, probably not—at least not for a long time. For me, yes, I could do it again. We may come back in a few years, but not for a while. We need time and distance from China right now—time to sort out what we have been through, time to reflect.

EPILOGUE

The Greek philosopher Epictetus said centuries ago: "What disturbs men's minds is not events but their judgments on events." Epictetus' wisdom has not been lost on me.

I'm glad I kept writing in my journals during those dark spring days in Nanjing. It pleases me to be able to look back on the first semester's entries----which confirms my belief in the power of the written word----and remember how normal I was. I know now, as I knew then in my mind but not in my guts, that there was nothing seriously wrong with me. Recently I had another stress/ thallium test, which turned out to be quite normal. My doctors tell me I have a strong heart and yet a potential for a fast, irregular heartbeat, not a highly unusual or serious condition.

For some time I had been acquainted with the notion that you can't trust the body after 50. But I didn't know it was also true of the mind. My heart scare and resulting depression amounted to a strong jolt of mortality. When I spoke to a friend and counselor after I got home, he said, "You've been humbled, Dave." I've tried denying my aging, and wishing it away, but nothing works. The plain, hard, inevitable truth is that I am no longer 30 or 40.

My depression has had at least one good result: It has made me understand my limitations a little better.

Jan and I are looking forward to returning to China. We want to see our friends again, and go to places and cities we haven't yet visited. China has changed us. It has given us new eyes, a new perspective. We hope, above all, that it has made us more tolerant. If so, the joy and the pain have been worth it.

DAE